T0418235

MASCULINITY, SEXUALITY
AND ILLEGAL MIGRATION

Studies in Migration and Diaspora

Series Editor:
Anne J. Kershen, Queen Mary, University of London, UK

Studies in Migration and Diaspora is a series designed to showcase the interdisciplinary and multidisciplinary nature of research in this important field. Volumes in the series cover local, national and global issues and engage with both historical and contemporary events. The books will appeal to scholars, students and all those engaged in the study of migration and diaspora. Amongst the topics covered are minority ethnic relations, transnational movements and the cultural, social and political implications of moving from 'over there', to 'over here'.

Also in the series:

Masculinity, Sexuality and Illegal Migration

Human Smuggling from Pakistan to Europe

ALI NOBIL AHMAD
Lahore University of Management Sciences, Pakistan

ASHGATE

Published by
Ashgate Publishing Limited
Wey Court East
Union Road
Farnham
Surrey, GU9 7PT
England

Ashgate Publishing Company
Suite 420
101 Cherry Street
Burlington
VT 05401-4405
USA

www.ashgate.com

British Library Cataloguing in Publication Data
Ahmad, Ali Nobil.
  Masculinity, sexuality and illegal migration: human
  smuggling from Pakistan to Europe. – (Studies in migration
  and diaspora)
  1. Human smuggling–Pakistan. 2. Human smuggling–Europe.
  3. Pakistan–Emigration and immigration–Social aspects.
  4. Illegal aliens–Europe. 5. Pakistanis–Europe. 6. Male
  immigrants–Europe.
  I. Title II. Series
  364.1'37'089914122-dc22

Library of Congress Cataloging-in-Publication Data
Ahmad, Ali Nobil.
  Masculinity, sexuality and illegal migration : human smuggling from Pakistan to Europe / by
Ali Nobil Ahmad.
      p. cm. – (Studies in migration and diaspora)
  Includes bibliographical references and index.
  ISBN 978-1-4094-0975-5 (hardback) – ISBN 978-1-4094-0976-2 (ebook)
1. Pakistan–Emigration and immigration–Social aspects 2. Europe–Emigration
and immigration–Social aspects. 3. Human smuggling–Pakistan. 4. Human smuggling–Europe.
I. Title.
  JV8753.A56 2011
  364.1'37–dc23

2011022580

ISBN 9781409409755 (hbk)
ISBN 9781409409762 (ebk)

Printed and bound in Great Britain by the
MPG Books Group, UK.

Contents

Masculinity, Sexuality and Illegal Migration

As stated by Ali Ahmad, this book's author, migration studies most commonly focus on an economic landscape upon which their genderless actors are propelled by economic forces. He considers this practice to be unsatisfactorily objective and one dimensional; presenting the migrant protagonists as merely foot soldiers in the global army of labour, one which is moved around in response to the emotionless demands of western society. The intention of this book is to dispel this approach and replace it with one which is more complex and which, accordingly, takes account of the emotional and sexual lives of male migrants, in the case of this volume, young men from Pakistan. As Ahmad explains, the originality of his work lies with its, 'specific focus on the driving dynamics of masculine ideology' – sexuality enhanced by affluence. Bearing this in mind, the author provides his readers with an all-embracing account, which has its foundations in a rewarding combination of a critical analysis of migration theory both past and present, together with an exploration of pertinent psychoanalytical discourses on gender and masculinity which, as he argues, provides a 'framework for the study of smuggling and migration'. For his actors are men from a society in which wealth and masculinity are vital constituents of perceived success, the need for which provides the incentive for submission to human trafficking and illegal migration as a means of entry into Europe. However, this is not just a theoretical work, and it is the empirical research carried out amongst first and second generation male migrants in London, Italy and Pakistan which provides the substance of the study. For those concerned about a gender bias the author does provide a contingent of female voices, for without the demands of the female, there would be less need for the displays of successful masculinity.

The binary to the abstract presents the empirical element of the book, one which is set within a political-economical context and one which has an historical dividing line created by the closing of the open door of migration into the United Kingdom. For the early migrants from Pakistan, illegality was not a factor. Until the immigration legislation of 1962 took effect entry was permissible and employment readily available. It is only in the past few decades that illegality and its hardships have become virtually the sole option for the ambitious male emigrant from Pakistan. If we link ambition with male sexual drive, then it becomes easier to understand why, even taking account of the hardship and risk to life, entering a country through its back door, as contraband, is the choice of many.

Though the majority of the migrants interviewed by Ahmad confess to having left their home country in order to grow rich, few admit to this having been to prove their manhood and bolster their sexuality. Perhaps some did not even make the connection, so deeply embedded can it be in their subconscious. The interviews reveal that migration and remigration are painful experiences. Few of those who settled in London in the 1960s and 1970s achieved the rewards hoped for: the streets were not paved with gold, and life in East London reduced rather than enhanced self esteem. What the migrants cling to now is a myth of return, one that day by day fades further into a distant dream; affluence and enhanced sexuality now being a part of the dream. Yet it is little better for many of the returnees, forced to demonstrate the success they never had, presenting an image of well-being and achievement by means of bank loans and car rentals. However it is this false picture and the conviction, 'I can succeed where others have not,' that encourages today's young men to make the sacrifice of being smuggled into an uncertain future. And it is an understanding of the motivations that ensure the survival of human smuggling across borders that makes this book an important addition to the library of migration studies.

Anne J. Kershen
Queen Mary, University of London

Preface and Acknowledgements

The Grand Trunk road is one of South Asia's oldest and most famous overland connections to the West. A short distance from the part of it that runs through Mandi Bahauddin, a district in Pakistani Punjab, lies a village called Chot Dheeran where towering minarets adorn the houses of Paris-based Pakistanis. These phallocentric symbols of excess built by men who migrated with the aid of human smugglers shame the nearby homes of those who cannot afford to send a family-member abroad. Empty and padlocked, sky-scraping émigré mosque-mansions are often surrounded by poor connecting roads, inadequate sewerage systems and brick-kilns worked by entire families (including children) earning little over a dollar-a-day.

The juxtaposition of private wealth and public deprivation in Chot Dheeran raises a series of pressing questions about the motivating drives, causes and consequences of human smuggling. What, for instance, is the relationship between wealth, religiosity and masculine power reflected in the construction of these homes that can be seen for miles, and what is their likely impact on aspirant young (and not so young) men in adjacent villages?

The argument of this book is counterintuitive. Its central claim – that human smuggling from Pakistan is driven by irrational forces – might well raise eyebrows given all the obvious reasons to leave Pakistan for a more 'secure' environment like London. On the other hand, scarcely has there been a more appropriate moment to highlight the idiosyncrasies in men's 'economic' decision-making: the spectacularly silly risk-taking that precipitated the recent financial crisis makes a mockery of neoliberalism's claim that markets are guided by benevolent, equilibrating, invisible hands.

Potlach is an indigenous American practice of escalatory gift-giving. It fascinated the French philosopher and writer Georges Bataille, who viewed it as emblematic of humanity's need for unproductive expenditure – its preoccupation with nobility, honour and rank above mere conservation and reproduction. Potlatch is about openly humiliating, defying and obligating a rival to respond with a more valuable gift, which must be returned with interest: a destructive form of ritual poker with no useful, rational or economic end in which each player risks and squanders wealth in organised acts of wasteful excess (1997: 172-4, 213).

For Bataille, Potlach explained the inflation of credit and banking systems.

I reckon it sheds light on the building of mosque-mansions in Chot Dheeran. An outlandish claim perhaps, but one supported by interviews with some 80 migrants whose narratives form the empirical core of this book. I hope I have done them justice: Saif Sahab, Aslam bhai and Chima will forgive me for mentioning their names. (Others might not.)

The following provided important assistance in the research process: Irfan Saleem, Saleem Sahab, Nasrullah Uncle, cousin Musa, Aqib (the leg-spinner from Pinner), Imran and the Lahore Kebab House family; Mian Aslam, Mirium Baji, Farida Khala and Nasir Uncle, Lado Khala, Khalid Uncle and Jimmy Chachu (sorely missed). Syed Habib, my colleague and gatekeeper in London deserves special mention.

Many individuals have shown great generosity by reading and commenting on earlier versions of the work presented here in different forms, above all Pnina Werbner, whose many years of care and support for my work and wellbeing are gratefully acknowledged. Most of the research was completed under her guidance together with Laurence Fontaine, my doctoral supervisor at the European University Institute in Florence. Annie Phizacklea has been extremely supportive since I met her at my viva in 2008. Ken Hully and Françoise Thauvin were extremely kind and helpful throughout my illnesses and administrative hassles; likewise Arfon Rees, Rita and Nicky in the History Department. Russel King, Nick Mai and especially Kaveri Qureshi provided important comments on articles, chapters and conference papers that went into parts of this book. So too Marlou Schrover and her co-editors on the IMISCOE book project.

I am grateful to *Migrance* (published by Génériques) for allowing me reproduce parts of Ahmad (2007) in Chapter 6; Sage for parts of Ahmad (2008a) in Chapter 6, the Introduction and 'Theoretical Framework'; Taylor and Francis (Routledge) for parts of Ahmad (2008b) in Chapters 5 and 6 along with parts of Ahmad (2009b) in Chapter 6, the Introduction and Overall Conclusion; Amsterdam University Press and IMISCOE for Ahmad (2008c) in Chapters 1 and 2; Ashgate for Ahmad (2008d) in Chapter 5; Oxford University Press (Karachi) for parts of Ahmad (2009a) in Chapters 3, 4, 5 and 6; CIDOB (Centro de Estudios y Documentación Internacionales de Barcelona) for parts of Ahmad (2010) in Chapters 3, 5, 6 and in my critique of migration theories which follows the Introduction.

Thanks go to my colleagues at UCL and Bristol on the Leverhulme project on Migration and Citizenship which generated an important part of the data I have used in this book: John Salt, James Clarke, Khalid Koser and Tariq Modood.

Lahore University of Management Sciences generously funded a research update in 2010. This was completed with the kind assistance of a bright young student called Amir Siddique who put me in touch with some interviewees in Punjab. Ali Khan has been a constant help, as have many other colleagues at the Department of Humanities and Social Sciences: Aimon Fatima, Maratib Ali Shad, Shamshir Haider, Ayesha Maratib, Noorya Hayat and Waheed Joseph.

I am grateful to Rasheed Araeen, Zia Sardar and the editorial team at *Third Text*, and to Sara Wajid for providing me with opportunities to write; so too the Scott Trust, which funded a stimulating year of training in journalism in 2008-9.

Friends: Luisa Brunori and Benoit Challand's kindness during my illness in Florence will never be forgotten. Sunil, Shehzad, Sach, Nils, FK, Jaspal, Renaud,

Rory and Willow – experts in reigning in my death drive – have borne its brunt for years. Sadaf Aziz and Asad Farooq are rapidly growing accustomed.

My siblings, Aamina, and Omar, have and helped inspired me in more ways than can be listed here. The same is true of my remarkable parents: Aboo migrated to London from Lahore in 1958, Ummy, from Karachi 13 years later – to them this book is dedicated with all my love.

All men by nature desire to know. An indication of this is the delight we take in our senses; for even apart from their usefulness they are loved for themselves; and above all others the sense of sight. For not only with a view to action, but even when we are not going to do anything, we prefer seeing (one might say) to everything else. The reason is that this, most of all the senses, makes us know and brings to light many differences between things.

Aristotle, *Metaphysics*

PART I
Introduction

Introduction

There's a curious complicity between researchers of migration and its protagonists. Both parties share an interest in representing migrants as asexual accumulators of capital, driven by little other than a narrowly defined, rational commitment to the material betterment of their kin and household.

Receiving societies propound this myth for its obvious ideological benefit of justifying the appropriation of migrant labour on favourable terms (the very term 'labour migrant' reduces the body in question to a pair of hands whose sole purpose is to work). It surfaces most obviously when this assumption is challenged by changing demographic realities – for instance, by the arrival of women and the settlement of families which often triggers a chorus of Malthusian concern about high rates of immigrant reproduction. The frequent association of immigration with housing shortages and strains on the welfare system amounts to balking at the idea that migrants themselves have emotional and sexual lives and aspirations which extend beyond the productive sphere: that they dare rise above their station to covet things we regard as normal for ourselves such as home ownership, domestic pleasures, family lives and, by implication, sex.

Thinking of migrants this way – as scrimpers and savers, embodiments of puritanical patience governed solely by the 'reality principle' – is comforting for societies which view themselves as progressive and tolerant, post-racial and democratic: sleep easy in the knowledge that the migrant who works nightshifts has no interest in pleasure; no *raison d'être* beyond survival and the material betterment of kinfolk.

Governments and communities in migrant-sending societies like Pakistan, for their part, are keen to project an image of their citizens and family members as pious and patriotic labourers whose sole objective is to serve their communities and countries with remittances that raise living standards and boost economic development. Migrants themselves, who play an important role in obfuscating matters, have little interest in challenging this image of themselves as martyrs. Nor indeed do their families, whose knowledge about the realities of life abroad is based on secondary reports rather than firsthand experience.

Then there is social science. Academic representations of labour migrancy, liberal and Marxist, have tended to carve up the migrant's social world into two distinct spheres. Economics and economic sociology, which dominate migration studies, foreground 'hard', quantitatively measurable causes and consequences. 'Cultural' drives, experiences and processes such as sexuality, supposedly less tangible, are relegated to the humanities and effectively ignored (for a discussion see Mai and King 2009). If anything, the emergence of a supposedly fresh set of concerns in the new millennium with paradigms such as 'transnationalism' and 'network theory' reflects the ongoing economism that pervades mainstream migration studies, a field in which the protagonists are only rarely discussed as complex, multidimensional social beings, willing and able to experience the full range of human emotions the rest of us take for granted.

There is, I reckon, a need for research that focuses upon the subjective nature of decision-making. The manner in which analysis is conducted in most sociological studies of migration networks and transnational economic practices effectively bypasses the individual; it assumes all actors within the 'migration network' to be objective rational actors and net beneficiaries of (labour) supply meeting demand in host countries. Very few, if any works produced in either of these fields question seriously whether migration is a profitable course to embark upon, and most do not address the question of motivation in sending contexts at all. This neglect is all the more perplexing given the growing importance of illegal migration and the rising death toll resulting from failed attempts to penetrate western borders. The difficult and sometimes terrible fate that awaits many of Pakistan's international labour migrants is one they engineer themselves at considerable cost, a fact which points to the need for a counter-intuitive explanation for *why* migration happens.

Gender and ideologies of migration

The novelty of this study lies in its specific focus on the driving dynamics of masculinity. The behaviour of men is placed at the heart of my explanation of why migration happens, in tension with the dominant paradigm that tends to take kinship's primacy for granted. Following Werbner's (2002: xxi) call for greater attentiveness to the dynamics of friendship, the research presented here demonstrates that decisions to migrate are forged amongst inner and outer circles of male friends, not the migrant's immediate family. Often they are mired in controversy, conflict, disharmony and discord between and across genders and generations within households, suggesting important tensions between friendship and kinship. The latter's primacy as a driving force of migration cannot be presumed; competing, colliding tussles between individual actors and their families suggest we need to think more carefully about who gets to migrate and what impels them to do so.

One important factor is the increasingly pervasive reach of consumerism in a country reputed for the purity of its religiosity (like the East more generally for its supposed spirituality). Commodity fetishism and lust for worldly status are intertwined with locally entrenched 'hegemonic masculinities' (Cornwall 1997: 11) and interpolated through advertising and television, driving large and diverse constellations of men to fixate obsessively upon seeing or making a career of the West in a manner that is, in some ways, a curious inversion of several European antecedents and equivalents – colonial adventure, the Hippy Trail and now the 'Gap Year' – each of which has successively institutionalised youthful intrepid exploration for middle-class Occidentals who continue to depart all year round in countless numbers on sensuous journeys to Asia and elsewhere where they wander, gaze upon and experience exotic cultural difference.

Such comparisons should not be, and are not pushed too far: what distinguishes Pakistani labour migrants most clearly from western travellers (and indeed the other great labour migrations of the 20th and previous centuries) is their subordination in travel, transit and destination to a structural edifice of state surveillance, discipline and control unprecedented in human history (the implications of which are examined in Parts III and IV). The sending context, moreover, is a violent, tormented society in which money equals power in ways that can have brutal implications: corruption, disintegrating institutions and corroding social fabric have taken a heavy psychological toll on the Pakistani middle-classes, for whom emigration holds the promise of purchasing – in some cases restoring – damaged masculine self-esteem in communities distorted by competition for status and power.

Sexuality

This book argues for an interdisciplinary understanding of labour migration's driving dynamics and consequences – one that considers its entanglements with disavowed and unconscious currents of sexual and erotic energy. Part II of this book explores the relationship between risk and fantasy in some detail, drawing upon Freudian and Lacanian psychoanalysis to underline the importance of libidinal investments and sublimated desire in shaping the decision to migrate.

Recent writing on the psychology behind insurance suggests that even the most seemingly conservative, apparently risk-averse acts of spending (purchasing indemnity) entails creative speculation about what one's future might resemble after incurring some loss that may or may not happen at an unknown point in the future (Patel 2007: 100, 102-3). It surely follows that human smuggling – a spectacular gamble that yields nothing but misery for some (injury or death for others) – must be embedded in imaginative processes worth understanding. What sorts of futures and pleasures are imagined before a person climbs into a small container of a truck or ferry in the hope of reaching Europe? The tragic circumstances under which these capsules of hope can become coffins are a reminder that, as with insurance, people don't always examine the details of their policies (what is paid for when someone buys insurance is not exact [Ibid: 102-3]). So too are the labour market outcomes of migrants who successfully reach intended destinations only to spend years trying to eradicate debts incurred in the process of trying to regularise their status.

The erotic energies that generate the drive to emigrate (Part II) must be seen in relation to the actual experiences and outcomes in transit, travel and work in receiving countries (Parts III and IV). Some bodies matter more than others under the present world order of capital, which has proved itself adept at appropriating and transforming the desires and energies of peripheral and marginal populations into useful production – labour power to be siphoned off, wasted and diverted elsewhere as deemed fit by core, rich countries as diverse as Britain and Italy. The former I call Afro-Eurasia which, following Georges Bataille, is conceptualised as part of capitalism's 'general economy' that includes, but is by no means restricted to Pakistan; the latter zones are synonymous with North Western and Southern Europe, conceptualised, again following Bataille, as the 'restrictive economy'.

Far from reflecting a loss of state control, human smuggling networks mediate the supply of Afro-Eurasian labour to demand in Europe's restrictive core. Their emergence is traced from colonial times to the present in a historical process of brokerage and commodification that has deepened as a result of restrictionist state policies since the early decades of the 20th century, culminating in the emergence of what is increasingly referred to as 'Fortress Europe'. The latter's relationship with immigrants who penetrate its borders is defined by labour regimes and laws that combine to thwart permanent settlement and work-life-balance for migrants who struggle to exist beyond the productive sphere; sexual desire (Part II) turns into sexual deprivation and deep-felt loss (Part IV). Corpses of those who die trying – the thousands drowned, suffocated and deported in the process of smuggling – are evidence of the gap in solidarity that confronts humanity in the 21st century. Part III ends by situating their lives and deaths in Afro-Eurasian history over the longue durée through connection with an older, universal spirit of travel, endurance and desirous, risky adventure dating back to ancient and medieval times: Xenophon's march and the Muslim invasion of Spain, like most of today's illegal migrations, are part of a Mediterranean history that elides the exclusionary notions of belonging which dominate contemporary myth-making and teleological histories of Europe based on its supposedly Christian, Greco-Roman heritage.

Conceptualising smuggling and illegality

Academic research on human smuggling is descriptive and dominated by high-flying technocratic, criminological and legal scholarship (important exceptions include Anderson 2007 and Andrijasevic 2009). Conferences, articles and books focus for the most part on the strategic concerns of policy-makers and officialdom in transit and destination states. Historical perspectives on smuggling are rare (for a notable exception see Schrover et al. 2008) and like the media, politicians and interior ministries to whom they tend to address themselves, case studies tend to treat smuggling as an unprecedented activity perpetrated by 'criminal networks' and 'trafficking rings' (a 2006 issue of *International Migration* contains no less than four articles on human smuggling, each of which focuses on the organisational structure of its operations: Bilger et al; Liempt and Doomernik 2006; Pastore et al. 2006; Neske 2006). The state and its role in producing illegality with restrictive policies is hardly anywhere to be seen in this work – predictably, perhaps, given its political coordinates and sympathies.

Theorisation of smuggling is sparse and premised on liberal and neoliberal assumptions – one-dimensional portraits of human behaviour dictated by narrow agendas of economic utility. Following Salt and Stein's (1997: 467-94) influential conception of smuggling as a business regulated by supply and demand, Bilger et al. (2006: 66-7) and Koser (2008) assume the existence of a trust-based symbiosis between smuggler and migrant, arguing, respectively that smuggling is a 'transnational service industry' which 'pays' – i.e. delivers in terms of net benefits to migrants, their families and agents. This book takes a somewhat different tack: if brokerage is a business, its 'customers', like all human agents, make decisions in political contexts – relations of power that shape transactions between migrants and smugglers in ways that are highly pronounced in travel and transit. Often there is very little meaningful 'trust' in smuggling networks: migrants are largely at the mercy of agents, who may or may not provide them with the service they require successfully.

Smuggling outcomes are uneven and erratic; networks do not necessarily deliver win-win-win scenarios for migrants, their families and agents. They are not nearly as uniformly profitable as the business analogy seems to imply because networks, like the human beings linked within the webs that compose them, behave irrationally. Even where they do thrive, net benefits are distributed unequally among their members. Leaving aside the mortal risks involved in border crossings and other perilous moments during the migration process which frequently lead to apprehension, imprisonment, extortion by corrupt officials, smuggling networks are subject to fraud and coercion: co-ordinating agents can disappear after payments are made up front, or abandon migrants in the course of the journey, dumping them in obscure locations without food and water.

Fixing responsibility on individuals and groups overlooks the fact that smuggling seldom involves a single 'agent', and distracts us from the policies and contexts that produce it. Historically, migrants and smugglers have always been permeable and organically linked categories; today they are more blurred than ever thanks to unparalleled restrictionism periodically punctuated by amnesties which create vast scope for profiteering among ordinary migrants who charge for 'help' in organising documents: extortion, blackmail, coercion, aggressive and blatant profiteering are rife in migration networks since the expansion of the migration business into regularisation in inhospitable host countries. The very term 'smuggler', as understood in media and policy circles, can thus be misleading: differentiating categorically between migrants and smugglers too neatly ignores the fact that many 'smugglers' are in fact migrants who facilitate illegal travel, entry and/or regularisation upon arrival of family members, friends, acquaintances and fee-paying strangers.

Boom-bust: cycles of prosperity and recession

Why and how do migration networks appear to benefit some migrants while having ambivalent and even negative consequences for others? To what can we attribute the success and failure of any given ethnic economy to provide a minimum of security for most of its participants? Part IV of this book makes the argument that ethnic economies, when analysed over time, reveal their vulnerability to cyclical fluctuations which are themselves the result of the dialectical relationship between the pull and push forces that generate migration networks, a fact that has important implications for individual migrants whose labour market and housing outcomes – more than class background and educational capital – are determined by *timing*. The point at which they are inserted into the enclave has fundamental implications for their position in relation to the broader migratory network and prospects in the context of reception. The ebb and flow of prosperity and recession can vary dramatically, abruptly altering newcomers' odds for achieving successful incorporation.

Economists might describe such fluctuations as markets correcting themselves through rational and inevitable operations of supply and demand: when the latter contracts, it is 'natural' that subsequent waves of redundant surplus labour experience unemployment. I prefer to think of networks as prone – like the bodies they connect – to generating excess energy that gets spent, redirected and wasted in ways that can have devastating implications for individuals who spend decades recovering losses when risks don't pay: embittered by their position of inferiority and subordination in cases where they work for and rent rooms or properties from more successful migrants within the enclave, these men face downward social mobility and subservience to those for whom the same risks proved lucrative.

Following several important (but relatively neglected) studies of migration in recent years, I focus on what happens once the supply of labour through networks begins to flow autonomously, irrespective of demand to create surplus (Light 2000; see also Knights' [1996] study of Bangladeshis in Rome). In such cases, when networks behave contrary to the utilitarian principle of balanced accounts, supply outstrips demand, leading to recession and unemployment. 'Enforceable trust' comes under threat in times of resource scarcity, exogenous shocks and externally imposed constraints, a fact that reminds us institutional environments (above all state policies and laws) and fluctuations in demand for labour determine the success or failure of migrant networks. The ability of a network's ability to generate social capital is contingent and alters over time in conjunction with broader transformations in structural context.

In short, history matters. The relatively positive outcomes of those who prospered under old migration regimes were dependent upon political-economic and legal-institutional conditions that have been steadily eroded. The extent of these changes between old and new migration have gone relatively unstudied in mainstream paradigms such as 'transnationalism', which fixates upon technological changes, telecommunications and supposedly cheap air-travel. The latter, I argue, are of relatively little importance when one considers the implications of human smuggling, illegal residency and illegal work, none of which are marginal issues or special cases, but rather have become increasingly central concerns to recent waves of Pakistani arrivals in European cities since the 1990s.

Political and economic conditions have also altered considerably: migrants today cannot count upon the availability of cheap housing which was abundant in the early postwar decades; nor are they supported by wives and children who, since family reunification in the 1960s, played a key role in bolstering ethnic enclaves across the UK. Finally, the labour process within new economic enclaves is increasingly based upon precarious service sector work that gives migrants little of the security they enjoyed in previous decades under Fordism. This has an adverse effect upon the network's ability to generate solidarity, credit and mutual aid schemes within the ethnic economies they forge. Trust, we are told by scholars of the ethnic economy, is its defining characteristic and the key to successful cultures of entrepreneurship. Yet the flexible economy leaves planning for the long term impossible; the flexible regimes of production which dominate the labour process into which migrants are absorbed are utterly inimical to collective values and commitments, as Richard Sennet (1998) among others have pointed out. If contemporary capitalism is rapidly corroding human society's most fundamental ethical values for the average citizen, my research suggests that it has particularly pernicious consequences for those who are extra dependent upon those values given their confinement to the ethnicised, relational sphere of the economy, in which informal arrangements govern social relations.

Time, loss and the labour process

In highlighting the costs of migration, this book serves as a corrective to what I regard as the unwarranted optimism that has clouded migration research since the 1990s. Many of today's migrants' experiences are closer, in certain respects, to migrant workers in previous historical epochs than those of the recent past (see conclusion to Part IV). An assessment of the historical literature on migration makes clear that Fordism and the brief interlude of relative security it brought for those who prospered under it was a historically exceptional period and can be seen, over the longue durée, as an aberration.

Life today for Pakistani migrants is distinguishable from that experienced by their predecessors under Fordism in several key respects. As Aglietta explains (1976: 158-9), Taylorism adapted to restrictions of the working day by increasing the intensity of labour and systematically compressing wasted time in the work place itself, with the result that 'increased exhaustion in the labour process had to be entirely repaired outside the workplace'. This necessitated a 'strict separation between working and non-working hours'. The post-industrial situation is quite different, as one might expect given the findings of numerous empirical studies which conclude that service industries have witnessed an intensification of the labour process due to growing competition with subcontracting, along with the increasing centrality of market imperatives under neoliberal capitalism (Rees and Fielder 1992: 365; Adam-Smith et al. 2003: 37).

Most new migrants employed in the service sector work between twelve and sixteen hours daily, six – sometimes seven days a week, often for months on end. They do so without any real respite at all in terms of holidays, free time in the evenings, weekends or even proper lunch breaks. They have less recuperation time at home than earlier waves of migrants did in the 1970s, a moment when factory workers tended to have properly allocated pauses and lunches and evenings and weekends off, along with wages negotiated by trade unions. Operations are small, and workers granted low levels of autonomy by employers who supervise their every move closely under what Burawoy (1985) would call a 'despotic' labour regime.

Smuggled migrants tend to deal with a specific set of constraints based on their higher costs of migration, which create a psychological burden: the constant possibility of being discovered and deported. Effectively, they travel thousands of miles across continents and vast migratory systems that span the globe, only to become prisoners of clock-time, locked in an endless cycle of work that confines them to a physical space of a few square metres both at work, often behind a counter which materially and symbolically segregates them from wider society, and home, in their dwellings, which are equally claustrophobic. If this applies to all labour migrants, it is particularly true of those with irregular status, for whom international travel is out of the question, and movement in space especially restricted. Theoretically, of course, they are relatively free to move around in anonymity in cities such as London. In practice, their enslavement to the clock ensures that they travel only between work and home. Harvey's 'time-space compression' (2001), if anything, captures the antithesis of their experience: if capital now moves across the globe instantaneously, labour's mobility is deeply reduced, not only in its ability to cross borders (Sutcliffe 2004: 261-80) but also upon destination, within the labour process itself.

The constant instability they experience in attempting to get settled gives the appearance of mobility: unemployment leads them to migrate secondarily and in some cases three or four more times in search of work; the need to regularise is another reason to risk further clandestine border-crossings. Their movement in space thus moves from one extreme to the other as they oscillate between spatial imprisonment and frenzied circulation. Most of the time, changing jobs and countries brings little other than a kind of horizontal (rather than upwardly mobile) sort of movement that seldom brings tangible long-term improvement in circumstances.

Migrants who enter Europe legally are able, in some cases, to purchase small properties and open businesses that bring them the psychological 'autonomy' that is often preferred by the working classes (Sennet and Cobb 1993: 235): for those who enter as spouses or manage to regularise their situations and call for their families, a minimum of emotional fulfilment awaits them at the end of a working day, however long their working-hours may be. For many migrants, however, (especially those who are unable to regularise their legal status), satisfaction of these basic human needs is, for the most part, beyond their reach. An all male constellation of uninvited guestworkers, they walk to work every morning from grotty nearby rooms rented privately and often, informally. Then, after a day's toil most of us would struggle to imagine, they trudge back to sleep in lonely, single beds where they crash, exhausted, into dreams of arrival and return.

Theories of migration: A critique

Theories and explanations of migration underwent considerable overhaul in the 1990s, an index of broader historical currents which swept away many of the political and intellectual bases of 20th century critical thinking within the academy. Once powerful overarching accounts of human behaviour such as Marxism lost legitimacy within the mainstream and by the end of the last millennium, a consensus developed which held that the new conditions of globalisation had exposed existing theories and assumptions to be outmoded, in some cases, embarrassingly so (Massey et al. 1998; Arango 2004: 15-35; King 2002: 89-106).

New questions and concerns replaced old. Mid-level units of analysis such as social networks came to be held as more significant than individuals and states in causing migration and understanding its effects. Social network theory, which had enjoyed a distinguished but by no means hegemonic position in the 1980s, became the dominant paradigm. Networking became synonymous with migration itself, so that Tilly's (1990: 84) claim – it's not individuals or even households but networks that migrate – became axiomatic in the noughties. 'Theoretical orthodoxies which prevail in the field of migration', wrote Arango in 2004, hold that it is no longer 'clear that investigating causes constitutes the most useful and interesting line of enquiry these days' (30, see also 15, 35); Foner (2001: 3-4), three years prior: 'migration can be thought of as progressive network-building'.

If 'old' approaches to migration are loosely identifiable by a preoccupation with the economic relationship of labour to capital, and a broadly separate view of 'cause' from 'consequence', the 'new' school rejects the dichotomy implicit in traditional explanations that emphasise either cause or consequence to the exclusion of one or the other, often bi-passing the issue of causality altogether, preferring to focus on the study of social processes over 'hard' 'economic' and 'political' structures in sending and receiving contexts. Any attempt to explain the causes of migration over time, they argue, is simultaneously an explanation of its consequences, because migration is fundamentally path-dependent; the abandonment of binaries such as 'sending'/'receiving' society, 'push'/'pull' in favour of analyses that emphasise their interaction is now something of a given.

New theories of migration can be loosely divided into three intertwined bodies of literature, each with its own broadly identifiable set of concerns. Below, I trace the emergence of each respectively, outlining their claims and conceptual bases and providing examples of their empirical usage in contemporary migration research.

Before doing so it is worth stating that 'old' orthodox, 'big' theories of migration
have somewhat stagnated in recent times, but continue to exist: neo-classical
economism as propounded by authors such as Todaro (1969), based on the familiar
economic tenets of rational choice, utility maximisation, factor mobility and wage
differentials (Arango 2004: 18) was revised by proponents of the 'new economics
of migration' who called for a substitution of the individual by the household as
the principle agent and unit of analysis (e.g. Stark and Taylor 1989: 1-14; Mincer
1978: 749-73). At the other end of the ideological spectrum, urban sociology and
updated world systems analysis (e.g. Sassen 1994) carried the baton from early
left-wing structuralist accounts which explained migration as a consequence of
the penetration of rural peripheral zones by advanced industrial capital, uneven
trade and development as conceptualised by authors such as Wallerstein (1974).
Though many of his core arguments remain true to their original spirit, Wallerstein
himself has taken to treating the household as a key unit of analysis within the
world system (Smith et al. 1984: 12-13), bringing left and right wing economists
into line through the use of a theoretical framework which shares some important
assumptions about the way income is pooled amongst kin.

1) Social network and/or social capital theory

Social networks, as Arango (2004: 27) points out, have figured in analyses
of migration for almost a century, but their newfound centrality in theoretical
explanations of migration since the 1990s is unmistakable. Social networks are
'sets of interpersonal relations that link migrants or return migrants with relatives,
friends or countrymen at home. They convey information, provide assistance,
facilitate employment and accommodation, and give support in various forms.
In doing so, they reduce the costs and uncertainty of migration and therefore
facilitate it' (Ibid: 27-8; see also Massey et al. 1998: 42-3). As Portes points out,
social networks are not in themselves 'social capital'. The latter is definable as the
'ability to mobilise them [and other forms of capital] on demand' (1995: 12). In
this sense, social networks and social capital are strongly linked to one another,
as indeed they both are to the 'moral economy', a concept developed by Scott
(1976) in a landmark study to capture the dynamics of 'affection' and 'mutual
self-interest' in redistributive strategies that ensure protection of the vulnerable in
subsistence-societies (Swift 1989: 8-15; Devereux 1999: 13).

2) Ethnic economies

The 'context of reception' approach pioneered by Alexandro Portes analyses
the economic and social clustering in space that is typical of new immigrants in
advanced capitalist countries. His conception of the MSI – 'mode of structural
incorporation' (1981) – is premised upon Granovetter's (1985: 481-2) Polanyian
conception of 'embeddedness', which famously made the case for treating social
ties and contexts as key to economic behaviour (Polanyi 1985[1944]). Portes

makes the useful distinction between 'structural' 'incorporation' of immigrants into the socio-economic mainstream of Western labour markets, and that which is 'relational' (1995: 6). The latter, which involves immersing oneself in ethnic networks, is prevalent precisely in contexts where the former is difficult to achieve, as is the case for most immigrants from Third World countries residing in the West. Kloosterman et al. (1999) have subsequently developed the notion of 'mixed embeddedness', which places greater emphases on the distinction between embeddedness in social networks and embeddedness in political and/or institutional contexts.

The new ethnic economy is composed of several strands of co-ethnics. Above all, Portes stresses the difference between EEs (ethnic enclaves) and MMMs ('middle men minorities'). The latter provide specific (often commercial) services to immigrant as well as wider communities and thus act as a buffer between newcomers and the host population; in contrast, the former are spatially clustered networks of businesses owned by members of a given minority that are based in proximity to the immigrant communities to which they supply a wide array of culturally specific services. By privileging members of their own ethnic group, MMMs and EE's create collective social capital and economic value and resources for newcomers. Some migrants can operate within both spheres of the ethnic economy; the enclave is controlled by a middleman-entrepreneurial class (Portes 1981: 292).

Another important point is that much of the economic activity within these ethnicised relational spheres takes place outside the ostensible orbit of state regulation, as it often does where small enterprise is concerned, a fact which requires reference to the concept of 'informal economy', a sub-field of economics, development studies and economic/urban anthropology that intersects at various points with the study of ethnic economies. Understood in its broadest sense by Castells and Portes (1989: 12) as 'all income generating activities … not regulated by the state in social environments where similar activities are regulated', the informal economy has come to be seen in recent years as a highly differentiated entity that takes multiple forms and overlaps with ethnic economies in complex ways. Governed by and dependent upon the logics of enforceable intra-ethnic trust that it produces and is based upon, informality often thrives on and complements the forms of social capital generated in EE's and MMMs: like 'intra-ethnic trust' or 'bounded solidarity', the informal economy is based on trust that is 'enforceable' (Portes 1994: 430-31).

3) Transnationalism

Pioneered by Glick-Schiller and colleagues (1992) in the early 1990s, the concept of transnationalism has evolved considerably over at least two waves of theoretical revision in a relatively short space of time, an indication of the excitement it has generated since its emergence. Portes (1999) once more, is at the heart of the intellectual movement that has brought transnationalism to the fore of migration studies, though its list of converts (as clear from a glance at the journal *Global Networks*) is impressive, and includes such names as Vertovec, Levitt and Landholt whose works are examined critically and interrogated here in some detail by virtue of their leading roles within the paradigm.

After extensive debate about the various kinds of ties that a meaningful and useful conception of transnationalism can reasonably include, its leading proponents have divided the practices of migrants ('from below') off from those of more powerful actors who intervene in the global arena 'from above' (Guarnizo and Smith 1998). They have also usefully distinguished between transnationalism that is 'comprehensive' (practiced by 'transmigrants') and that which is 'selective', 'periodic' and 'occasional'. It can take place alongside 'assimilation'; its rhythms are shaped by class and lifecycle (Levitt et al. 2003: 571). Smith (2002: xii) has pointed out that there are 'many different ways of being transnational and that these are linked to distinctive types of social space'.

Like network theory and the 'context of reception' approach to embeddedness, to which it is closely tied, the transnational perspective proudly 'removes the focus from the motivations of migration' (Al-Ali and Koser 2002: 3), fixing its attention upon socio-economic ties and other connections between sending and receiving contexts that, according to its proponents, have reached historically unprecedented levels in the context of new technologies of travel and communication.

New theories of migration: A critique

New theories of migration, then, consider the original motives for emigration unimportant; path dependency is the driving force of labour flows, networks a form of collective resource-pooling that maximise individual and group potential. Rationality in intention and benefit in consequence are taken as self-evident by virtue of the existence of such pathways and networks: migration happens, so it must be worthwhile for its various protagonists.

The philosophical problems with economistic notions of rationality are discussed in greater detail in the next chapter. Our present concern is with migration theory and the empirical studies which flow from it – a vast historical and sociological literature in which international movements of labour are assumed to occur for the best. Gabaccia's benign portrait of Latin patriarchy, for example, argues that 'international family economies developed out of rational, shrewd choices' (Gabaccia 2001: 203) based on the fact that there were work options for women at home. 'Separation', she suggests, 'made economic sense' (Ibid: 195). Men sent remittances; women worked tirelessly for the family's consumption (Ibid: 197). Shaw's (2000) study of Pakistanis in Oxford typically states that 'the primary motive for migration from Pakistan to Britain in the late 1950s and early 1960s was socio-economic' (Ibid: 13) without unpacking what this means. (See also Delaney 2001: 217.)

Historians tend to take economic cause as their starting point and put everything else down to a combination of social networks and kinship (which are themselves bound up with the goal of material betterment) along with historical contingencies specific to their chosen case study. Manchuelle's (1997) study of Sonike labour diasporas is a good example. The author begins by dismissing 'colonial' explanations associated with non-economic factors ('bright lights big city') on the basis that they patronisingly represent Africans as non-rational. He firmly asserts that the Sonike were in fact 'looking for cash' and therefore 'not unlike modern European, rational economical beings' (Ibid 1997: 4). His intentions are noble enough, but he takes little interest in what that 'cash' may have signified and what impulses lay behind its pursuit. The possibility that neither Africans nor Europeans are always 'rational' (a term he does not define) gets left unexplored, and like most scholars of migration, his analysis of cause goes no further than listing the familiar litany: kinship, networks ('channels') which 'were themselves causes in their own right' and various contingencies (Ibid: 6, 222). This despite the fact that his own data raise compelling issues such as the desire of youth to break away from patriarchal authority (Ibid: 145). The latter, regrettably, do not get incorporated or theorised in any of his general explanations of the 'economic determinants' of migration (Ibid: 5).

Cultural anthropologists, meanwhile, have tended to treat migration as a rational process even when ostensibly writing about non-economic behaviours. Khan, Ballard and Ballard write of a process in which 'honour' is rationally accumulated by the family (Ballard and Ballard 1977: 27, 69; Khan 1977: 71), the interests of which are represented by a gender-neutral 'South Asian villager': 'the primary social unit' 'is the household' within which 'roles are precisely and clearly defined into a pattern of ... individual subordination to the group' (Khan, 1977: 60-61; see also Dahya on this point, [1974: 82]). The household and even the wider tribal clan is assumed to be an undifferentiated entity with a single collective voice:

> The decision to emigrate is made by family and kin ... The head of the household, or of the immediate *biraderi* grouping selects the emigrant and makes the preparations. The joint decision reinforces the ties with kin and community, thus cementing feelings of affection and determination. The migrant knows he has support (Khan 1977: 70).

What these accounts share is a tendency to conflate household *izzat* with material wealth and treat it as a collectively owned commodity in which all members have an equal stake. They reflect, in other words, the widespread axiom in much social science research on migration that 'the household is an unproblematic unit that allocates time and labour, pools income and distributes it fairly evenly among its members' (Fontaine and Schlumbohm 2000: 3). This tendency requires correction by examination of the strategies of individuals both 'within households' (Ibid: 5), as well as processes that occur *outside* them as I demonstrate below. It also requires that we broaden and complicate our understanding of honour and social standing which, as the testimonies in this book reveal, cannot be reduced to the acquisition of capital and land, as it implicitly is in some of the above-cited early accounts. As I show in Chapter 1, we would do well do question which members of the household experience what kinds of deprivation, and in what contexts? Whose self-esteem does migration serve to boost?

Seldom in any of these accounts of the migration process is the *quality* of the information passed through network ties examined in sufficient historical, sociological or ethnographic detail. Rarely are the objectives of actors who transmit knowledge and facilitate migration rigorously interrogated. Analysis, rather, is often conducted as if the multiple motivations of the very actors who compose a given network – and the enormous complexity of their interactions as social beings – can somehow be treated as an irrelevance.

The problem with this kind of mechanical exposition of network theory, replete as it with unexamined assumptions about rationality, is not specific to works that deal with migration, and indeed has been highlighted by critics working within the wider disciplines of history and historical sociology such as Emirbayer and Goodwin who argued as early as 1994 (1413), in a ground-breaking intervention, that network analysis

> all too often denies in practice the crucial notion that structure, culture and human agency presuppose one another; it either neglects or inadequately conceptualises the crucial dimension of subjective meaning and motivation – including the *normative commitments* [their italics] of actors – and thereby fails to show exactly how it is that intentional, creative human action serves in part to constitute those very networks that so powerfully constrain actors in turn… [It therefore provides] no more than a description of social reality… [and fails] to grasp in concepts the dynamic processes that shape reality over time.

Migrants' recourse to networks is hardly in itself proof that they are the force behind migration. Excessive stress on ties *between* migrants on the move can lead to a neglect of the very agential forces and motivation that actually drive the movement itself. Indeed, networks may facilitate migration but it is people who migrate. A full understanding of the migration process cannot afford to ignore the interiority of the very subjects who make up the network.

Nor can it do without attending to relations of power. Network theory in all its manifestations discussed above tends to be premised on an assumption that social ties and associations between ethnic and national groups form a 'natural' source of social capital (Dahinden 2005: 205) – that social networks are benign and rational in intention and consequence and hence *necessarily* reduce the costs of migration. In a typical exposition of network theory, Levitt, for instance asserts that the 'risks and costs for subsequent migrants are lower because there is a group of experts already in the receiving country to greet newcomers and serve as their guides. Because these well established migrants help new arrivals find jobs and housing', networks invariably 'increase migration's economic returns' (2001: 8).

Foner reels off the same reasoning: 'Network connections lower the costs, raise the benefits, and reduce the risks of migration'. She goes on: 'by allocating most immigration along family lines, US immigration law *reinforces* and formalises the operation of migrant networks' (2001: 3-4 [my italics]). This last assertion – that state control *reinforces* the importance of migration networks (taken to mean cost-cutting strong bonds) is also made by Arango when he presumes that 'the capital role that networks have usually played in migration flows is usually enhanced nowadays in a world in which circulation is widely restricted … the importance of social networks is bound to increase as entry into receiving countries becomes more difficult, on account of their capacity to reduce the costs and risks of moving' (Arango 2004: 28).

In truth social networks operate under various sorts of constraints. They have complex and ambivalent effects that must be contextually unpacked. Others have argued this in disciplines such as development studies, where a growing fatigue with the somewhat simplistic and naïve aspects of 'social capitalism' has been articulated from various quarters. Critics have pointed out that the prevailing view rather misses the point that networks are shaped by the institutional practices and values embedded within them – their linkages to society and state (Meagher 2005: 224-5). They are structured by political and economic contexts – above all borders and the macro economic forces that shape national and local labour markets. Many of the most important questions surround the specific character of ties within given networks, and the manner in which networks create processes of social exclusion and class formation (Blokland and Savage 2001: 221-6). Accepting this argument means treating the migration process as one that is embedded in capitalist social relations and configurations of power. 'Networks do not necessarily fuse the self-interest of different actors into a harmonious and egalitarian whole; they may be characterised by inequalities of power, strategic coalitions … and opportunistic collaboration … power asymmetries as well as a sense of moral obligation. What appears to indicate trust may be largely a consequence of domination or lack of alternatives, or simple mutual dependency (Sayer 2001: 699).

Take, for instance, the inequalities that exist within ethnic economies – seldom analysed in new theories of migration as labour markets – in which there is a labour process and changing labour regimes. Now it may be true that orthodox marxism's tendency to reduce all history to a dualistic struggle between capitalist and worker (Knights and Wilmott 1990) is of limited use in analysing the situation of service sector immigrant workers today, for whom the very idea of industrial 'relations *of* production' (between worker and capitalist) have little meaning. To foreground ethnicity, however, is hardly likely to yield a more accurate portrait of ground realities. A better approach would surely be to rethink class through and in relation to the ethnic economy, making use, perhaps, of Burawoy's relations *in* production (1985: 13). These refer to relationships between workers with one another and their employers in the labour process, and allow for an understanding of the boundaries between workers and capitalists in small businesses that, no matter how contingent, fluid and permeable, continue to exist in any capitalist labour process (Part IV).

Transnationalism and its discontents

Although it is not always stated explicitly, the upbeat tone of recent literature on migration inspired by the new theories described above is an important general feature. Despite its preference for the study of networks over individual subjectivity and agency, transnationalism tends to represent new labour diasporas as an example of the ways in which migrants from the global South have been able to overcome structural barriers such as national-state boundaries to shape the world economy in important ways. Several well-known scholars have posited transnational migration as a rebellion against global capital and the state. Portes has been fairly unambiguous about what he sees as the 'success' of transnational migrant initiatives, which supposedly 'stand as a tribute to human ingenuity and create a partial counter to the hegemony of international and multinational actors on the world stage (Portes 2001: 191-2). In this same vein, Roger Ballard has described transnational Mirpuri social networks as 'successful in subverting one of the principle instruments whereby global structures of inequality are sustained in the post-imperial world: immigration control' (Ballard, R. 2002: 24).

The impact of new theories of migration has thus been to inject a note of optimism into discussions of migration and development studies which have become popular for restoring the importance of collective agency in fields of study that have traditionally been overshadowed by gloomy accounts of the constraints imposed by structures. All this is very much in line with the political climate of the 1990s, when international fiscal, financial and developmental agencies and organisations became increasingly interested in the transformative power of international labour migration in sending societies. Having attracted the interest of institutions such as the World Bank as a potential alternative to western foreign aid, remittances have been hailed by mainstream magazines such *Newsweek* (e.g. cover story by Johnson and Contreras 2004: 38-40) and newspapers including *The New York Times* (e.g. DeParle's 2010, republished in *The Observer*). Parallel and interrelated trends at the opposite end of the ideological spectrum include Hardt and Negri's (2000) keen celebration of the supposedly transgressive political potential of undocumented migration as a trope for anti-systemic radicalism in cutting-edge social theory; in cultural studies, the preoccupation with (and celebration of) 'hybridity' and 'metissage' (Ahmad 2001).

Despite their diverse disciplinary roots and political orientations, each of these sets of arguments might reasonably be lumped together under what Anthony Messina (1996: 130-54) has termed the 'loss of control' thesis: a belief that unbridled or at least expansive in-migration, despite restrictionist policies in the contemporary West, is a reflection (and determinant) of the supposed erosion of the powers of the nation-state. This kind of argument, he asserts, envelops the whole field of political science on immigration and citizenship in Western Europe. Following Gary Freeman and other cited authors, he points out that, curiously, 'few scholarly works supply much hard evidence that the capacity of West European states to control unwanted immigration has significantly waned' (Ibid: 140-1), with authors opting, instead, for 'hyperbole and exaggeration' (Ibid: 152).

Levitt et al. (2003: 598), to their credit, concede that 'much of transnational studies … is conceptually blind to those areas where no transnational communities form amongst migrants'. By the admission of its own adherents, where there is no transnationalism, the paradigm is of little use.

Just how important is it, then?

Portes himself seems to have conceded considerable ground in a telling but damaging admission that the paradigm emerged on the basis of research that 'sampled on the variable': the new theoretical lens of transnationalism 'is grounded on the activities of only a minority of the population' (2003: 876-7). This last statement, which explicitly posits transnational migrants as an elite minority, goes further than Vertovec has been willing to with his rather more guarded concession: 'not all migrants develop transnational practices, and many do so in one sphere of their lives' (2004: 5). Levitt et al. appear to fudge the issue by using the term, 'not all', which could be fewer or more than Portes' 'minority': 'Not all migrants are engaged in transnationalism practices and those that do, do so with considerable variation in the sectors, levels, strength and formality of their involvement' (2003: 569).

The discrepancy in these accounts lays bare the fundamental ambiguity of transnationalism's claims. Proponents of the concept seem to be well aware, on one hand, of the 'danger of ignoring the majority of migrants who cannot be described as transnational' (Al-Ali and Koser 2001: 14). Yet despite such admissions and awareness about the first wave of studies, including an acknowledgement of its 'technological determinism' (Wimmer and Glick Schiller 2003: 596), its leading scholars cannot appear to let go of the questionable twin claims that lie at the heart of their framework: firstly, that the paradigm they have developed offers the most appropriate way of framing international migration today; secondly, that transnationalism is a reflection of new communications technology and therefore takes new, specific, intense forms under contemporary globalisation. Landolt's (2001: 220) emphasis on the 'growing tendency among migration populations to avail themselves of space-time compressing technologies' which 'exhibit an expansion in the realm of what is possible' and 'the scope of who is doing it' is but one example of the continuing hold of the latter of these two ideas, despite it being disowned in the very same collection of essays that his article appears in! Approvingly, Vertovec cites Brettell (2000: 104) in a passage that underlines his adherence to both grand claims:

> As a theoretical construct about immigrant life and identity, transnationalism aptly suits the study of population movements in a world where improved modes of transportation as well as images are transmitted by means of modern

telecommunications which have shortened the social distance between sending and receiving countries (Wimmer and Glick Schiller 2003: 642).

The first wave of studies on transnationalism's lack of attentiveness to the ways in which migrants' ability to engage in transnational activities is varied and conditioned by all manner of restrictions and political and institutional contexts has been recognised by Glick Schiller, Portes, Vertovec et al., each of whom has admitted that the earliest studies of transnationalism and migration networks underestimated the role of the state. It has now become customary to concede that although 'earlier research in this area ... speculated that state sovereignty had diminished' it is now clear that 'states continue to exert a strong influence on transnational migration'; that 'state policies still matter'; 'the state is here to stay' (Levitt et al. 2003: 568). Some of the best more recent studies asks a more set of nuanced set of questions about who benefits from transnational migration, under what circumstances and why. Transnationalists now understand that 'long standing patterns of privilege and access do not disappear merely because they are recreated across borders', with Levitt's work (2001: 13) in particular showing how it recreates gender and class inequalities and creates new frictions between parents and children. Smith (2002: viii) prefaces an important edited collection on transnationalism with the sanguine note that, rather than pleasurable 'hybrid subjectivity', migrancy can just as easily be experienced as tension and pain, uneasiness; as being 'neither here nor there'.

Upon close inspection, however, transnationalism's ongoing alignment to the loss of control thesis remains powerfully evident, and is most visible where it draws equivalences between movements of capital and people, as if the laws which govern each are somehow the same. 'Not only corporations but common people' too, Portes tells us, 'can now cross borders in large numbers and with great flexibility' (Portes 2001: 191-2). Landolt (2001: 220) makes a similar claim, invoking Harvey's (2001) general analysis of new technologies and capital flows under contemporary globalisation, when she explains that transnationalism is down to the 'growing tendency among migration populations to avail themselves of space-time compressing technologies'. Citing authors such Keohane and Nye (1971), Rosenau (1980) and Held et al. (1999) who have written on transnationalism and globalisation in relation to capital flows, business, NGOs, private individuals and tourists, Vertovec makes a similar conflation, melting factors of production, technologies and all manner of networks together in a generalised account of 'improved transportation and telecommunications' that have 'enhanced the extent, velocity and impact of other modes of global interconnectedness' (Vertovec 2003: 642-5). In the same volume, Guarnizo claims that transnationalism, as it stands, 'underestimates migrants' agency and their influence at the global level'. Pointing to the role of corporations in profiting from remittances, he impels us to study this as a case of 'capital following the lead of labour (rather than the other way around)'; as an example of the way in which 'migrants' transnational engagement has significant influence... on global macro-economic processes, including international financial arrangements, international trade etc.' (Guarnizo 2003: 667). The fact that corporations now control the remittance market is thus taken as an index of migrant agency. The following statement sums up the ambiguity of his overall position: 'migrants are still unaware of their tremendous economic power (or at least are unable to make use of it)' (Ibid: 688-9).

The trouble with this desire to represent migrants as highly influential players in the world system, empowered (with a power they are 'unable to make use of') is that, at bottom, it stems from a desire to avoid talking about what migrants spend most of their waking hours doing. *Work*.

The labour process has no place whatsoever in the theoretical framework espoused by transnationalism. Surveying the literature as a whole, the unmistakeable absence of discussions of employment would seem to imply that migrants have little interest in anything but forging all-important ties between sending and receiving societies. Indeed, 'transnational living' is described by Guarnizo as a kind of life-style choice that stems from 'migrants' drive to reproduce their social milieu from afar' (Ibid 2003: 667); by Levitt (2001: 5) as a consequence of the fact that 'They do not shift their participatory energies from one country to another ... they remain connected to the country they leave behind.' It is this general assumption that migrants themselves prioritise transnationalism that allows its authors to present it as of greater importance than the labour process.

Where new theories of migration do make fleeting theoretical reflections on the role of the labour process, they are generally so wide of the mark that one begins to understand how profoundly they misconstrue key aspects of the migrant experience today. Levitt et al. (2003: 569) claim that 'more uncertain labour market demand and employment encourage the maintenance of ties to resources back home'. My own data on transnationalism, which there is not space to present in this book, would seem to suggest the very opposite: long settled old migrants in the UK who enjoyed more secure employment were able, on the basis of their relative prosperity, to invest in entrepreneurial activities, travel and the purchase of property in Pakistan. Is this really that surprising? Surely only very well-established migrants are likely to be able to take advantage of 'cheap air travel' (a relative concept if ever there was one – at six hundred pounds, a flight to Pakistan is hardly cheap for someone earning three pounds an hour).

The new migrants I encountered were far too busy scraping by to construct sustained social ties with the homeland. They had neither the time, nor the money (nor the legal right in many cases) to travel. Contrary to Levitt's portrayal of archetypal international migrants, they had indeed shifted their 'participatory energies' from Pakistan to London, Italy (and France and Germany and elsewhere) where they were desperate to establish themselves. They worked long hours and were preoccupied with their current lives abroad rather than 'recreating their social milieu from afar'. It is difficult to reconcile their testimonies with the following passage, which reflects the full extent of transnationalism's misrepresentation of the new migrant experience. My italics highlight the causal relationship between precarity and the maintenance of ties to the homeland posited by the author:

> *Because* contemporary migrants are often incorporated insecurely into the labour market, *it is easier for them to maintain a transnational lifestyle than workers with steady employment.* Because their jobs pay less and provide fewer benefits than blue-collar jobs of the past, poor migrants today face more limited prospects, a condition that *may encourage* long-term transnational ties (Levitt 2001: 26).

This dubious argument – the reverse of which seems more likely to be true – is presented as self-evident, and accompanied by the equally unlikely claim that today's high levels of transnationalism are reflective of 'greater cultural tolerance' and higher levels of 'diversity' now accepted in Western societies (Levitt et al. 2003: 569). The two assertions would seem to be difficult to reconcile. Is the growing insecurity migrants face – in large part a consequence of their continued exclusion from the primary labour market, stiffening legal entry rights and the growing criminalisation of illegal work – really likely to reflect greater tolerance? Few Pakistanis, or indeed other commentators speak of the US as a more tolerant place than it was in the 1980s (Gerstle 2003: 31-8; Paden and Singer 2003: 8-14). Levitt herself regards these claims as doubly applicable to the European context (without presenting any evidence): 'The social and political context of the new European Union is *particularly* favourable to long-term home and host country attachments' (Levitt 2001: 16).

The point is not to suppress discussion of cross-border social and commercial networks and exchanges. Quite the opposite: of the migrants I encountered, I learned that much of their energies are spent negotiating ties and networks that bind two or more locations in the global North, a fact which illustrates that the transnationalism paradigm's privileging of one kind of cross-border network – ties between migrants and their homelands – effectively obscures many of the most important actually existing transnational networks and processes that take place in contemporary migration. These do not necessarily involve a singular, sustained connection between the sending and receiving society.

For all their rhetoric of novelty, virtually all of the scholars mentioned above speak of transnationalism (and study it empirically) in a rather old fashioned way, as if it must consist exclusively of a connective circularity between two discrete locations (Caglar 2001: 607; Vertovec 2004: 3). Meanwhile, the whole question of transnational transit, which I discuss in Part III, is completely ignored. Guarnizo (2003: 668) makes a rare reference to the need to study North-North/South-South connections, though his advice remains unheeded by a paradigm fixated upon the binary relation between two rigidly conceived nation-states; a reification that reinforces the very 'theoretical nationalism' (Wimmer and Glick Schiller 2003: 576-7) it claims to have overcome. Existing approaches to migration stand accused naturalising the global regime of nation-states and unwittingly endorsing reactionary assumptions about the normal process of assimilation by which immigrants are expected to shed their pasts and ties with home (Wimmer and Glick Schiller 2003: 576). Yet transnationalism merely inverts this logic, fetishising migrants' ties with home in a manner that undermines their preoccupation with employment and residency elsewhere.

In reality, what is required is a framework which understands that labour migration forges global pathways and global landscapes that criss-cross each other, centred in quite different parts of the world, and which understands that these are hierarchically ordered (Werbner 1999: 19, 23). The insight, advanced by Levitt as if earth-shattering news, that 'migrants social and economic lives are not bounded by national borders' (Ibid 2001: 5) is true but banal, and adds little to our understanding of world migration that we do not already know from studies of migration that take *migration systems* as their starting point. The latter – defined as geo-spatial formations formed over time, connecting movements of people to concomitant flows of goods, capital and information sustained and reinforced by social, political and institutional networks and relationships which make possible and encourage migration along certain paths and not others (Kritz et al. 1992) – allow us to study all of the ties that transnationalism claims to have discovered along with many others too.

Most of the authors I draw upon in this book are less fashionable than they are astute. Some argue, conversely to the current orthodoxy, that international migration is in fact very limited when viewed within the context of the world's population and against a backdrop of other indicators of globalisation such as trade, finance and capital flows (Sutcliffe 2004: 264). Indeed, a balanced assessment of world history questions seriously whether it can be claimed that migration in proportionate terms is now significantly greater than it was at the beginning of the 20th century. Comparing volume alone, in any case, 'is meaningless if we do not understand the broad patterns and distinctions that shape migration, and have been used to ... control migration' (McKeown 2004: 184-5).

Nowhere is the lack of attention to power, institutional constraints and capitalist social relations in migration sociology of the 1990s more clearly reflected than in the absence of sustained engagement of by transnationalists with the question of irregular migration, which despite its growing importance throughout the decade, was left relatively unstudied. This is no coincidence, of course: the realities of borders raise serious questions about the viability of transnationalism as a way of life for the many thousands of migrants from the global South who enter and/or reside and/or work in rich countries without legal authorisation, and potentially renders the insights of its theorists less important than they might otherwise appear to be. The latter parts of this book are precisely about the consequences that unprecedented levels of restrictionism have had and are having for new migrants, increasing numbers of whom in Europe are in fact losing the battle with borders to control their lives in a global political and institutional context quite different to the one encountered by migrants of old.

Psychoanalysis, marxism and base materiality: A framework for the study of smuggling and migration

Gender, masculinity and the household

For most of the 20th century, the importance of gender in households, networks and institutions in studies of migration was largely overlooked by academics in all disciplines (Phizacklea 2004). The same was true of the spatial configurations they produce – migration *systems* (Kritz et al. 1992) – until feminist interventions brought about a significant redress to the imbalanced sexual distribution of academic literature with a flurry of work on the feminisation of migration (Yinger 2006). The importance of this now substantial literature as a corrective to the masculinist blindspots of early migration studies cannot be underestimated.

However, critics have pointed out that studying the gendered dynamics of migration has too often meant studying women in isolation rather analysing the processes which produce and reflect the social and power relations between and among men and women (Phizacklea 1988; Pettman 1996; Pessar and Mahler 2003: 812-46; Ryan and Webster 2008: 4). The sudden proliferation of conferences, edited collections and published research on gender and migration in the latter part of the last decade has begun to address this shortcoming in existing work, but there remains a scarcity of empirical literature dealing with the construction and experience of masculinity in the migration process (important exceptions include Charsley 2005: 85-105; Keeler 2008).

Overlooking masculinity is especially problematic in cases where independent migration is the exclusive preserve of men. Pakistan is a case in point: despite the strikingly imbalanced sexual division of migratory movement, the role of gender in driving it has been ignored, naturalised and effectively reified in most existing studies, none of which beg the simple question: why is it that women do not migrate independently? Or to reverse the question, how do we explain the fact that only men migrate independently?

If the study of masculinity remains somewhat neglected within migration studies, a voluminous body of work on men and men's history has accumulated since feminist interventions in mainstream history exposed the fraudulence of most history-writing's claims to universality in the mid-1980s, establishing the study of masculinity as central to the feminist project (Ditz 2004: 1-35). Extrapolating from the insights of this work as a basis to study international migration is not, of course, without its problems. For one thing, of those masculinities that have received attention – migrants and especially Third World men of Muslim origin – seldom feature at all (a state of affairs that mirrors the early development of feminist women's history, which has been extensively critiqued for its Eurocentrism (Brah 1996; Afshar and Maynard 2000: 805-19).

Indeed, any such extrapolation of the concept of masculinity from this body of work must take into account the specific set of problems that position non-Western male migrants as economically and politically marginalised and racialised subjects, as well as beneficiaries and perpetrators of structural domination over women. It must, in other words, be socially located: informed by the complex geometries of global power relations that organise human subjects hierarchically along multiple axes of difference. Sensitivity to the complex and often contradictory social positions occupied by men of the global South – what Avtar Brah (1996) has termed the politics of intersectionality – is particularly important in thinking about international labour migrants. Whilst the latter often experience systematic exploitation and discrimination in host countries, their frequently elevated status in communities of origin often places them in positions of power over women *and* men who stay put.

The relation of the individual migrant to the household is at the heart of these contradictory intersections; unfortunately, the relevant literatures are of limited help in understanding its complexity. Proponents of 'social choice theory' and the 'new household economics' propounded by Becker (1976) take households (interchangeably with families) to be unitary collectives of individuals whose interests are tied together rationally by a 'benevolent despotism'. This orthodox conception of the household, which grants the migrant no individual interest beyond that of working for the material betterment of all its members, was first challenged by espousers of 'game theory', who looked at intra-household conflict and the family as sites of 'bargaining' between individuals from the 1980s (see Agarwal [1997: 3-4] for a discussion) and then more fundamentally in the writings of Sen (1985, 1990), whose sustained critique of the foundational notions of rationality within mainstream economics problematised conventional notions of the household as an aggregation of individual preferences (Agarwal et al. 2005: 4-5).

The power of Sen's argument lay in his insistence on comprehending agency in relation to a given actor's subjective 'aims, objectives, allegiances, obligations and – in a broad sense, the person's conception of the good' (Sen 1985: 203). This was based on his appreciation of the role of social norms and experience in shaping motivations, wants and outcomes, which are in turn premised upon marketised notions of value that distort the perceived contribution of women's labour (Sen 1990; Agarwal 1997: 11). As Peter (2005: 21) explains, Sen rejects the exclusive focus of conventional economists on objectively calculated measures of well-being as the sole objectives of actors, defining agency instead as the ability to set and pursue one's own goals and interests, of which pursuit of well-being may be only one. Sen's insights have been incorporated by feminist theorists of the household, and thus far have focused primarily on their implications for viewing women's agency in the context of specific social conditions and perceptions (Peter 2005: 15-34). Yet they could equally apply to making sense of male motivations, behaviours and agencies which are equally shaped by context and subjectivity.

Take risk

Defined by Ulrich Beck (1992, 2000) as *uncertainty* rather than actual 'damages incurred', risk, according to Beck, assumes new importance under conditions of late modernity; a kind of 'peculiar intermediate state between security and destruction' which is ever more pervasive as a governing concept of thought and action. Risk's meaning, that is to say, is increasingly manufactured in subjective ways and thus 'fictitious' (2000: 16), the world we live in as a result 'artificial' (Ibid: 221). Geeta Patel makes a related argument about insurance which belongs to the same 'subjective objective' realm occupied by risk: indemnity policies may be premised on mathematically calculated probabilities but their meaning for those who purchase them is reflective of fantasies and speculations anchored in the imaginative. They are, after all, protection of possessions and capital that may or may not be accumulated at some future point in time against losses that may or may not occur (Patel 2007: 101, 104).

The notion of risk as socially constructed has particular salience in thinking about irregular international labour migration which, in the context of restrictive state policies, is increasingly expensive, perilous and sometimes catastrophically disastrous for the individuals who decide to migrate. Migration scholars have tended to assume their subjects are driven by objective, rational, utilitarian calculations oriented towards security and betterment of the household. Sen, Beck and Patel's insights compel us to look more closely at the cultural, subjective perception of risk in migrant-sending contexts – places such as Pakistan in which unequal increases in wealth, technological change and the deepening hold of consumer culture have altered social aspirations and eroded traditional notions of what constitutes a good life. How are these perceptions bound up with culture, imagination, ideology?

Psychoanalysis

Until recently, academic research on human mobility has resisted the insights of psychoanalysis (King and Mai 2009). Migration studies protagonists have tended to be cogent, conscious, Cartesian selves and households: pushed, pulled and motivated by clearly identifiable economic forces and calcualtions, they migrate therefore they are. This is quite the opposite of Freud's portrait of humanity: a desirous, deeply confused species of sexual beings unwittingly engaged in the relentless pursuit of unhappiness. The Self in psychoanalysis is unstable and incomplete, the ego truncated at the point of its formation by a foundational act of sexual repression in childhood: a process of demarcation from exteriority that entails severance from a limitless 'oceanic' feeling of being bound up with world outside oneself (Freud 2007 [1930]: 4-5). This originary break between subject and object produces alienation in the former. Repressed memories of a blissfully fulsome state which existed prior to the establishment of selfhood haunt adult lives spent yearning unconsciously for its recuperation. It remains elusive thanks to the imposition of an endless array of other boundary formations – civilisational taboos that discipline sexual behaviour and temper individuals' claims to pleasure: we trade happiness for security, leaving us unsatisfied and generating powerful currents of attraction towards objects which promise return to the moment of Oneness before separation between self and object (Freud 2007 [1930]: 15). Invisible but ever-present, this is the 'pleasure principle': not an outcome, but a force of desire – for people, things and imagined pleasurable states, the achievability or obtainable extent of which is usually doubtful.

Desire makes bad decisions. Its source, along with its most important consequences, lie not in its objects but in its foolish subjects. The invariable overestimation of the former by the latter, and the utter desolation felt when desired targets prove elusive (not to mention the emptiness where they do not) connect psychoanalysis with older conversations about love. Since Plato, writers, poets and philosophers such as the Muslim polymath Avicenna have debated the nature of different kinds of love, and noted the variously elevating, maddening and disturbing effects these can have on the 'sufferer'. 'Unrequited love' commonly appears in ancient and medieval literatures as a kind of incurable sickness that can even bring physical changes in the body, most famously in English by Chaucer's Franklyn in the *Canterbury Tales*. Freud's observations about love as a form of self-inflicted misery, the point is, have important antecedents, giving psychoanalytic desire a universal relevance.

More precisely, what exactly is desire?

The question misses the point: the absence of any concise, satisfactory definition is in many ways appropriate, since desire is constituted by what it does. Desire drives. As Lacan and his followers are at pains to emphasise, Freud's notion of desire is visible only in its effects. Not a thing but a force of impulse that manifests sexual needs and wants, the sating of which is impossible since satisfaction is fundamentally unsatisfying to desire, its point is not to achieve some happy ending in which tender contentment is reached but rather to reproduce itself as desire.

This goes some considerable way to explaining the pessimism of 'Civilization and its discontents' (2007 [1930]), in which Freud warns against conceiving of humans 'gentle creatures' in search of actual love as an outcome: desire is driven as much by natural hostility and murderous intent towards our fellow man as it is by love (55-61). This is the death drive, which reflects humanity's will to destroy. Whether its effects are outwardly (sadistically) or inwardly (masochistically) directed depends on the extent to which civilisation, acting as conscience, manages to divert its orientations and energies into self-loathing guilt through the imposition of behavioural restrictions (Ibid: 61).

Thanatos (a term Freud himself does not use in this essay but which nevertheless has come to stand for the death drive) rules the world jointly with Eros, impulses that respectively produce aggression and love in dialectical tensions that mirror, to some extent, the conflictual relationship between the pleasure principle and the 'reality principle' (the latter holds gratification in check in the interests of our own and other people's safety). However, an important caveat complicates these dialectics, which are not simply parallel and conflicting, but intertwined and overlapping. The drives seldom 'appear in isolation' and tend to manifest themselves in complex alloys and conflations of desire (Ibid: 54-5). The confused nature of our resulting hybrid yearnings is compounded by civilisation's externally imposed sexual prohibitions which cause human subjects to pursue the wrong targets: objects we think we want and love are often fetishes – substitutes for things we (don't know we) actually want. Hence Freud's conception of sublimation – a way of denoting the process by which repressed desire finds displaced forms, and the 'possessive', 'proprietorial' sentiments associated with 'cathexis': investment of sublimated libidinal energies in things and people. The upshot is a counter-intuitive tautology: Thanatos equals Eros; love *is* aggressivity in that it represents our will to kill in sublimated form.

Against the rational optimism of economics, then, psychoanalysis is profoundly pessimistic about the human condition: what hope of happiness for a species prone to chasing chimeras, the attainment of which would anyway be unsatisfying? Life, according to Freud's haunted ontology of loss, is a miserable and alienated affair spent howling unconsciously for an impossible recuperation of a long lost connectivity we aren't actually aware of. A kind of amputated limb we never knew we had, and that no longer exists. The bleakness of our predicament is most apparent in sublimation: the ways we pursue worldly success and other inadequate substitutes for this impossible return to some remote condition, the memory of which is implanted within the depths of our being but cannot be consciously thought (Bollas 1987).

For a while after Freud's death, some relatively optimistic currents of ego psychology and its postulated cures enjoyed prominence but these were soon challenged by Lacan's restatement of Freud's vision, an even bleaker portrait of the troubled relationship between the Self and its desired objects. If classical psychoanalysis made clear the particular configurations of desire produced by the drives are unknown to us, Lacan went further, arguing 'us' is itself an unstable product of the objects we desire: the unconscious itself is structured by language; selves and others relate through a 'dialectic of inter-subjectivity' (Lacan 2002 [1977]: 40). Ruling out conventional notions of healing and recovery, he contested the existence of knowable subjects and with it shattered the possibility of return to some authentic, comforting truthful sense of identity prior to the individual's immersion in discourse.

Lacan's argument rested on the way bodily personhood is first experienced when a child begins to (mis)recognise itself as a being through its reflection, confirmed by the presence of the mother. The 'Mirror Stage' (Ibid: 79), in which 'the specular 'I' becomes the social 'I' through a 'dialectic linking socially elaborated situations', gave psychoanalysis a social significance and wider applicability. By inserting 'other people' (the mother) into Freud's account of subject-formation, it explained how identity and meaning are produced in a 'triadic' space of 'specular communion' linking subject, object and social context (Ibid: 92). The latter, termed the realm of the 'Symbolic', mediates the way in which the subconscious ('Imaginary') relates to materiality (the 'Real'). Desire, it follows, is subject to the machinations of language and culture (the 'radical defile of speech' [Ibid: 40]).

Lacan's novel emphasis on the erotic dimensions of looking – the way individuals fixate on images (Ibid: 92) – as a means of identification also represented an important advance. Drawing upon the 'informational function' of images in Freud's writings, where they figure time and again in discussions of memory and intuition (Ibid: 71), he conceptualises a Symbolic order that encompasses and highlights the importance of visual discourse. The Self's encounter with it is the key to understanding how we apprehend, are attracted by and assimilate the Real through specular inscriptions of difference – an insight that has been keenly embraced by students of cultural representation (Hall 1997: 237, 266-8, 317-8) and above all, scholars of cinema, who have found it invaluable for thinking about the intensely voyeuristic way desire functions in cultural settings (Mulvey 1975).

A vast literature on the uses of psychoanalysis in interpreting colonial discourse and western racism pioneered by scholars such as Bhabha (1994), Mercer (1994) McClintock (1995) and Sehshadri-Crooks (2004) takes its cue from this idea of desire as a form of voyeurism: post-colonial theory draws attention to the way in which 'the white gaze' objectifies and fetishises non-whiteness through the projection of eroticised tropes of sexual difference. They wed Lacan's ideas on specularity to older Freudian concepts of experiencing selfhood through seeing and wanting: 'scopophilia', 'object cathexis', 'projection', and above all, *fetishism* – desirous 'looking' that invests objects with libidinal energies.

This literature will be of some interest to the arguments developed in Part II. The remainder of this book is less about subjective perception than it is about experience and affect grounded in materiality. For this reason, the framework advanced here relies as much on materialist traditions of psychoanalysis as those associated with cultural and literary studies. To these we now turn in a discussion of Marxism and its entanglements with the writings of Freud and Lacan which have been adapted, deployed and integrated into critiques of capitalism that are especially useful for thinking about borders, labour and international migration in the contemporary epoch.

Marxism

Prior to interest from cultural and cinema studies, it was the French philosopher and theorist Louis Althusser who, in an important innovation, first incorporated psychoanalysis full-scale into his study of class, institutions and ideology in the 1970s. It was by no means an obvious solution to Marxism's theoretical impasse at the time: Freud's dismissive treatment of social context and silence on divisions of labour remains indisputable. His reduction of economic activity to a sublimate of repressed sexual drives is directly at odds with Marx's belief that work is the fundamental expression of human creativity and nature (For a discussion see Wolfenstein [1993: 35-6, 43-4]). Marx, for his part, had always been read in reductive ways arguably traceable to moments of rigidity in his own thinking. Still, the impetus for dialogue came from within the Marxian tradition, which had at least attached a minimal degree of importance to human perception. The 'mystical', 'mysterious' character of commodities as they are described in Volume I of *Das Capital* (1994 [1867]: 26-7), for instance, suggests material objects can have 'qualities' that are imperceptible by the senses', an insight that brings imagination, fantasy and cultural representation into play.

Drawing inspiration from Freud and Lacan, Althusser argued ideology 'has little to do with consciousness' and is in fact 'profoundly unconscious' – that it consists of 'the imaginary relationship of individuals to their real conditions of existence'. Class positions, he explained, are 'interpolated' subjectively. The term 'subjectivity' thus entered Cultural Studies to link psychic interiority directly with social context, a considerable break from the truth-claims of Marxist orthodoxy at that time (Althusser 1994 [1970]: 88-9, 101). The exchange was two-way: marxism served as a corrective to the reductionism of psychoanalysis which, for its part, had tended towards exclusive focus on the family in the formation of the unconscious. Freud's analysis of isolated bourgeois individuals in interwar Vienna, as Deleuze and Guattari argued as early as 1972 in *Anti-Oedipus*, ignores the social and economic production of desire (For a discussion see Barrett 1991: 117).

Althusser's intervention also raised the question of context and its implications for the way in which 'historical variation in kinship and ideology might materially affect some or other aspect' of the theories delineated by Freud and Lacan (Althusser 1969: 64). In questioning the universality of particular aspects of psychoanalysis, his insights compel reflection on how its main concepts can be extrapolated and put to use within non-Western contexts. In India, debates about cross-cultural psycho-civilisational differences between the western and Indian 'Self' have a long history (Kakar 1978). Far from neutralising the validity of psychoanalysis in non-Western contexts, the existence of such differences or rather, specificities, adds credence to the fundamental insight of psychoanalysis that 'heterosexual object-choice' and the 'fantasies' of 'man' and 'woman' on which these choices rest need to be explained rather than assumed (Rose 2000: 53).

Unfortunately, much psychoanalytic criticism has been characterised by a certain insouciance when confronted with unfamiliar terrain exemplified, for instance, in Susan Sontag's throwaway parenthetic remarks on 'the Orient or Moslem world' (undefined, of course), which she asserts somewhat sweepingly, without explaining why or how, has an imagination that is 'very different' (Sontag 2001 [1967]: 115). Freud's own interesting but brief reflections on Moses have recently been the subject of in-depth debate about the extent and of the doctor's own biases (Said 2003; Rose 2003). For the most part, attempts to theorise Islam and psychoanalysis have been few and far between (e.g. Khatibi 2009 [1989]). Most are textual analyses of Islamist political subjectivities attempting to address the urgent problem of contemporary fundamentalism's 'terrifying wish for vengeance' (Benslama 2009: 9-10).

Against this backdrop, empirical research on lived experience and everyday sexualities in Muslim contexts make an important contribution, above all by demonstrating that religious influences have always been, and remain just one among many that shape the lives of Muslims in South Asia. The remarks of India's most prominent psychoanalyst (himself originally from Lahore) on this question are unequivocal: 'there is no difference between the home of a Muslim and that of a Hindu, Jew or Christian'; 'the sickness of television' and 'ungodly entertainment' has entered all of them, reflecting and reinforcing modern preoccupations with 'worldly wealth and success' (Kakar 2001: 335).

My preference is to emphasise how bodies across the world are subject to comparable socially and economically determined flows of desire produced and in an increasingly culturally homogenous, deterritorialised global capitalism. Interpolated through television advertising and other kinds of media, its ideology of commodity fetishism imparts similar notions of beauty and value (and hence desire) around the surface of the planet, driving labour to capital – often, in familiar directions, producing the same old equations of surplus extraction. What does cultural difference matter in determining desire when we all want the same things: big houses, fridges, cars and other gadgets? In migrant-sending contexts, the mythical promises made by consumerism outweigh differences in ethnicity and religion, education and generation. And whatever cultural specificities and differences might mark out a 'Pakistani' from a Punjabi Sikh, Moroccan or Pole, subjectivisation takes places in accordance with the imperatives of a singular force (capital) which positions their bodies in time and space, generating similar experiences of commodification throughout the migration process – experiences that are modern and universal aspects of the human condition we all recognise. To the extent that Pakistani migrants' fates are marked by specificities, these relate more to the general condition of Europe's migratory proletariat than any national or cultural designation.

Time, space and the politics of production

Understanding alterations in the structure of temporality have long been seen as crucial in making sense of historical change and the development of human experience in the modern epoch (Adam 2004: 37). Marx wrote extensively of the compression and commodification of time in the labour process in his analysis of the changing length of the working day, patterns of shift work and other developments ushered in with the arrival of industrialism. Implicit throughout his polemic against the subjugation of natural time to abstract, quantifiable clock-time governed by the logic of accumulation, is the assumption that time is historically constructed, and experienced differently throughout the ages (Adam 2004: 38-40).

This premise has informed many classical critical analyses of capitalism's evolution. It is central, for instance, to Georg Lukács' (1971 [1968]: 88-9) account of 'reification' in the transition to capitalism, by which the worker loses contact with the product of his labour through its increasing commodification, his work 'reduced to the mechanical repetition of a set of actions'. Likewise, in a rich empirical study based on ethnographic research conducted in Algeria, the French sociologist Pierre Bourdieu (1979) similarly placed temporality at the heart of his account of agrarian precapitalist Kabyle's evolution into a society governed by modern logics of accumulation. His starting point: all economies are 'tied to a system of dispositions towards time' and above all 'the future' (Ibid: 6-7).

If Marx, Lukács and Bourdieu all addressed, in different ways, the changing quality of human (and particularly proletarian) experience in time and space as a consequence of capitalism's rise, contemporary critical social theorists have turned to the problem of time under post-Fordist 'flexible' labour regimes. The writings of Richard Sennet, which explore the corrosive personal consequences of late capitalism's temporal structure, assert that 'No long term' is the motto of the new 'flexible' economy. Underscoring its incompatibility with linear life narratives in which cumulative achievement brings rewards, Sennet describes the ways in which it gnaws away at all the things that bring meaning to human existence: character and relationships, ethical values like trust and commitment; work as a career rather than a series of fragmentary episodes (1998).

The transition to post-Fordist work patterns are exemplified by the differences in contemporary migration from the old Fordist model in which migrants settled into a job and a single location. Today, ongoing mobility in the migration process – a politically engineered outcome of restrictive regimes that now produce illegality – has reached such an extent that the myth of return has been replaced by a myth of arrival. 'Winner takes all markets' (Frank and Cook 1995) dictate that the few profit whilst the many are left feeling strong currents of pressure to move from one position to another so as not get left behind, an activity which, in the absence of clear vertical career paths, lends itself to 'ambiguously lateral moves' and even perilous gambles (Sennet 1998: 84). Liberal economic approaches to the study of illegal migration tell us 'smuggling pays' (Koser 2008). And yet, even where a migrant is 'successful' – that is, where he reaches his destination and graduates to being an illegally resident worker – he is stripped of rights and entitlements in the labour process. Insecurity becomes a kind of ontological condition (Ahmad 2007). It is no coincidence that 'illegal' migrancy is often seen as the emblem of precarity in critiques of flexibility (Mezzadra 2001; 2004; Moulier-Boutang 1998).

The coining of the term precarity marks an important development in the emergent dialogue between new literatures on migration and class. Although there are few clear, concise definitions in circulation, its significance is generally understood to lie in 'being continually available for work, to regard life outside waged work as a time of preparation for and readiness to work' (Mitropoulos 2005). The implications of this, as one Italian activist has succinctly put it, include 'being unable to plan one's time, being a worker on call where your life and time are determined by external forces'. What concerns workers in an age of precarity, unlike previous epochs, is thus not merely the issue of pay or safer working conditions but control of one's time: the right to plan one's future with a minimum of security and job certainty; the right to the minimum degree of 'predictability' that is necessary 'to build social relations and feelings of affection' (Foti 2004).

This is hardly an entirely unprecedented set of problems, and classical Marxist concepts such as 'commodity fetishism' and 'alienation' provide ample scope for exploring the deeper, subjective and psychological experience of repressed sexual desire within a materialist framework. There is, indeed, a growing appreciation of the ways in which labour regimes structure experiences of intimacy for certain groups in society – love and sexuality's relationship with mobility (see Mai and King 2009). New work linking emotions to the economy is of particular relevance here: thinking of emotions as forms of capital which accumulate over time raises interesting questions about how feelings are produced in relation to bodily circulation across social fields; how they function as fetishes implicated in the erasure of histories of production (Ahmed 2004: 11).

Part IV, which focuses on the labour process, is about making sense of migration's consequences. As in all human experience, this consists of being made to forego satisfaction of the drives and is tied closely with feelings of sinfulness, guilt and a need to punish the self (Freud 2007 [1930]: 61-3). For illegal migrants, however, loss takes acute forms due to specific forms of spatial confinement, downward social mobility and sexual deprivation. The first task, to identify these, is tricky enough. The second is harder still: how to describe the affective consequences that flow from these material realities when they are not always explicitly articulated? Freud's (2005 [1917]) reflections on mourning and melancholia offer clues as to how sadness and depression work themselves out in dreams and behaviours that latently (and in some cases manifestly) convey repressed sexual desires. His notion of melancholia as loss that cannot be mourned is especially useful in making sense of how the political and economic conditions of contemporary capitalism denude self-esteem.

Bataille, experience and base materiality

Migration as an emotional journey – detached from material considerations, social contexts and relations of power – is not the story. A return to the culturalism of postmodern tracts on nomadism that became fashionable in the 1990s (see Ahmad 2001) would be lamentable. What we *are* arguing, rather: the material, emotional, spiritual and psychological realms of migratory experience are not easily or usefully separated; love, sexuality and romantic sentiment should form part of the mainstream economic sociology of labour migration. Migration is about connections between production and reproduction; materiality and fantasy; exterior social conditions and interior psychological processes.

George Bataille can help us. Less a theorist than a thinker, writer and philosopher, his legacy derives from an eclectic body of intellectual work – essays, fiction, empirical researches and highly original reflections on political economy which, despite their variation in form, return time and time again to several key interrelated themes centred on the disavowed extremities of human experience, and the way these are grounded in economies of expenditure and erotic desire. Bataille's starting points are often Freudian, his conclusions gritty materialist extensions of psychoanalysis. His ideas, initially associated with the Surrealist art movement (from which he broke ranks) are rarely situated within the lineages of either psychoanalysis or Marxism, but their incestuous intermingling with both traditions is plain enough (and reflected in his life: Bataille's ex-wife, actress Sylvia, married Jacques Lacan in 1953).

Freud saw civilisation as the disciplining of desire in individuals for the sake of society. Shame, repugnance of genitalia, guilt and other feelings that control and prevent pleasure are discontents produced by the trade-off of 'security for happiness' (Freud 2007 [1930]: 50-51). They are held in place by a series of taboos prescribing acceptable sexual attitudes and behaviour – restrictions generative of sexual want: 'the attraction of whatever is forbidden'. He hints at the way regimes of denial make the satisfaction of wild instinctual and perverse impulses incomparably more intense than the sating of 'tamed' ones (Ibid: 17).

But there little sense in Freud that transgressing prohibitions is especially meaningful, or that it brings anything more than the kind of 'episodic', 'luke warm comfort' associated with other kinds of happiness that ultimately prove disappointing (Ibid: 14-15): transgression in classical psychoanalysis is a kind of cheap thrill that operates like the pleasure principle – a compulsion that promises more than it delivers (In terms of actual happiness, 'only very little results from the condition itself' [Ibid: 15]). Pleasure is an illusion. Love, it follows, nothing more than a projection that seeks to overcome the alienation of Self from object. It may lead to a blurring of the border between them. But never union: a person in love 'asserts that 'I' and 'you' are one and is ready to behave as if this were true.' (Ibid 2007 [1930]: 5). (Notice the insinuation of emotion as fetish: the phrase, 'as if this were true', underlines the ultimate foolishness loving behaviour; the infinite dimensions of the gap it seeks to bridge).

Bataille offers an antidote to the determinism of this pessimism. For although he affirms the irrationality of Freud's love-subject ('there is a sickness in desire that often makes us perceive some gap between the object imagined and the real object' [1997: 94]), there is meaning in the self-inflicted suffering it brings: the sacrificial dimension in 'wanting to die from this love' (Ibid 1997: 96). What psychoanalysis diagnoses as humankind's deepest malaise, Bataille celebrates as the key to unlocking its potential – the capacity to undergo extreme, uncontrolled emotional states. Desire and its suppression might drive and distort behaviour. But what happens when it bubbles over, unbridled? Eruptions of ecstasy, horror, anguish; intoxicated yearnings and agonies, archaic and modern – experiences that materialise the one-dimensional subject shackled in Lacan's linguistic prison.

And what generates these affects?

In a word, risk. There is, Bataille observes, unparalleled joy in overturning ascetic orders held in place by taboos – planks of the repressive, 'restrictive' economies that produce sensible, 'useful' behaviour and tastes. Transgression, in this narrative, involves non-productive activity that can result in catastrophic loss – of wealth, of Self. Carnal love, like Freud's foolish love, involves excess suffering and rendering oneself vulnerable (Ibid 1997: 96). But where Freud saw only misery, Bataille argues that jeopardising the stability of our own identity renders visible the contours of a return to our estranged oneness with alterity. The one meets the other in authentic communion (Direk 2007: 98-100). No cheap thrills, no guarantees of self-preservation. Finally, a bridge to ecstasy, across the gap Freud thought insurmountable.

Eroticism is a materialist account of human sexuality in which death is at the centre. As in psychoanalysis, it is generated by prohibitive disavowals, and heightened with proximity to the border of taboo. Ecstasy lies in reckless transgression, even – indeed especially when danger is involved (Bataille 2001 [1962], 256). Death is the ultimate anathema. Fear of it thus feeds the possibility of life and sexual excitement like nothing else. Sex and death are hence intimately connected, even though the latter 'may appear to be the opposite of a function whose purpose is birth' (Bataille 1997: 242). Just as 'the growth of plants presupposes the amassing of decayed substances', death is the 'source and condition of life' and 'ensures its renewal'. Its 'luxurious truth' is revealed in the way 'spent organisms give way to new ones'. Death is 'the most luxurious form of life' (or to put the other way around: 'life is the luxury of which death is the highest degree' (Ibid: 245-6). Excretions, in psychoanalytic terms, are conjoined (Ibid 1997: 172); eroticism is the sum of these associations, a point made by Bataille's infamous encounter with the divine through the anal orifice of a prostitute, Madam Eduarda, in arguably one of the most profound works of pornographic fiction ever written (his *Story of the Eye*, first published in 1928, is another contender).

Proximity to the unknowable depths of Eduarda's void – an erotic abyss of profanity and death personifying the infiniteness of alterity – brings unimaginable excitement and mystical joy. The implications are more than sexual: that we can be drawn so passionately to risk loss of life in pursuit of experience that takes us to the brink of death upsets theories of rational utility and economic instrumentalism. Bataille's specific contribution to political-economy is thus to theorise the non-utilitarian component of expenditure: a sexual-economy of irrationality; an extended reflection on the substantial elements of our activities that make up the 'accursed share' (Ibid: 240) – the part of us that *must* waste: expend energy in a manner that does not produce value but rather, uses it up in acts of consumption in which 'the accent is placed on loss' (Ibid: 169-72). Eroticism is about the gambler in humankind, whose proneness to anarchic destruction arguably pervades and explains the most dramatic aspects of all history – from the madness of war to the destruction of the environment and risk-taking that led to the 2008 banking crisis – events, processes, behaviours that defy the rational. He dares us to think about perilous forms of risk-taking in ways that complicate orthodox marxism's representation of man's existence as a desperate search for security and material advancement; to confront the perplexing yet undeniable fact that relatively comfortable individuals willingly place themselves in positions of life-threatening insecurity. Human society must have an interest in catastrophic loss: our savagery, our insistence on living at the brink of annihilation (not least during the 20th century when Bataille was writing) led him to conclude we don't want peace (Ibid: 168).

What are the politics of all this?

Bataillean political economy offers a virulent critique of ideas that subordinate man's activity to ends other than the useless consumption of their resources: 'servility of thought', its 'submission to useful ends' is an 'infinitely dreadful abdication' (Ibid : 238). His contempt for 'SERVILE MAN' [his capitals] (Ibid: 238) is a deep-felt loathing of institutionalised instrumentalism, whether utilitarian productive systems such as capitalism, or oppressive moral norms that govern and demand useful (reproductive) sexual behaviour. A communist with anarchic tendencies, Bataille's damning view of bourgeois liberal economics as being responsible for modernity's discontents is at the heart of all he writes. He refused to accept the idea that man's natural tendency is towards 'the principle of producing at the least expense', which is 'not so much a human idea as a narrowly capitalist one' (Ibid).

'We must make consumption the sovereign principle of activity'. The optimism, urgency and ideological polarities of the 20th century pervade his ambitious advocacy. (For an interesting discussion see Grindon 2010). What relevance could it possibly have today? Despite the seemingly bizarre glorification of massive expenditure, anguish and death in writings, it must be remembered he was neither a nihilist nor an idealist but a gritty materialist who refused to accept the separation of economic and sexual spheres. He understood perfectly well that 'the anguish of death', and death itself are the 'antipodes pleasure', (Bataille 2001 [1962]: 102). His 'strangely ethical' vision understood that human needs defied the logic of utilitarianism – to engage in costly and often ruinous risks. He would never have valorised tragic waste and social suffering of any kind, let alone that rooted in and responsible for global inequity (Stokel 2007).

His point, rather, is to make us conscious of our wastage and consumptive expenditure: 'The thing we desire most ardently is likely to drag us into wild extravagance and ruin us… men seek out the greatest losses and the greatest danger. Anyone with the strength and the means is continually endangering himself' (Ibid : 86). None of this is an apology for eroticism, the consequences of which are diverse and contingent. It is, however, an 'apology for humanity' and its need to expend excess (Ibid : 240). Because our tendency to waste relates to our need to feel the entirety of our being – which in turn affirms existence in the fullness of its affective potentiality. 'The question is how to consume the energy we have at our disposal … we need sovereign 'useless values' (Ibid: 239; see also 240).

Ignoring the connectedness of sexuality and violent catastrophe impoverishes comprehension of all manner of social discontents, an analytical flaw that mirrors, and is rooted in humanity's deep horror (and resulting disavowal) of death, fear of which continues to result in our refusal to confront political problems as diverse as war and work. Herein lies the most radically material aspect of Bataille's materialism: its base component. Rather than capitulate to our fear and loathing of nothingness by shunning death (which, in contrast to life and birth, receives nothing but execrative contempt) Bataille forces us to confront the biggest taboo of all. He mounts a defence of death, and insists we acknowledge its place at centre of sexuality in human life. 'Death is no less ignoble than birth', but death is castigated as life's unspoken alterity, evident in humanity's repugnance of corpses and the stench decay, its aversion to substances where life ferments: eggs, germs, swarming 'maggots make our hearts sink and turn our stomachs'; forms which thrive on mortification – in wounds – at the intersecting, corporeal materiality of live flesh and dead meat (Bataille 1997: 242-4). Death's excoriation parallels the abject status of revolting substances: ejaculated fluids are thus connected on account of their centrality to the domain of prohibitions: bodily excretions, menstrual blood: 'excrement is analogous to corpses'. The place of its emission being close to the sexual parts is not coincidental. These things are all inextricably linked through a complex of expulsions and assimilations (Ibid: 242).

If sexuality must be understood in its relations to, and proximity with death and its disavowal, so too must other human activity. Bataille sketches the general economy from the perspective of that which is horribly excluded through expulsion from the productive system. His insistence that we must look to the history of expulsion directs us to the disavowals within any given 'restricted economy' we wish to understand, and to the ways in which energy circulates throughout the *general economy* to which it is connected, offering a powerful metaphor for the relationship between abject subaltern labour and capital. Bodily abjection – jizz, shit, blood and corporeal decay – have their political-economic equivalents. For the researcher of capitalism, this opens up unsettling but interesting possibilities. Lie next to the decaying corpse. Peer into the toilet. Fish condoms from history's dustbin. Ruminate on their pasts. Gaze at manifestations of waste that disturb us most and contemplate why. To read human smuggling through Bataille is to reconstruct a history of the giddying, vertiginous extremes of migrant experience in all their violence and ecstasy; narratives of expenditure from the bowels of Europe's restricted economy.

FIELDWORK AND DATA

The research presented in this book is primarily based on some 90 semi-structured interviews conducted over a period of six years. All but a handful were in Urdu, the remainder in English and Punjabi. The bulk (fifty three) were conducted with Pakistani migrants in East London in 2003-4 (Appendices I and II); a further 20 in Florence-Prato, Italy, in 2006 (Appendix III). I conducted them and transcribed them myself, with the exception of the final round of interviews conducted in 2010 as a research update: three of these were in London; ten in Lahore and Peshawar (several with migrants whom I had met in London in 2003-4, including a two who had been deported). A research assistant was present at several of the Lahore interviews and subsequently helped with transcription. Note that the appendices listing details about most (but not all) of the respondents referred to in the text can be found at the end. Where a piece of information is unknown, such as a migrant's age, it is left blank.'

A one-month research trip to Pakistan in December-January 2003-4 provided the opportunity for some participant observation in Islamabad and Lahore, where I interviewed a smuggler and some prospective clients. I also conducted sixteen interviews with Pakistani officials, NGO and social workers and journalists. These yielded useful background material, as did interviews with two voluntary-workers at a charity organisation that provides support for Afghan migrants in West London, a significant number of whom enter the UK after having spent time in Pakistan.

Of the East London cohort, a total of ten interviews were completed with 'First Generation' male migrants who came to Britain in the early postwar decades, mostly in their homes. These were lengthy, tape-recorded encounters with men approached at a local community centre and mosque. A further nine women were interviewed, most of whom were contacted at an equivalent ladies' group where they were interviewed. These women were younger than their husbands, most of them having arrived in Britain as teenagers and in their early 20s during the 1970s. Some of these interviews were shorter and part of focus groups, which facilitated a more relaxed setting. Most but not all were recorded and took place at the venue of their regular meeting.

My position as a young, single male of Pakistani origin shaped the kinds of information generated in the research process in obvious ways. Access to the female members of the Pakistani population, for instance, was problematic; on the other hand. I was able to broach issues of sexuality with men with a degree of frankness that would have been difficult for a female researcher. Indeed this is one of the reasons my research evolved into a study of masculinity. I did, however, try my best to avoid elision of women's role in the migration process – critical for understanding the material base of patriarchal masculinity. A cohort of seven (mostly tape-recorded) interviews with Pakistanis who migrated to Britain as young dependents, along with five who were born in Britain in the 1970s proved indispensible given the sensitive nature of women's work among the 'First Generation' (its potential to undermine the status of household heads as breadwinner renders it taboo). These encounters with the 'Second Generation' and child migrants (now in their thirties, forties and fifties) yielded good information on the economic activities of their parents, though of course, they were filtered through memory and represented in accordance with each group of actors' varying gendered, subjective perceptions.

These data on old migration in London were juxtaposed with the results of a separate study for which a total of 26 interviews with 'new' Pakistani migrants were conducted, all but two of which were with men. These respondents were approached in their places of work and quizzed in nearby cafés about their experience of the contemporary labour market. Their responses were noted primarily by hand, as many of these individuals were living or working illegally and accordingly insecure about tape-recorders. They included seven 'Mangeters' (marriage migrants), six 'students', two 'visitors' and nine individuals who entered the UK illegally.

A different set of problems was encountered in this phase of the research process. Statistics and interview data on illegal migration are notoriously unreliable and problematic given the obvious difficulties in accessing and accurately counting the populations in question. Ensuring trust was critical in order to ensure the reliability of the information gathered, as was interpreting interview data in conjunction with newspaper reports and secondary reading. Initially I faced difficulties in persuading migrants and employers to participate in the research given the sensitivity of the subject matter. Hardening policies and media coverage in the UK have succeeded in attaching high levels of stigma to irregular migrant workers, whose economic activities and networks have been pushed deeper underground, their dealings with the state and its institutions reduced to a bare minimum. Contact between migrants of 'illegal' status and the older, more settled, 'law-abiding' members of their own respective communities have deteriorated as the stakes for providing assistance to irregular migrants have been raised by the government (Home Office 2002: 81): 'ethnic' and migrant community organisations are increasingly run by individuals whose ties to irregular migrants are weak. They cannot be relied upon to provide access to the relevant populations. Projects such as my own, which work with Muslim populations, must deal with the added pressure of disassociating their endeavours, in the eyes of migrants, from the growing surveillance of the Islamic community that now exists in relation to the issue of so called 'terrorism'. The latter has, as is well known, had a deeply alienating impact on all British Muslims in particular.

Having found myself operating in an institutional vacuum, the strategies I adopted, which evolved somewhat organically in the course of their practical execution, were by necessity diverse and involved a number of stages and strands. The first one entailed developing a series of non-institutional links with migrants and employers through my own existing contacts which, as a British Pakistani (and researcher of Pakistanis in London) ranged from old school friends to relatives and individuals I had already interviewed in the course of previously conducted research. Secondly, and rather more importantly, I developed a new set of contacts for the purposes of this project by approaching migrant workers and employers directly, without an intermediary, in their places of work. This last method proved more effective than any other, and allowed me to reach sections of the groups in question that would have otherwise not been accessible (my existing contacts were of limited use given their class/and or generational differences in relation to new migrant workers).

The third, Italian sample is based on 20 semi-structured interviews conducted with migrants in Prato and Florence in Tuscany. Of these, 18 were tape recorded before being transcribed and analysed. The other two were conducted using a note pad (one at the request of a nervous interviewee in an irregular situation, the other due to technical difficulties which emerged with the tape recorder). Most of these interviews were in-depth, some well over two hours. They were spread over a number of different venues – either in workplaces, in the houses and flats of migrants themselves or in the open air (parks, piazzas and even street corners…).

Migrants in Italy were recruited for interview through standard snowballing techniques, which began through contacts I made whilst resident in Florence in 2004-5 (I met my gatekeeper by approaching him directly in his place of work). Some anthropological participant observation was also carried out with migrants in their places of work, as well as in their free time while they relaxed in their houses or wandered around town.

In terms of the geographically situated biases of this sample, it may well be that Tuscan settlements contain fewer of those Pakistanis who entered Italy via the Mediterranean than those in the South (only one such individual is interviewed here, despite the fact that we know from media reports of border apprehensions that increasingly, Pakistanis are entering Italy from there). There is little reason to believe, however, that those who enter from the Mediterranean are a cohesive group that radically differs in profile to those in my sample, most of whom arrived by air and overland from the continent or directly from Pakistan. Nor is there any reason to believe that Pakistanis in Tuscany are in any way different to those settled elsewhere in the country (many of those interviewed here have themselves lived in cities and towns elsewhere; many men I encountered during my time in Florence moved on to elsewhere). That said, Italy is renowned for its highly uneven economic structure and development and my data may well be marked by specificities relating to the Tuscan context. The full extent of locality's importance, however, remains unclear until further research is conducted in other sites within Italy.

In its defence, interviews were spread over two locations (Prato and Florence) and two sectors (industrial and service). The migrants who feature, moreover, have lived and worked in various parts of Italy, which allowed me to deduce various features of the Pakistani experience elsewhere up and down the country. Many, moreover, have lived and worked in other countries, which allowed contextualisation of the Italian experience in relation to the situation of Pakistanis beyond Italy's borders.

Qualitative research seldom leads to exhaustive or categorical pronouncements informed by any great deal of quantitative precision. This book is no exception, though I have sought to collate and analyse enough new factual information with enough rigour to establish some important, verifiable and objective processes, facts and transformations in the history of human smuggling.

Its principle contribution, however, lies in its focus on the imaginative and experiential dimensions of migration: the subjective, the psychological. Most of the men I spoke with provided me with oral history life stories in semi-structured interviews, many of which lasted up to three hours (most were around one hour) – time spent 'remembering, repeating and working through' (Freud 2003 [1914]: 33-4) in which the goal was partly recuperative: to reach forgotten impressions, scenes, experiences. These seldom came to the fore immediately or chronologically since, as is now widely accepted among oral historians, 'unconscious psychic processes are timeless' (Ibid: 67). The sequentially ordered triadic structure of this book, in which the sending context is discussed at the start, is a teleological imposition of my own, in order to render the subject matter intelligible.

The extent to which the material generated in interviews was indeed forgotten and/or previously unconscious was not always clear. I am okay with this. Freud's own view of the subconscious was somewhat more complex than is often assumed (patients, he said, would often add after a session of analysis: 'I've always known that really I just never thought about it' (Ibid: 35). Nothing, the point is ever really lost or completely forgotten in psychoanalysis; some things are known and yet somehow still disavowed.

On the other hand, I report things that 'never have been forgotten since they were not conscious, noticed in the first place' (Ibid: 41). These utterly unconscious and sublimated desires and anxieties including cathexis and melancholia respectively emerged mostly in the process of my interpreting the data, sometimes long after the interviews were conducted. Are they my impositions?

No doubt the eclectic nature of my methods, together with the license I have taken to build my own models based on the thinking of Bataille, who was certainly not a professional therapist of any sort, will fail to impress some practitioners and critics of professional psychoanalysis. Fair enough. Non-professional (some would say amateur) psychoanalysis of the sort that is increasingly integral to oral history is not without methodological conundrums. However, if a genius like Freud was happy to concede he might be barking up the wrong tree, why should those of us who dabble with his conceptual tool kit have any shame in doing the same? His response to scepticism about psychoanalytic 'guesswork' or 'speculation' – exemplified in two well-known passages from Beyond the Pleasure Principle (2003 [1920]) – displays a disarming humility, openness to criticism and lack of defensive sentiment I shall try and take comfort from should this book be dismissed as nonsense:

> People might ask me whether and to what extent I myself am convinced by the hypothesis set out here. My answer would be to that I am not convinced myself, nor am I trying to persuade others to believe in them. It seems to me that the emotional factor of conviction need not enter into it at all. One can certainly give oneself over completely to a particular line of thought, and follow it through to wherever it leads out of sheer scientific curiosity, or out of a desire to act as devil's advocate – without signing oneself over to the devil (97-8; see also 6; 67).

Research design and terminology

The fields selected for study are strategically divided case studies, each represented by a cohort of interviews. My objective is to understand the specific pattern of each particular unit, so I have sought to maintain a minimum of symmetry in comparing the three contexts (East London in the days of Fordism; East London today; Prato-Florence). Inevitably, however, discussion of each case is balanced differently, giving comparison an apples-and-orange-like quality at times. Aspects of my research in the sending context moreover, are impressionistic when compared with the more embedded work I did in London and Italy. Writing this book in Lahore several years after the bulk of the research was conducted makes the shortcomings that result from this Eurocentrism all the more frustrating, but I take comfort from the fact that a final round of interviews conducted last year in Lahore and Peshawar threw up relatively few surprises. Even so, I have had to rely on newspaper reports from the Pakistani press to support, elaborate and supplement interview data.

Part III makes reference to events and processes that span several cities, continents and countries it would have been impossible to visit. Human smuggling connects a dizzying array of cities in West Asia, North Africa, Eastern Europe and indeed beyond. Time limits and resources did not permit extensive primary research in these sites; other means of study were adopted to back up interview data, above all, secondary reading and press accounts. Questions will inevitably be raised as to whether reliance on migrants themselves is sufficient to discuss these issues. Clearly, the picture I paint of smuggling networks in Part III would have been fuller had I been able to conduct inquiries in Turkey, Poland, the Czech Republic etc. It is hoped that the material presented here encourages researchers to pursue further study in these locations.

On a similar note, the London and Italy case studies vary in relation to the degree of my own embeddedness within these respective contexts. As a native Londoner, inevitably, I was more familiar with the terrain and acquired an understanding of the economic, social and institutional context that would be difficult to replicate in Italy, where my research was, in any case, conducted over a much shorter space of time. The differences in my knowledge of each context were compounded by the relative scarcity of secondary reading material on migration in Florence, which pales in comparison to the many volumes written about migration to East London dating back to over a century. It should also be pointed out that the community in London is far older and has more layers. The terminology I use in the London study, which is based on gender and generation, reflects this, as does the temporal scope of historical change: discussion of long-term processes and outcomes, in contrast to discussion of the Italian context which is based upon outcomes in the short and medium term.

Use of the term 'Pakistani' is, at best, an approximation – no better or worse than any national or ethnic epithet can claim to be, but given that it is applied to identify and describe highly diverse groups of embodied subjects whose members identify with it in different ways, some clarification is required.

Mine is not a totalising account of all migration from Pakistan. Such an account would have to include migration of the highly skilled, refugees and various other groups whose experiences were outside the scope of my inquiries. The very existence of a unitary Pakistani diaspora, like the notion of a unitary South Asian diaspora, is barely tenable (Markovits 2000: 4). Indeed, I take it as given that the term 'Pakistani' is mediated by all manner of additional identifications and social relations based on other kinds of ethnic and regional belonging in both the Italian and London contexts of study. The importance of language, region, religion and country of origin at any given time is contingent upon context. The usefulness of the term 'Pakistani' in the smuggling process, therefore, varies from high (for instance, in sending contexts, and in destination countries where 'ethnic enclaves', networks and labour market niches are often identifiably Pakistani) to low (for instance, in illegal travel across the Mediterranean, where Pakistanis are one of many groups sharing a particular experience).

I have developed my own terminology based on the relation between labour and capital at the world level, and use these alongside (sometimes interchangeably with 'Pakistanis' and 'Europe'): 'Afro-Eurasia', following Georges Bataille, is conceptualised as part of capitalism's 'general economy' that includes, but is by no means restricted to Pakistan (North Africa and the rest of the global South are equal members); 'the restrictive economy', is synonymous with North Western and Southern Europe, the European Union, 'Fortress Europe' and even 'rich countries' (terms used interchangeably and somewhat loosely). Eastern Europe is on the cusp of these two systems.

Caste, clan and religion barely get a mention. These are treated impressively by Werbner (2002), Shaw (2000) and Ballard (1983), each of whom have shown that social structure, 'religious' marriage practices and levels of social capital and education have an important impact upon the long-term social consequences of migration during the phase of 'consolidation'. My own study looks at the long-term in rather less detail. However, a key implicit argument of this book is that caste and religion are negligible in explanation of why, how and with what consequence migration happens. Nor are rural-urban distinctions helpful, as Shaw (2000: 30) and Aurora, who made the point as early as 1967, point out (Aurora 1967: 16-17). Following Kalra's (2000) typology, this book connects age and position within the household to gender distinctions. It also draws on Manheim's notion of generation as historical location: dividing migrants into 'old' and 'new'; Fordist and post-Fordist is far more useful than the somewhat culturalist usages of 'First' and 'Second Generation' applied to immigrants in everyday discourse.

The term 'irregularity', as I use it, refers to a status into and out of which individual migrants can move over time throughout the migration process: it can, of course, occur at the sending context if the endorsement or bureaucratic procedures stipulated as necessary by the sending state in order to emigrate are not respected (Gosh1998: 1-4). This book is mostly about migrants whose status is irregular from the perspective of destination countries due to the fact that they either enter without compliance with the legal procedures required by the reception country, and/or do not comply with the legal conditions attached to their residency and/or employment. As Gosh underlines, the relations between these different sorts of irregularity are complex: they are not mutually exclusive, but nor does the existence of one imply that any of the others will necessarily follow.

The terms 'clandestine', 'undocumented' and 'undeclared' (De Tapia 2002: 13-14) are considered imprecise, even if they are less coloured than 'irregular', 'unlawful' and 'illegal', which are preferred here, and used interchangeably. That some of those who enter/and/or reside and/or work without legal sanction are 'undocumented' is besides the point, as is the fact that irregularity is a construct of (arguably socially unjust) state policies. Of interest to governments and the public is the fact that they are in various ways breaking the law. Following Black (2003: 41-2), it is held that an approach which looks specifically at the effects of this reality for them and society is justified, so long as it is understood that what we are studying is 'not illegal migrants' but migration (and work) that is 'illegal'. Many of the problems they experience, after all, arise specifically from the fact that their actions contravene national laws, and are not simply a consequence of their lying outside the 'formal', regulated sector. This is especially true of smuggled migrants.

'Smuggling', incidentally, is itself not an unproblematic term. If there was little consensus about its meaning in the 1990s, there appears to be a growing acceptance of the analytical and/or practical need to distinguish between 'human smuggling' on the one hand, defined by the Vienna Protocols as the 'procurement for profit for illegal entry of a person into and/or illegal residence in a state of which the person is not a national or permanent resident', and 'trafficking in persons' which, on the other, is specified as 'the recruitment, transfer, harbouring or receipt of persons, either by the threat or use of abduction, force, fraud, deception or coercion ...' (Salt and Hogarth 2000: 153). Nonetheless, the two terms remain heuristic devices, the applicability of which in any given situation on the ground is unlikely to ever be complete. If anything, they are best seen as two ends of a 'continuum', in which there is 'room for considerable variation between the extremes' (Graycar 1999: 3).

PART II
Drives

Introduction to Part II

Britain emerged as a significant migratory destination for South Asians in the 19th and early 20th centuries, during which a constant trickle of Indians to London and other English seaports laid the foundations of today's European South Asian diaspora. The content of these flows were already fairly complex and included members of the educated elite, above all students and a small number of domestic servants, many of whom were women (Visram 1986: 2002; Lahiri 2000). The most numerically important and historically significant in terms of paving the way for the post-war mass migrations which followed was made up of *lascars* – seamen who worked in the British Merchant navy, often as sweepers and cleaners on emigrant ships carrying indentured labour to the plantation colonies. Ambitious individuals who deserted ship in search of economic opportunities (much to the irritation of the British authorities), lascars sowed the seeds of most of the substantive Pakistani and Indian settlements in Britain today though at the time they were seen as little different to their fellow 'Asiatic' Chinese, Arab and Malay equivalents (Salter 1873).

The earliest lascars were first recruited from Surat District in the North of Bombay and Sylhet in the North East of what is now Bangladesh in the 1800s (and was once East Pakistan); then Mirpur in what is now Pakistani Kashmir around 1900. The genesis of Sikh (and some Muslim) migration from Jullundur and elsewhere in the Punjab is as much associated with military recruitment as it is lascar migration. Its origins date more to the interwar period, when regiments of engineers and mechanics stationed (and in some cases discharged) in various locations across the empire began to explore ways to earn money abroad. They were swiftly followed by individuals from their villages of origin who financed their own migrations and worked as peddlers (Ballard and Ballard 1977: 23-4, 27). Indications are that the earliest migration from those areas of Punjab that are today in Pakistan is likely to be tied up with both lascar recruitment into the merchant industry and navy and military recruitment from those areas dating to the First World War (Khan 1977: 65), though disentangling the chronology of the various threads which compose these flows is difficult since they tended to overlap.

Around three thousand lascars a year were flowing into Britain by the 1830s. Like most Indians in Britain during this period, they often returned home after periods of living and working in Britain as migrants (Visram 1986: 34, 48). Their numbers grew at a steady pace in the early decades of the 20th century, hardly surprising given that the percentage of Indian British maritime labour rose from 20 in 1919 to 26 in 1938 (Visram 2002: 225). By 1932, the Indian National Congress estimated there were over 7,000 Indians in the UK, though this was most probably an underestimate (Visram 1986: 190). The flows that produced this small community prefigure post-colonial mass migrations from Pakistan (and, of course, India and Bangladesh) in important ways, and their development has had a significant bearing on much of the subsequent historical geography of those flows, as we shall see.

Visram's historical research on the crucial interwar years leads her to conclude 'the underlying reason [for migration] was economic' (2002: 255). Her argument is based upon the fact that they apparently had plenty of objective reasons to migrate. Whilst the labour conditions of western seamen steadily improved after the International Labour Organisation was founded in 1919, the wages and employment terms of lascars remained appallingly low throughout the interwar years (Visram 2002: 225). Even the lowest incomes they managed to attain in shore industries such as one pound a week as porters in Jewish tailoring firms in East London would have been more attractive than seamen's wages (Ibid: 259). Economic pull factors are also deemed to have been important: the demand for cheap labour within British industries played a critical role at key moments in the interwar years, to the extent that private firms such as Tate Sugar refinery in Silvertown were accused of encouraging lascar desertion by various government agencies (Ibid: 68).

And yet, many of the details within Visram's own superb research raise important questions about the 'underlying economic' motivations she takes for granted. By her own admission, the degree of voluntarism in lascar migration varied. Often their contracts didn't give them passage back. Some didn't receive their wages and found themselves stranded in London or Liverpool; others stowed away from ships after being ill-treated and exploited (Visram 1986: 51). Demand for labour was in fact intermittent, and dried up at regular intervals. Britain was in many ways a hostile environment where race riots were not uncommon. White working-class resentment towards the growing Indian presence manifested itself in many British cities (Ibid: 256), and the authorities were deeply unnerved by the sight of 'half-caste' born children of Indian fathers in East London and elsewhere (Ibid: 274). The Home Office did all in its power to halt lascar desertion: launching or attempting to launch schemes of deportation and voluntary repatriation (2004: 199-202); posting notices warning of the perils of migration to England at Indian shipping offices in India (Ibid: 218); restricting the granting of passports in India to those with a 'low standard of education' unless they could provide proof of an offer of employment (Ibid: 222); discouraging the award of peddler licenses to Indian applicants (Ibid: 217).

In such an unwelcoming environment, it is hardly surprising that the net profitability of migration to *Vilayat* is unclear. Most of Visram's own evidence points to the fact that, in the deeply hostile climate sketched above, many lascars would have experienced much hardship and insecurity. If they were motivated by commercial gain, there would have been little guarantee that they would succeed in fulfilling their objectives: of those who migrated, a lucky few got jobs in factories; most were self-employed peddlers who experienced poverty and even destitution;

some died beggars (Visram 1986: 51), facts which surely raise the question of whether migration was indeed a rational course of action.

My interview data adds little to what we currently know about this phase of migration (I encountered or learned of no surviving lascars). The question of what a fuller, truer account of their motivations might look like, however, is addressed implicitly in my discussion of what motivated those who followed in the paths they carved out in subsequent years.

The historical-structural context is well known: in 1947, a distinct Pakistan-UK migration system was established. Partition was a key migratory push factor in Punjab in the post-war period when Britain opened its doors to the New Commonwealth; the British Nationality Act of 1948, which defined Commonwealth citizenship for Great Britain and the colonies, left something of an Open Door for Commonwealth populations to enter the UK (Hiro 1973: 103).

Only a relatively small proportion from South Asia took up the opportunity to migrate at this time. In contrast to the contemporary picture, the newly formed states of India and Pakistan were, at this point in the historical evolution of the Asian migration system, far from uniformly enthusiastic about emigration from their countries to the world centres of capital. A regime of stringent control of emigration, which contrasts significantly with today's attempts to mobilise out migration as a form of generating foreign currency through remittances, hindered movement of Indian and Pakistani citizens abroad (Hiro 1973: 107). For various reasons, then, until the early 1960s, the rate of labour migration from Pakistan and India into Britain was low compared to people movements from other countries and regions.

This changed following a joint international venture led by British and other Western enterprises to build the world's largest hydro-electric earth dam at Mangla in Mirpur in 1960: 100,000 people (18,000 families) were displaced (Khan 1977: 66). Some were given vouchers facilitating their migration to the UK as compensation for losing their lands and employment; a sizeable number would have migrated to join relatives in the UK (Kalra 2000: 63, 68). By the late 1960s, passport offices opened in Rawalpindi and Mirpur itself (Khan 1977: 67).

Political developments at the receiving end too played an important role in boosting immigration. The 1962 Commonwealth Immigration Act stimulated NC-British migration to hitherto unseen numbers, as thousands rushed to 'beat the ban', a number of whom may never have migrated had it not been introduced. In 1960, migration from the subcontinent had been only 7,500. The tide turned in 1961 when 48,000 entered Britain as rumours of impending anti-immigration legislation circulated (Hiro 1973: 108; Shaw 2000: 30-31). Instantly, a much more sizeable community of permanent Pakistani residents was thus created than had previously existed as a direct consequence of restrictive state policy. Its composition, in terms of sexual ratio, would become increasingly balanced, as secondary annual marriage migration flows of women soon reached thousands and have remained so ever since.

What then, drove migration?

Shaw offers a complex explanation, emphasising diverse historical contexts, themselves products of colonial policies and physical geography: Mirpur in Kashmir, where the rocky terrain and low agricultural output shaped an environment of poor infrastructure and economic stagnation is clumped with nearby Northern Punjabi sites such as Jhelum, Gujrat and Gujuranwala where irrigation is also poor, and contrasted with canal colonies such as Faislabad and Sargodah in the heartlands of Punjab, characterised by high agricultural yields and levels of infrastructural development in the 19th century (Shaw 2000: 20-21, 26). Kalra, meanwhile, stresses the centrality of political factors in his account of emigration from Mirpur, making a claim that migration was initiated by the need to subsist rather than commercial ambition following the region's exploitation by political leadership before partition, and then accentuated after it by the building of the Mangla dam, which was also a product of Mirpur's political marginalisation (2000: 58-9, 63).

My own research effectively collapses the differences implicit in these explanations in order to explore the question of causality from a different angle, beginning with the assumption that cause ought not to be confused with context: emigration from Mirpur, for instance, took place from a context of poverty; elsewhere, it was encouraged in a setting of prosperity. What these regions have always shared are interrelated histories of movement: local men traditionally supplied labour to British shipping lines, and personnel to the British army, which famously preferred recruits from the Northern, 'martial' races of the subcontinent. This culture, the chapters that follow argue, was in fact the basis of a powerful ideology of travel, the interpolation of which is central to understanding subject-formation in migrant-sending areas of Pakistan.

Chapter 1
Gender, the Household and Migrant Masculinity

At some point in the 1950s, the lascars appear to have blended gradually but increasingly clearly into another wave of émigrés who, for the most part, were slightly younger. In many cases, they had never done paid work. Unlike their predecessors, to whom they were often related as sons and nephews, they were not necessarily lascars or military men. Some migrated secondarily (they were brought over by fathers and uncles).

A good deal has, of course, been written about 'Babas', as Virinder Kalra calls them, along with the lascars, with whom they are effectively lumped together by the somewhat misleading and epithet, 'First Generation'. Beyond academia, they are associated with the fiercely patriarchal protagonists of a number of widely diffused cultural and artistic representations of the Asian diasporic family (above all, Ayub Khan-Din's *East is East)*. There exists, that is to say, a pervasive body of assumptions about who these men are and what motivates them. Most of these postulates have been constructed on the basis of a distortive presentism. Traits they display in their lives as 'respectable' community-elders, as witnessed by their offspring and the host society, get projected backwards into their pasts, so that their motivations are viewed exclusively through the prisms of religiosity, conservatism and claims about their self-sacrificial heroism.

In this chapter, I have sought to explore the recesses of their memories, taking them back to the moment of the decision to migrate in order to explore what triggered the impulse to pack their bags and leave. Our focus is on the motivations of individual migrants leading up to the point of migration rather than subsequent events (apart from where these reveal something about the former). I take seriously the ways in which they articulate their own histories and trajectories, but analyse their testimonies critically, interpreting them with a view to unpacking the often unstated, psychological forces at work.

The Babas are a socially differentiated group. Even the small sample of men interviewed in East London can be distinguished by ethnicity, regional, social and economic background as well as the point in their lives at which they migrated, as will be discussed where individual accounts are explored in detail. For the most part, however, I focus on certain commonalities that emerge in their narratives, beginning with an exploration of the degree of choice and voluntarism they indicate.

Throughout my research it was only very rarely that I encountered men who felt 'obliged' to migrate or spoke in terms of having been 'sent' by a collective decision made within their households. If poverty was often acute in the emigration context, respondents made clear that the capacity to migrate internationally even from Mirpur was conditioned by power relations and access to resources in the form of social and material capital. Though formally uneducated, Baba Malik (who does not know his exact age) was of a prestigious and powerful family within his village in Mirpur, his grandfather a village elder who would be called upon to administer justice when arbitration was needed to solve a land dispute.

Baba Sarwar, who migrated a year after he did, suggested that those who migrated after the lascars were often the most educated within their families: 'At that time, those educated, doing matriculation [GCSE equivalent], were going. They were looking for relatives they might have here'. In short, though many would have wanted to emigrate, differential access to social and economic capital (wealth and status in the village) meant that migration abroad was an option for some, but by no means all, and certainly not the poorest.

The same is true, according to Baba Malik, of those who were displaced by the Mangla Dam. As Kalra (2000: 63-5) points out, political forces and state policies created the conditions in which emigration from Mirpur became imperative. Mangla residents were literally forced to leave their homes. However, as is clear from the following account, they still had to go to considerable efforts to ensure their arrival in the UK, a country to which they are often assumed (erroneously) to have been given automatic rights of entry and free passage.

> Our Pakistani brothers think that Pakistan gave Kashmiris compensation because of the dam. This is a complete lie. Those of our people who were there – they didn't immediately give us a passport to go to England. None of those people got a passport free. You had to give at least 5,000 … for the passport, 1,500 rupees for the ticket. Those who came behind them, they came, some of them, via Iran, some via Kuwait … so there was not such a passport issued whereby the Pakistan government said, 'Ok, you are effected by the Mangla Dam, you can go to England. No, it didn't happen like that.'

There are hints here that illegality in migration – or at least legally complex, circuitous travel routes and a business in migration brokerage to the UK were firmly in place by the 1960s. London-based newspapers quoted by Aurora (1967: 41-5) confirm this: *The Daily Star* reported as early as 15th August 1958 that the Indian Prime Minister complained to Indian MPs: 'of the 17,300 Indians who reached Britain in 1955, 1956 and 1957, only 4,964 held passports issued by his government, the remainder being forged'. They also confirm how expensive it was to travel from India even at this time: 'the cheapest fare in those days was around £60. A conservative estimate of an additional expenditure of £20 per immigrant took the total to around Rs.1,070 in Indian currency. Even for a middle-class farmer's family to mobilise this amount must have been 'a great feat. In many cases this sum was collected from the sale of family valuables and probably a proportion of the land as well.'

Migration from South Asia to London, the point is, has long been somewhat costly, risky and difficult – always one of several options, seldom the easiest. It needs, therefore, to be explained beyond reference to generic structural causes, in a manner that accords due weight to agential drives. The testimonies of migrants from Mirpur with relatively low levels of social capital are illuminating precisely because they articulate little sense of having been forced to migrate. Baba Sarwar claims he 'didn't have much ambition', yet he retained, in his own eyes, a sense of control over his own destiny, which he expresses through a clear rejection of the idea that he was somehow compelled to migrate:

> AA: *Did you want to come, or was it obligation, or did someone send you or ...*
> *What was your motivation?*
> I had a cousin here in Sheffield. I was studying, doing matriculation. Amongst
> our lot everyone was poor. I was the head in my family. Only I was educated.
> My cousin said, 'Do you want to come here?'. The choice though, was mine. No
> one forced me. It was for the betterment of my life.

The unmistakeable appearance of personal ambition here ('the betterment of *my* life'), suggests that even from a backward and peripheral economic context, the forces which motivate men to leave for the metropolitan centre of global capitalism are *not* exclusively a sense of obligation to the family or household. Nor are they explicable by some abstract force of cumulative causation powered by the anonymous momentum of kinship networks, though these are present in the story. Baba Sarwar's cousin facilitated his migration, but the choice to go, he claims, was his own.

A final illuminating issue that arises from his testimony emerges from a discussion he had with a schoolteacher prior to departing from England.

> When I told my headmaster, an ex-soldier, he said: 'Don't go! You're a good
> student.' He said: 'What are you doing? Don't leave your education half-way!'.
> I said, 'Headmaster, I need to go'. [Laughs]. And so I came here.

The literature on migration emigration from Mirpur (e.g. Kalra 2000) refers to poor infrastructure and lack of schools that, it is implied, created an environment of desperation from which migration became imperative. Certainly the infrastructure was very poor in Mirpur; Baba Malik says there were no schools in his area. Yet here we have a migrant who abandoned his education despite having been begged to stay by his headmaster: personal will enters again, this time *against* the advice of a senior figure within the community.

As is indicated by a note in the text, the respondent laughed after telling this anecdote. Some of the men I interviewed began smiling as they recounted their original reasons for migrating. Others chuckled.

What's so funny?

As migrants recall, with the benefit of hindsight, their original reasons for departure from sending contexts, a chasm between their former and current selves opens up. This distance represents the gap between past fantasies about imagined futures and present realities of loss (discussed in Part IV): a space in which irony enters discourse. Laughter signals self-reflexivity, a kind of knowledge gained through experience. Freud would have approved: there's no cure for the sadness human beings bring upon themselves, but as Mark Edmundson's (2003: viii) preface to *Beyond the Pleasure Principle and Other Writings* points out, the creation of a sceptical distance from desire and its effects is considered healthy in psychoanalysis: 'an ethics of irony and renunciation' that understands, without ever suppressing, the passions that our shape behaviour.

Irony seldom surfaced at the start of interviews. Few men had ever considered why they had migrated in any great detail. Almost all had a kind of 'official version' which began to unravel as we began digging through their memories, tugging on loose threads in their initial sets of claims. The testimonies of men who migrated as husbands and fathers in their thirties were especially interesting given the number of voices within their households seeking to influence the course of their lives.

At 30, Baba Rashid, a former Partition refugee from Jullundur had already been married for some eight years. Despite being better educated than some villagers, having matriculated, he was struggling unsuccessfully to find the sort of employment he wanted (a clerical job) in 1961, when he migrated:

> We were five or six brothers and sisters ... I thought, 'I've done my matriculation, but I can't get work.' People were saying there's work abroad, [they were leaving] for good jobs, to improve their situations. So I thought I should go too. At that time I was married and had four children.

In addition to underlining the difficult material conditions, unemployment and indeed poverty that would have marked the context of many of the Babas' decisions to leave, this passage appears to raise the importance of kinship in the decision-making process, and at a glance would appear to confirm the saliency of 'the household' as the primary force behind emigration. As the eldest, most educated of his siblings and a father of four, Rashid, we might assume, would have migrated out of a sense of responsibility to provide for and ensure the household's future security: the decision would have been a rational, collective survival strategy pursued by the household as an income and resource pooling unit in times of poverty.

Closer examination, however, reveals a more complex picture. Rashid refers to his family as the backdrop against which the decision was made, but there is no causal link between his feelings of responsibility for their wellbeing and his decision to up and leave. Upon being probed as to where the latter really stemmed from, an ambivalent, less harmonious set of circumstances emerges.

AA: So what did your father feel and think about this?
He didn't say anything to me. In fact, he didn't like the idea of his son leaving. But he thought 'This man is trying to make a living for his children who are getting bigger, and if he wants a good job, it's fair enough … '

His wife, too, was unhappy at the prospect of his leaving, though as he states below, she was fairly powerless to exert her will over his. Notice how, when describing her feelings and those of his family, he switches to using generic personal pronouns twice within a short passage, perhaps to indicate the typical nature of the responses he is describing and deflect attention from his personal culpability:

> There is a lot of bad feeling amongst the family, especially the wife. The children were so small they didn't understand – they were just three or four. But the wife felt bad … They do. But they have to compromise.

Though they agreed to support him, then, the decision to migrate seems to have been Rashid's own. Even if it was made in the context of feelings of responsibility to the household and family – indeed even if they figured in his considerations as a predominant force – these obligations are analytically separable from, and not reducible to his desire to leave. This, we learn further on, surfaced in discussions with other young men with whom he conversed *outside* the household. These exchanges were not necessarily with returnees or even individuals who had been abroad – just 'people' ('people were saying'). Rashid's calculations, in other words, were premised on rumours. Rumours spread by men who may or may not have themselves migrated drove other men to pursue their own autonomous migratory agendas. The speculative nature of the risk involved in making this kind of judgement is underlined by the following quote, which suggests his wife and family – far from constituting a group whose future he migrated in order to safeguard – was rather the opposite. The household provided the security for him to risk migrating:

> I was not worried because we were a joint family: mother, father, brothers, sisters, and children. We all lived together. No man would like to leave his children without that [kind of arrangement]. This provided a safety, so I felt I could leave the children.

A similar kind of tension between pursuit of personal fulfilment, on one hand, and commitments to the household on the other emerges powerfully in the testimony of Baba Anwar, a science teacher at a prestigious, private, English medium school in Sialkot some time after the Commonwealth Immigration Act in 1962. For a number of reasons (discussed below), Anwar Sahab developed an avidity to migrate. The following account of an initial attempt to do so that was aborted due to pressure from his wife underlines the lack of unanimity that can characterise the decision-making process. Like Baba Rashid, conversations with friends outside the family led him to make an application for the relevant papers and even make travel arrangements, but here, the discordant nature of interests within the household is more pronounced:

> Within six months they sent me vouchers ... Then everything [was] gotten ready – the ticket and everything ... But when I said, 'What do you think?', she was not happy. She just started crying. I said, 'Alright, it doesn't matter. I won't go.' I never came. She stopped me. No, she didn't stop me as such, I felt she was not happy – that she will feel lonely ... So I never came. That seat was cancelled.

Like Rashid's wife, Anwar's was unhappy at the thought of being left to live with her in-laws and bring up the children with an absent father. She was able to exert enough emotional leverage to prevent him fulfilling his own individual wish to leave on this occasion, compelling him to reverse his decision. However, she was relatively powerless in the face of a subsequent change of heart some months later following an intervention by another female figure within the household. As with Baba Rashid's wife (who had to 'compromise'), she was, in the end, compelled to defer, but this time to the combined will of her husband and mother-law. The decision not to migrate was overturned:

> Some time passed, a few months. My mother said, one morning when I was getting ready and having my breakfast: 'Son, your brother and sisters are very little, if you go it's a good thing. Perhaps it will help – for [their] education.' We were seven brothers, at that time.

Anwar Sahab never asked his mother where her conviction that he should migrate surfaced from, but reckons the fact of her brother's migration to London some years prior would have influenced her to decide that her own son ought to leave his job for the material betterment of the household's interests as she perceived them. He speculates:

> I don't know. Maybe some money was coming in and ... she would have realised ... her brother's wife would have told her. I'm sure she would have asked: 'Now he's gone there, how much money does he send?'. She definitely would have asked, and then worked out that what you get here is worth 10, 15 times more.

The implications of this information sharing between households through women are noteworthy. Women appear to have had their own subtle, situated ways of asserting their agency, as they are known to in contexts where they occupy subordinate positions (Sen 1990: 126; Agarwal 1997: 23-5). Baba Anwar's wife employed emotional pressure directly; his mother also drew on her own social networks (a form of social capital) and elevated position within the household to exert influence directly.

Women within households, the point is, did not speak with a single voice, or even express a shared interest against those of men. The young wife's position at the bottom of the patriarchal hierarchy merely confirms what we know to be true from other contexts: maintenance of any gendered order that favours men requires mediation through some women, with whom men forge alliances in pursuit of their objectives (Ditz 2004: 19; Shaheed 2002: 355). It also illustrates how gender is lived through and in relation to age, generation and other social categories that can run counter to its overall workings. The positioning of subjects within the household is a complex process, manipulated and contested by different women in ways that are visible upon close examination of men's testimonies. On this occasion, an outspoken mother appears to have had the decisive say. The benefits of this particular (legal) migration in the early 1960s, for her, seem to have been rationally calculated on the basis of material considerations. She learned of the money to be made in *Vilayat* through gossip – an imperfect form of information that tends to circulate within tightly knit groups and is thus more reliable than rumour. The latter spreads unsubstantiated information more widely across the social field (Harney 2006: 376).

And yet, it should not be assumed that Baba Anwar was himself driven to migrate only or even primarily as a consequence of this pressure. Even if their agendas coincided, his mother's wishes revived a desire that, as will be discussed in the next chapter, was already in place. If networks figure prominently in migrant testimonies, as new theories of migration predict, it is also the case that networks are multiple, and reflect conflicting interests and agendas that need disentangling.

They are also inflected by ideology, the gendered dynamics of which relate to male status within the sending context, and may well be important in understanding assessments of acceptable risk. Much of the information upon which actual decisions to migrate were made was circulated through interactions between men in non-domestic public spaces, *outside* the domain of feminine. The significance of this emerges in Baba Anwar's testimony.

> In our area there were nine or ten villages. From one of them, a businessman's son or brother came to England to study, and he went back while I was still studying in college, in the early 1950s. It was a big thing for the pupils and for us, who were in the college at that time: 'This bloke has gone to England! He's an *England Returned*!' He used to be a big gun. For the family itself and the person who went there, the *England Returned*, it was a really big thing.

For men, to travel was associated with a certain worldliness and mastery of the globe associated with modernity; an accumulation of cultural and experiential capital that raised one's status among male peers. Returnees would enjoy their elevated status over men like Anwar Sahab, and swagger around town, making the most of it. The myths they spread would have reached far and wide, inspiring men of all sorts of ages and social backgrounds to find a way 'to see' for themselves what all the fuss was about.

New migration

The 1962 Commonwealth Immigration Act and subsequent installation of a voucher system in Britain represented a historically unprecedented and unusually early attempt to curb unskilled migration from the global economic peripheries in Europe. Restriction of people movement from Turkey to Germany and from the Maghreb to France, to name just two other parallel examples, was to become an increasingly common trend within the post-war European continental migration system, into which Britain became increasingly integrated as the 1970s progressed.

At the world level, the 1973 oil shock and subsequent global recession made full employment a vexing political issue throughout Europe. Even in France, which has historically feared demographic decline, immigrants were no longer seen as needed, and became increasingly perceived as a social problem to be controlled (Massey et al. 1998). After his election to power in 1971, Prime Minister Heath passed the Immigration Act of 1971, which limited the right of entry to Britain of individuals without parents or grandparents born in Britain, reinforcing the preference for movement from the 'Old' Commonwealth. The Act, which was made effective from 1973, introduced a system of annually renewable work permits for those non-Brits granted entry to work, thus ending the automatic right to settle that NC workers had enjoyed if they were allowed in under the voucher system. Then Margaret Thatcher instituted various measures to curb transnational subcontinental marriages including the British Nationality Act of 1981, so that by 1982 policy had already altered the composition of stocks in terms of the ratio of workers to dependents, and men to women. Flows in general, meanwhile, were substantially reduced: even the number of dependents declined from 50,000 in 1972, to a mere 21,000 in 1983 (Anwar 1995: 275). It was in the context of these developments, which appeared to have ended the era of primary migration from the NC, that the social scientist Muhammad Anwar concluded that 'large-scale immigration from the colonies is now over and that the unification of undivided families is the main source of immigration' (Ibid 1995: 275). Less than two decades after this pronouncement, a glance at the statistics in Britain and Europe would suggest that Anwar's assertion, based on data up to the early 1990s, needs careful qualification. (The International Passenger Survey reveals that total international immigration from Pakistan to the UK from 1995 to 2004 was 29,100 (ONS: table 2.3, p. 6), up considerably from the figure of 17,600 over the corresponding period from 1992-2001 (ONS: table 2.3, p. 6).)

A series of parallel and intertwined changes at the world level and sending context has seen the development of 'new' migratory patterns and configurations: the infusion of petro-dollars, which transformed the Gulf into an immigrant-receiving region following the 1973 oil crisis and subsequent emergence of West Asia as the primary destination of international migration from South Asia, especially Pakistan (Massey et al. 1998). The obviously expanding widespread desire to emigrate (distinguishable from actual flows) amongst large chunks of the population is for many, an index of Pakistan's broader downward descent into political and economic chaos bordering on state failure and social disintegration. Like so many post-colonial Third World countries, which, since independence, have experienced deepening poverty, population explosions and unemployment crises, Pakistan's history since the 1970s, from virtually every perspective, is catalogue of disappointments and tragedies.

The importance of emigration in this process has grown exponentially with its descent into chaos, with overseas remittances having long constituted the country's principle source of foreign exchange. Dependency on the West Asian diaspora has become part of an overall strategy of high growth-oriented policies that placed income distribution, poverty alleviation and human resource development firmly on the back burner (Naseem 2002: 251). At the start of the current millennium, the 1990s was referred to as 'the lost decade', economically 'the worst in the country's history' (Sayeed 2002: 230) thanks partly to a disastrous exchange rate liberalisation in which the rupee was effectively devalued by 100 per cent over the course of ten years, ushering in severe inflationary pressures (Ibid: 232).

How might historians describe the decade that followed? Floods, wars, proliferating terrorism, soaring crime, crippling power cuts, ever-greater chunks of the population enveloped by poverty, with inflation biting harder than ever. In the midst of all this, the IMF (which gobbles up around a third of Pakistan's budget revenues to cover the interest on debts run up by its kleptocratic military dictators and venal politicians) and World Bank relentlessly demand privatisations and the ramming of various other neo-liberal medicines down the throat of an ailing economy already on its knees by the end of the Musharraf years. (It remains prostrate.)

Decades of catastrophic war in neighbouring Afghanistan, meanwhile, the world's biggest sender of refugees in recent years, has had direct and far reaching consequences for the Pakistani migration system, for years a passage to the West for many Afghans. Though impossible to calculate, there is every reason to believe a substantial proportion – probably more than half – of Afghani immigrants to Britain would have passed through Pakistan, or indeed come directly from there. (Some are probably Pakistani Pushtoons who posed as political refugees in order to acquire residence rights.) Leaving aside the Afghan/Pakistani-Pushtoon contingent, the number of Pakistanis recognised as refugees by the UNHCR has also climbed steadily every year since 1992 when it was just 1,100 to 12,400 in 2001 (UNHCR 2001: Table A.6, p. 89). Though the grounds for their claims are unspecified in the statistics, these are likely to include persecuted minorities such as Ahmedis, along with miscellaneous victims of state and societal repression – trade unionists, women, ethnic minorities, artists facing censorship, individuals fleeing sectarian conflicts.

There are, then, new political and economic problems – and no shortage of new rational reasons to want to leave Pakistan. To what extent do they explain new migratory flows?

Freshies

Politically incorrect but barely possible to resist, the above epithet refers to new migrants from Pakistan: men 'fresh off the boat', so to speak.

Who are they?

A glance at Home Office 'control of migration' statistics in the new millennium would appear to confirm King's (2002) thesis that the forces which shape contemporary migration are more diverse and complex than those of their predecessors; different sorts of immigration are gaining added importance. Student migration and the number of tourists are up: of the 212,000 Pakistani nationals admitted into the UK in 2004, around half were visitors; six per cent (12,600) were students (3.5 per cent (7,590) were spouses). So too asylum claims, which hovered between 1,710 in 2004 and a peak of 3,165 in 2000 over the period 1996-2004 (Home Office, 2004: table 3.2, p. 43). The number and proportion of Pakistanis entering the UK on work permits is also notably on the increase, again in line with general trends since the mid-1990s. At 3,265 (Ibid: table 2.2, p. 34-5) it is higher than at any time in the post-war period – even the 1960s, which is often regarded as the era of the work permit. In 2002, the number was 2,254, up from 1,614 the previous year, itself around double the year before that (Ibid: 785). Half were in IT and Nursing, with a good number of the remainder in catering (source: work permits UK).

My own table of respondents (Appendix II) also reflects an apparent diversity in composition. Profiles reveal increased marriage migration, a mix of asylum and refugee flows, students, tourists and visitors. That these migrants are better educated is noteworthy: many Babas were barely matriculated. Legal and many illegal migrants today, in contrast, often have Bachelors degrees.

And yet, there are important continuities with old migration, as this chapter seeks to demonstrate. (They don't show up in statistics.) Before sketching these, it is worth pointing out two obvious and important points. Firstly, five decades since mass migration got underway, the key sites of emigration remain remarkably close to the pathways that connected Kashmir and the Northern Punjab to *Vilayat*, as is clear from Appendix II, which indicates that most men hail from districts such as Gujrat and Mandi Bahauddin. Secondly, educational profile need not represent a fundamental difference in likely motivations between old and new migrants: possessing a formal education is hardly indicative of having acquired a radically different set of priorities. (Nor, incidentally, is it always necessarily an indication of possessing an actual education in Pakistan, where a recent series of media investigations into Pakistani politicians' purported educational backgrounds revealed scores of fake degrees.)

Despite its apparently higher educational background, then, today's Pakistani migratory proletariat in Europe is in many ways structurally comparable to yesterday's Fordist 'guest-workers', and originates from similar localities within Pakistan. There is, furthermore a sense in which legal classifications can be misleading even within new channels of migration, as the all-encompassing term

'Freshies' implies. These become evident upon close inspection of testimonies which, once again, are wrought with similar kinds of silences and contradictions when it comes to addressing the question of why they migrated. Pakistanis across Europe are quick to point out the political-economic context back home is one which would appear to encourage emigration; that migration's purpose was to support and build families; 'that we are here, sacrificing our lives for our families'. But as with the old migrants, these claims about the broader picture seldom tally with their own individual situations when closely examined. Macro-contexts, once again, do not determine causality mechanistically.

This becomes particularly evident when one considers the extraordinary costs of migratory travel to places like London from Pakistan, a good deal of which is now irregular. The status of networks as cost-saving, rationalising mechanisms cannot be assumed; strong bonds do not necessarily reduce the cost of migration (Part IV). Given the mortal risks involved in attempting to penetrate Fortress Europe illegally, migration can hardly be explained as some kind of path dependent, natural consequence of prior emigration.

It is, however, linked with a deepening of consumer culture which is in part a consequence of capital in-flows resulting from prior migrations: the transformative impact of remittances from the UK since the 1950s; the Gulf since the 1970s; North America and Europe since the 1980s, has been considerable in the North West, Kashmir and above all Punjab. Among certain classes in specific districts, men from families that have for generations worked in agriculture increasingly find this beneath them as a career trajectory. As with studies of Gulf returnees in India, a sudden jump in economic position has effectively created new classes of status-conscious individuals ... unwilling to take up their previous [agrarian] occupations which they now consider as low status' (Sekher 1999: 202). Migration to the Gulf, meanwhile, has become more difficult and, for the crème of peasantry, lacks glamour due its association with the previous generation and a certain mediocrity in relation to westward travel.

Freshies I interviewed in London included Pushtoons from relatively small, semi-rural towns (which they often refer to as 'villages') in Pakistan's North West Frontier province (recently renamed Khyber Pakhtunkhwa). Like the other migrants from that region I met, they belong mostly to families that benefited from the vast, continuing migration to the Middle East that has sucked in and transformed the lives of millions across South Asia since the 1970s. They each grew up with fathers leading transnational existences between home and the Gulf, and in some cases, spent some of their most important formative years abroad. Twenty-four-year-old Khan Sahab, whose family is from a town called Kohat, initially claimed he had the encouragement of his father, a truck-driver in Qatar: 'Dad said "I don't want you to do that [drive trucks]".' He went on to place his own choice at the centre of his narrative: 'I decided I'd come here. I liked the idea of coming here rather than Qatar'. Asad, a 23-year-old rice farmer from a small town near Peshawar, was similarly insistent on an English destination:

> Two or three years ago, people from my village who had been in Manchester and Bradford since '96-'97 and had made lots of money sent it back. They had quite an impact. Their families got big houses and moved to Peshawar and Islamabad. I thought, 'I want more money. Qatar's not good enough'.

When, exactly, are the final decisions to migrate taken, and by whom? Khan Sahab recounts: 'It was my responsibility to keep things going. In 1999 I decided I would come. They didn't say anything – it's better not to put your parents in the position where they have to ask [you to migrate].' The so-called 'family decision' appears to have been taken by an individual exercising his personal will in the interest of a collective. It is difficult to know exactly what his father would have felt about his travelling since Khan Sahab's initial representation of his father's position as encouraging is contradicted by the more modest, passive sort of support implicit in his subsequent phrase, 'they didn't say anything'.

On women, who barely feature in his life-story, Khan Sahab's silence was broken only when I explicitly asked him about how the migration process affects them. Their status ('izzat', literally honour) is incomparably lower than a man's, he told me, pointing to his foot to explain the whereabouts of its extent. A woman who dares suggest a preference to her male relatives on the question of whom she might marry is promptly shot, he added (nodding to indicate the propriety of this policy). He expressed opposition to education for women, yet sees it as entirely natural for him to want to improve himself. The desirability of men's mobility – geographic and upwardly social – is a given, an attitude that reflects the gendered, international social relations which tie households to foreign destinations through a single male migrant:

> We live together with four of my father's brothers. One has two wives. I'm one of seven siblings – we're 40 people … Every family is supported by someone abroad; each man who leaves feeds 40 people. My father and three *chachas* [paternal uncles] are in Qatar – they have been there since before I was born. Dad and his brothers drove trucks there. I was born in Qatar [and lived there] until the age of ten when I went to Pakistan.

Khans Sahab's testimony confirms what we know about from evidence gathered on the impact of Middle East remittances upon gender relations in Pakistan, most of which demonstrates conclusively that the 'capital-rich' (Ballard 2003: 72) developmental consequences of emigration are at best, ambivalent. If anything, it is not uncommon for women to experience greater seclusion and confinement to their homes when their households are lifted out of material poverty by overseas male migrants, who tend to deploy their resources to impose stricter purdah and increase their own social standing within patriarchal communities, in which confining womenfolk to the home confers honour and prestige upon the household (Lefebvre 1990: 82-4; Gardezi 1995: 100).

Historically, this is unremarkable and by no means specific to any country or culture. In 18th- and 19th-century Portugal, for instance, the emigration of young women was rejected as a household strategy because 'to be forced to send a daughter out into service was an indication of poverty, a factor that made…[them] that much more undesirable as potential spouses' (Brettell 1986: 137). Women in Khan Sahab's community, however, appear to have less room for manoeuvre than their Portuguese counterparts who, like Italian women (Gabaccia 2001: 190-208), played a pivotal role in the agricultural economy: there was no shame in working in the fields. This important economic function helped to preserve their status in society, reflected in the fact that there was little stigma attached to spinsterhood (Ibid: 139). High rates of illegitimacy (Ibid: 211, 249-50), as Brettell (1986) points out, probably reflect women's agency: having children may have been a way to avoid spinsterhood without care.

This difference may go some way towards explaining why they continue to express such ambiguous sentiments about the decisions of their male household members to migrate illegally (see also Gardner 1995: 227). Despite their limited clout in shaping assessments of acceptable risk – their marginal role in 'relations of definition', to use Beck's (2000: 214, 224) terminology – wives are likely well aware of the fact that they are directly affected by the risk entailed in the process. (It is not unusual for them to contribute to raising the requisite capital directly through the sale of their jewelry (Koser 2006). Perhaps female scepticism is borne in some measure from the distinct possibility that, where benefits do accrue from migration, they are seldom distributed equally within the household. Bilal, a Punjabi textile worker in Prato since the 1990s, admits:

> No wife wants her husband to go away. Sensible women don't want their husbands to leave the country. If he makes money, it stays with him! As far as women are concerned, money stays within the hands of men.

As was clear in the testimonies of old migrants, wives feel the departure of a husband can leave them in a weaker position within their household. When asked what his 'missus' said about his coming to Italy illegally, Faizal, an unemployed, middle-aged Punjabi migrant in Florence said: 'Wives in Pakistan say nothing. They say, "You know what's best".' When probed, however, it emerged that his wife had been against his emigrating, but that he had ignored her wishes. 'When a man leaves', he explained, 'he goes for two years at a time', leaving his wife living alone with her in-laws 'not knowing when he'll be coming back'. If this applied to men such as Baba Anwar, this state of uncertainty is heightened for many Freshies given that irregular migration does not afford migrants or their wives the luxury of knowing when (or if) they will return (or indeed arrive), a point elaborated in Part IV.

Parents are even more ambivalent about the departure of their sons, and in some cases express outright opposition to their plans to emigrate. The following fairly typical accounts of parents' reactions to being told about (illegal) migration decisions, recounted by Freshies from Punjab and the North West suggest that this is the case across a diverse range of social contexts in Pakistan:

> *Asad:* I decided myself to leave, a long time before I did ... Agents say don't go this way, they warn people against it, they say there are many dangers, but people go to them anyway ... My father told me not to go, 'It's very dangerous, come to Qatar and look after my business with me,' he said. I didn't listen to him. I wanted to come here.

> *Chima:* From the beginning Dad said 'What's the need to go abroad?', 'What do you want for here?'. I told him [I was going] him three days before leaving. When he found out he swore at me!

> *Farhad:* I got the money off my parents and paid an agent. It was difficult to get them to agree. We don't have that much money. I made a fuss and they had to give in the end. Parents do their best to fulfil their children's wishes.

Chima and Farhad are FA-educated [A-level equivalent], unmarried, middle-class men from semi-rural Punjab. I interviewed them in Italy where they had migrated illegally in 1998 and 2002 respectively. Asad, a Pushtoon from a village near Peshawar, worked with his parents in agriculture prior to migrating illegally to London. All are beneficiaries of a patriarchal family system that controls but simultaneously spoils its young males, a fact they understand and consciously profited from. Farhad and Chima confessed to '*zid*' and '*nukhra*' – having made a fuss and thrown tantrums in order to manipulate their parents. I learned of several decisions to migrate being made without the knowledge of the household, and then enacted *against* its wishes. It is the household, remember, that must finance migration, a complicated process that can require carefully organised bouts of pressure. Chima used his father's elder brother to persuade him into financing his first bid to migrate to Europe in 1996:

> The first time I told my *Taya* [father's elder brother]: 'I want to go abroad. My friend went and he says it will cost this much and earned lots of money, please persuade my father, tell him he wants to go, he's doing nothing here' ... He talked my father into it with great difficulty. My father agreed and said: 'I'll give him the money, tell him to arrange it.' He gave me a lakh rupees. I talked to my friend.

Arrested, imprisoned for three months and deported, Chima eventually ended up back where he started. His agent turned out to be true to his word and offered him the option to try again rather than have his money back. His father, relieved to see him, was even more adamant that he forget the whole thing. 'Thank God you're back', he said, before, laying down the law: 'You are not to go abroad again, forget it.' [He said]: 'Go and get the money back'. This time, however, Chima did not even consult him, knowing that he would never agree. He chose, instead, to present him with a *fait accompli* just prior to leaving.

> I told him three days before leaving. I organised the plane myself ... When he found it he swore at me. I asked him for money, saying I need it for clothes. I need dollars. He swore at me and said: 'Get your passport back! I told you, you are not to go, there's absolutely no need for it. Last time look what happened, jail. And we had to be thankful you got back in one piece. You have everything here! Get working here! Get to the village and start a fish farm! Our own work here isn't getting done, What are you going abroad for?'. I listened to his insults for about half an hour, and then left. The next day I went out. Aboo thought, 'Maybe he's gone to his friend's house' ... I went and bought a few pairs of trousers and stuff.

The household head's powerlessness here is quite remarkable. What appears to be the most rigidly hierarchical of contexts, is, upon close inspection, one in which young men have considerable license. Though careful not to voice rebellion, the disdain with which Chima listens to his father's lecture is plain. The patriarch can do little to block his desired course of action, and is even presented with requests for spending money.

A number of important messages emerge from the narratives of these migrants, the first of which is that smuggling from Pakistan to London is a highly expensive endeavour embarked upon only by migrants from families unlikely to be reliant on remittances from the West for 'coping'. Many already have breadwinners stationed in the Gulf. Even for migrants from the most peripheral areas, international migration can thus be considered an 'accumulation strategy' (Devereux 1999: 8). It is not necessarily triggered by unemployment (all these men appear to have had jobs or job options in Pakistan), and certainly not by the poverty that surrounds them. If anything, the close proximity of less fortunate, often wretchedly impoverished constellations of the rural populace appears to provide them with no great sense of threat to their own relative wellbeing. They look instead to their neighbours – those within their own social milieu who have benefited from remittances from abroad, and become consumed, it appears, with an avidity to acquire more.

Privileged within their own societies, Pakistan's male emigrants enjoy levels of mobility unimaginable for the female members of the households that finance their migrations. Family reunification has gone some way toward evening up the ratio of males to females amongst long regularised and settled populations in Western Europe, but generally international migration from these districts remains powerfully gendered – monopolised by men who risk household savings and cash raised through the sale of property (not to mention their own safety) in pursuit of their own personal autonomy. It is by virtue of their powerful desire to migrate, and relatively high levels of agency that such individuals make it to London (and other cities) illegally.

This is all the more significant when we consider what has taken place at the lower end of the Pakistani migration system, and how it has affected women and other vulnerable groups in these and other regions of Pakistan. Gender, that is to say, determines global patterns of movement in such a way that renders international irregular migration almost unthinkable for women of all classes, and leaves many of the poorest vulnerable to the worst kinds of trafficking. If the women folk of the men I interviewed do not belong to the classes of women that end up in trafficking situations, they are part of a constellation of women for whom the basic freedoms of mobility remain highly problematic (Shaheed 2002: 353, 364). Their confinement to the home has not been altered by their brothers, husbands and sons travelling the world. As with colonial migration (Omvedt 1980: 195-7) and the 'old' fordist migration from Mirpur (Ballard 2002: 52), new migration has, if anything, reinforced the rigidity of existing customs and traditions in relation to the gendered division of movement in space.

Chapter 2
Sexuality and Migration: Thinking Beyond the Economic

A second line of argument taken up in Part II relates to sexuality and the ways in which psychoanalysis can enrich our understanding of labour migration from sending contexts such as Pakistan. This chapter argues psychological push factors, although difficult to identify and quantify with any precision, play an important, hitherto relatively unstudied role in motivating individual migrants to up and leave. Once again, I begin with an exploration of the Babas' testimonies, before moving onto those of the *Freshies* and then hazarding some comparative reflections that focus on the growing importance of human smuggling.

Anwar Sahab, we noted in the previous chapter, migrated partly at the behest of his mother's concern about the material wellbeing of the household. He had an agenda of his own, however – quite independent of her wishes. This, his discourse reveal, were less obviously utilitarian:

> I had very good job, I tell you. Enough money for those days. I was getting pay over there which was a heck of a lot of money, and I had people asking me for tuition, but I was happy with my money. I wouldn't do tuition, which I could have done easily (people asking me …). But I said: 'No, I've got enough money'.

Anwar Sahab's own personal initial interest in migration, then, was driven not primarily or even remotely for cash and what it might buy. He had, by his own reckoning, a perfectly good job that paid well, and even brought him elevated social status, prestige and fulfilment.

How then, did he first develop an interest in migrating?

> I had a colleague working with me. He happened to [go to] a government agency that provided people with jobs, an 'employment exchange' ... So he told me to have a look. He said: 'The employment exchange has received information that they want teachers, they want nurses, they want doctors, so go!'. I said, 'What do I want to go there for, I just got married recently.' He said 'Go on ... If you don't like it come back after six months or a year.' I said, 'Alright, let's find out about this.' I went to the employment exchange ... and confirmed there was demand. [They said] 'Take this [form], fill it up.' I did that and took it back after a week.

> ... Within six months ... I started preparing [to leave] ... There was a secretary of a school. In the process of this enquiring and filling in an application form, I learnt that he had gone. I thought, 'Many people are going now.' Mr Bashir Ahmad was not the only one. I thought, 'Others must also be going'. And that was it really. No motivation at all, I would say.

In recounting the events leading up to his migration, Anwar Sahab himself appeared to have difficulty explaining what it really was that made him want to leave in the first place. He kept shrugging his shoulders, scratching his head and frowning as he thought it through, perhaps for the first time in his life. 'No motivation at all', he kept saying:

> *AA: What do you think motivated you?*
> Nothing really motivated me, just that man telling me.

The lengthy ramble that follows provides clearer clues as to what was really at stake, and what precisely it was in his friends' discourse that appealed:

> It was his suggestion – nothing else: we will roam around and have a good look at England. When I did my degree at that time, in English, I remember we used to cram some things, a few things which you would find fancy. Something interesting ... going around, seeing the world ... Curiosity. Travelling. Journeying ... He said, 'If nothing happens, we will go, look around, travel around. Have a look at London and then come back' ... I think that one point stuck into my head. Go and *see* what England is. Not just, *hear* about it: go and *see* what it is!

Migration here is plainly seen as a means of travelling the world, motivated by curiosity about far away places that are imagined as exotic and different. The desire to enter the ranks of those who have *seen* and not merely *heard*; a rejection of dependency upon others for knowledge of the world – a rejection of relegation to the lowly status, within one's community, of one who relies upon the testimonies of an emergent international class of global travelers for understanding the Occident. To remain dependent in this way, of course, is to share the status of women, for whom travelling is out of the question: it is, in this sense, a typically masculine, symbolic repudiation of femininity (Ditz 2004: 18).

Many middle-class Pakistanis migrated to London in this period from big cities along age-old colonial pathways of movement that existed long before mass labour migration from the villages got underway. The forces that drove them too tended not to be economic in a narrow sense; a high proportion were of families involved in economic and low-level administrative activities of the British Empire; many came as students, but ended up staying on for longer than they had intended (Ahmad 2006). Their experiences echo the accounts of Indian travelers to London in the 19th and early 20th centuries (Burton 1996; Lahiri 2000, respectively).

Of course, the experiences of a group that includes such individuals as Jinnah, Ghandi and Nehru can hardly be conflated with Europe's lumpen Pakistani workforce. Yet, there are more parallels between the motivations of highly educated individuals and their rural and semi-rural counterparts than one might assume. Differences between the two social groupings are, for one thing, not always clear-cut, as Shaw (2000: 19) points out in her discussion of migration from Pakistan since the 1960s. Baba Anwar himself, though a schoolteacher, is very much of agricultural origin and did farm work as a boy. Moreover, colonial ideology was widely diffused through institutions such as the army which inculcated the myth of white superiority and established London as *the* epitome of modernity – an imperial metropolis to be seen – for sizeable constellations of rural, working-class and lower middle-class men. Baba Zia, a Punjabi (originally from Amritsar) who spent most of his working-life running a grocery shop in Newham told me his desire to emigrate sprang from when he

came here in 1953 – when I was in the Pakistan airforce ... to attend the Queen's coronation. We stayed here about two months. We participated in the parade, which started in Kensington Gardens, through Marble Arch and around the Thames to Buckingham Palace. We were honoured to be in Buckingham Palace Gardens, where her Majesty Queen Elizabeth came and expected the soldiers, about 75,000 soldiers from different commonwealth countries. We were awarded different medals ... I was very much impressed by the attitude, the behaviour of, especially the police. They were very helpful when I forgot my way. I said I wanted to go to Kensington Gardens. He said: 'I'll help you'. He started walking with me. I said, 'It's alright,' but he brought me all the way to Kensington Gardens, in front of camp! I said, 'That's very good, thank you very much.' Then I thought, 'When I complete my air force contract, I think I would like to come and live in this country.' And that's how it happened. When I finished my Contract in 1959, December, in January I came over here.

The fact that he knew only one individual in England (an ex-airforce friend) suggests his migration had little to do with kinship networks, as do the details of his story: he initially lived in a hotel, before contacting the embassy, which sent him the address of a hostel for students in central London SW1, where he stayed for some time before finding his way to East London.

Zia's testimony is unusual in that his decision to migrate was based partly on a concrete experience of travel. For most men it was fostered through an imaginative process, in which they constructed fantasies about what their prospective futures might look like after migration. Visions of life in *Vilayat* were fed by imperfect economic intelligence discussed in the previous chapter (including gossip and rumour), but also various kinds of cultural and visual information. Less tangible and even harder to quantify than the impact of returnees' advisements and purported reckonings, these were likely, nonetheless, to have been influential. Indeed, the importance of looking or 'seeing' in the contemplation of migration was already alluded to indirectly in the previous chapter. Baba Anwar's choice of words in describing the origins of his original motivation to travel – to 'go *see* what England is' – is palpably infused with sensuous imaginings of a future visual experience.

Drawing upon Lacan's ideas about the structuring of the Self through desirous encounters with alterity, the remainder of this chapter explores how visual experience can contribute to understanding the driving forces of migration.

Desire and alterity

Global consumer culture, disseminated through visual technologies like cinema and television nourishes fantasies about migration in peripheral economic locations (see Mai 2001 for a discussion of Albanian perceptions of Italy). In the course of so doing it makes promises about what life at the heart of capitalist modernity looks like. Part IV of this book is about the immense disappointment that follows when these break. For the moment, we are concerned with how they are made.

Consider the testimony of Nasir (not listed in the table of respondents), whom I interviewed for a previous research project (Ahmad 2006). A retired South London-based dentist born in Jhang, his family lived in a *kacha* house (made of mud or clay bricks). His father, an Urdu and Pharsee teacher, was 'a religious man, suspicious of British culture', who would not let his children have breakfast until they had read a few pages of the Koran. And yet, during his upbringing he remembers being drawn Westward after watching Hollywood films in Lahore as early as the 1950s.

> I knew quite a lot about England and about London actually. I even knew all the streets, most big streets like Piccadilly, long before I decided to come over (from library books). Even before I came, I was watching films in Lahore. There were three or four cinemas that showed non-stop American and British pictures.

The power of film and other media including commercial photography and advertising to transport South Asian publics – to tantalise their senses by immersing them in immensely pleasurable and glamorous imaginary settings – has a history that extends back at least to the early and middle decades of the 20th century. The powerful attraction Nasir developed for England through cinema is illustrative of this. How might we develop a broader understanding of visual perception – one that accords reality itself a filmic quality? (If Lacan teaches us anything, it is that interpreting the world is itself a process of filtering, organising and misunderstanding things and events). There are countless ways in which London, England and many other symbols of alterity were encountered in migrant-sending contexts – as images, coveted objects and in observable embodied forms: flesh and blood people whose actions, words and practices triggered desire in those who witnessed them. This last claim requires an imaginative leap from the European reader: a reversal of the hegemonic assumption, implicit in the discourse of the political Right everywhere, that it is only ever immigrants who intervene and intrude into the lives of Europeans and never the other way around.

Anti-racist campaigners in Britain have long emphasised the importance of colonialism in triggering migration ('We are here because you were there'). True enough. But there are other, more recent examples of metropolitan travel to the global economic periphery intervening in the lives of Asia's immobile on-lookers, spreading various kinds of economic information (and misinformation) about the West. Tourists, for instance, indulge in material processes of consumption that might well have played a hitherto unstudied role in generating the production of migratory desire.

A recently published journalistic account of the hippy trail presents anecdotal evidence of its impact upon locals in countries as diverse as Turkey, Iran and India (MacLean 2006). The indelible impression left by the 'intrepids' and their 'liberal values' on youngsters is apparent throughout. A man in Turkey is quoted as saying: 'Their liberal values ... spread in a soft way throughout Turkish society. Our women began to feel they had the freedom to act as they wished' (MacLean 2006: 13). Another recounts: 'I remember the parties most of all ... drinking wine, playing guitars ... our mothers told us, 'Don't go near the ... infidels' (Ibid: 51). A former Iranian conscript remembers spying on a young woman through binoculars as she crouched behind a small bush to relieve herself in 1967 at the Afghan border: 'That sight was like the first bite of a forbidden fruit. Next I heard about an oasis... where hippies stopped to sunbathe and swim'. He spied on them there too (Ibid: 107).

The word 'spying' carries deeply negative connotations in liberal, sexually open societies where mass consumer culture and liberal values have rendered the naked body mundane. Without questioning the invasive, uninvited nature of the creepiness in the scenarios described above, the dynamics of capitalism in regulating such interactions need sketching in here. It is a mystificatory trick of cultural imperialism that manages to classify voyeurism, exoticism and hedonistic consumerism as harmless forms of tourism when the subject in question is indulging from a position of material privilege. Hippies meant no harm. But they contributed to an emergent ideology of consumerism in Asia that triggered various kinds of desire in people they encountered; their 'cultural' activities must be seen as part of network of travel and material exchange connected with migration (and as I discuss below, human smuggling) in unexpected ways.

Now retired, Nadir – a degree-level educated former bank manager – is from a village called Dinga in Gujrat district, a locality from where (together with neighbouring Mandi Bahauddin, and Gujuranwala) human smuggling rates to the West are known to be the highest in the whole of Pakistan (Raza 2004; Ali, W. 2004: 6). In describing the experiences that led him to want to migrate as a young man, he makes clear there is more to understand about 'spying' on the hippies than meets the eye, so to speak:

I remember European people would go by road through Iran, Afghanistan and the Khyber Pass through Pindi and Lahore, from the UK. We would see them on the GT road – the motorway starting from Peshawar, Pindi, Jhelum, Gujrat, Gujuranwala and Lahore. From there they would go to Delhi. These were small vans. [We saw] their free style of life, their capacity to spend money and enjoy life. They were hippies, tourists. Hundreds would pass through daily, Americans, English, French. They would stop in Kharian, Jhelum, Gujrat, and stay there, wherever night fell. They would stay in hotels and use tents. We had a fascination to meet them. You would go and talk to them in bars, cafés, tea places on the GT roadside. *The fascination with the white colour, the women.* 'What sort of people are they?' [we wondered]. This was the early 60s. They were individual tourists. Also we'd see them on the trains, up to the 1970s. For youth, this inspired one to leave.

Epidermal or 'racial fetishism', to draw on Mercer's (1994) conceptual vocabulary, has some relevance here, but the reference to 'spending power' is equally important. Whiteness is about more than skin colour: the 'free style of life' that western travelers were clearly enjoying as they passed through the subcontinent at the height of the sexual revolution – making journeys that fulfilled their own desires to travel and discover what they thought of as 'India' – had quite an impact on at least some of the young men into whose view they crossed; so too the sight of mobile, autonomous, female sexuality embodied in 'white women'. Cultural and perceived racial difference melded with social alterity – a class of people for whom leisure was a lifestyle – to produce an alluring blend of objects giving impetus to desire. Whiteness, that is to say, is concocted as a symbol of access to material *and* sexual pleasures: an imagined sovereignty, in which consumption can be enjoyed without work – without re-investing surplus back into production (Bataille 1997: 23-4).

The issue of class might compel us once again, to qualify this generalisation. How is desire for alterity and scopophilia experienced by men who'd never seen flesh and blood white people? What relevance could mythologies of whiteness have had for the earlier waves of Babas, some of whom hadn't ever watched television or been to a cinema? Historical, anthropological and literary accounts suggest that working-class men routinely ended up in relationships with white women before large-scale family reunification and spouse migration (Visram 1986; 2002; Shaw 2000; Hussein 2000). This in itself, of course, is not sufficient to say that such sentiments triggered migration in the first place.

There is, however, evidence that among the peasantry too, there was clearly an element of mystique surrounding the West; an element of curiosity and wonder at what lay behind the *purdah* that separated them from the outside. Though seldom explicitly articulated, this is hinted at in memories recollected by some of the working-class men I interviewed. From a place like Mirpur, the closest contact men would have to metropolitan Europe would be through returnees who had been there. The representation of these actors, who appeared to possess unusual powers upon their return to communities of origin as early as the late 1940s in the following vivid portrait of the emigration context, suggests that their having been to the UK, coupled with their new found affluence and exposure to metropolitan urbanity effectively whitened them in the imaginations of the young and immobile, and added to the appeal of travelling to Vilayat:

> *Baba Malik:* Their colour and clothes were different. It was nylon. At that time nylon was a very bright cloth: *white* nylon and yellow *shalwars. And the men's colour was white.*

Whiteness here hints at the presence of class, caste and 'race' as markers of social distinction between members of the same 'racial' community which, to some extent, can be acquired: affluence and proximity to the perceived heart of economic modernity through migration can bring about a kind of bodily metamorphosis in the desirous eyes of immobile onlookers. White complexions and clean lightened clothes blend into a single object of social and corporeal alterity in the minds of rural youth.

Indeed, a closer look at the way communities of immobile men look at, fetishise and exotify commodities and bodies connected with the world outside is suggestive as to how sexuality is experienced and lived in the village: displaced and projected through alternative forms, it manifests itself in outwardly non-sexual preoccupations and energies – acquisitive sentiments towards commodities and related feelings these trigger for those who possess them. The way immobile male villagers look at and describe material goods that have come from (or returned from) abroad, and want these for themselves, in particular, invites psychoanalytic readings: as interviewees revisited these, entering the recesses of their own memory, they would clasp at their own bodies with a hand or fold their arms, underlining the personal importance of the incidents they were recounting, and demonstrating the intertwined basis of corporeal and social identity in complex histories of selfhood.

Despite the apparent absence of femininity, women or indeed any explicit articulation of sexual desire, these acquisitive sentiments suggest sublimated sexual desire. Several of the men I interviewed recalled specific instances of seeing returning visiting migrants wandering about town. They confessed to having coveted the wealth and status of these returnees: above all their 'gadgets' and consumer goods. These commodities, it seems, brought the bearer amplified status within the communities of men that comprised their social worlds. This much, perhaps, is relatively uncontroversial, and not incompatible with many classical accounts of the migration process. A closer reading of the precise terms in which they describe the moment at which the desire to migrate entered their consciousness, however, reveals a more complex set of forces, and suggests that part of the reason for the enhanced status of returnees relates to a process by which they become the focus of desire for the immobile. Understanding the full extent of their allure, however, requires consideration of the way in which it was tied up not only with the material or worldly appeal they held.

Though it belongs more to the testimonies grouped with later waves of 'new' migration, the recollections of Faizal, a middle-aged respondent from Italy, echo Baba Malik's account, in which returnees appear to the immobile youngster as some kind of different, superior race. Having matriculated, Faizal's background is typical of many old Pakistani labour migrants from Punjab who left early on the in the 1960s. Asked why he first emigrated at the age of 17, a young man growing up in a village in Gujrat in the 1970s and 1980s, he stressed that he and his younger brother 'were comfortable', then recounted seeing returnees in the bazaar, a public and largely male space, far removed from the feminised domestic sphere of the home and away from the fields, both of which are associated with parental supervision (Chopra 2004: 49):

> Our thinking was this: whichever guy comes from outside, you see them wearing white clothes. He's holding a good suitcase in his hand. Whether he's really got money or not, when he comes, he's going to have money then – even if he's been cleaning toilets to make that money. No one knows that! But he'll wear white clothes, and be wearing a gold watch.

> *AA: Do you remember seeing these guys?*
> Absolutely. When I passed my matric I thought I should go. 'What's the point in staying here, working the land with your parents. You'll get nothing'. I'll go outside and make good money. I'll come back wearing watches and stuff.

> *AA: What's this about white clothes?*
> When a man returns from there he wears good clothes.

> *AA: What does white mean?*
> White meaning good. Good clothes, beautiful clothes. A man who works and lives in Pakistan, he'll work, sometimes he'll have good clothes. Sometimes he won't. But who comes from outside, he won't work there. He wakes up in the morning, bathes and puts on good clothes, and goes for a stroll in the bazaar. When we would see them, it felt as though we should go as well. We felt stuck there. We thought we should go too.

> *AA: Where would you see them?*
> We would see them when we were going around in the market.

> *AA: So you would know they were from outside just by looking at them?*
> Everyone knows what everyone is doing there. You know so-and-so is back from England; so-and-so is back from Saudi or an Arab country.

Faizal makes no explicit reference to white people but the symbolism of his constant references to white clothes – like 'white skin' and the clothes of Babab Malik's Mirpuri returnees in the 1950s – invoke diverse kinds of alterity. 'White' clothes and complexions, in the minds of rural youth, are associated with affluence, power and exclusivity; they denote novelty, newness and access to consumer luxuries: 'watches' are associated with automated time and suitcases with travel – both of which are synonymous with modernity and having left behind the unglamorous world of agriculture where people work for a living. Through the effect of visual demonstration as well as gossip and rumour, the latter comes to be perceived as the plight of the immobile – the lot of those condemned to a dull and mediocre existence, bound – like women – to families and households. Returnees understand and exploit this perception in order to enhance their own self-esteem (several men confessed to putting on their 'whitest' clothes and deriving satisfaction from splashing money around in front of the immobile, deliberately giving the impression that their disposable income is greater than what it in fact is).

There is an obvious sense in which acquisitive sentiments for commodoties invite Freudian readings of 'object cathexis', a process by which 'things' are invested with libidinal significance. An approach which goes beyond classical psychoanalysis, however, would be attentive to the ways in which the very act of looking at these 'things' was intertwined with gazing upon the bodily alterity of return migrants, into which the magical powers of these commodities melted within a local masculine imaginary, activating and projecting various forms of unconscious and repressed sexual energy. The specular dynamics of this process, which sometimes took place in the complete absence of verbal exchange between observer and observed, were central to the production of the desire to migrate. Scopophilia, here, is not just a psychic process but a two-way social relation: just as there is enjoyment in looking, there is also pleasure in being watched: returnees are cognisant of their admirers and actively participate in how this process unfolds in all its theatricality. When they strut through the bazaar, they are putting on a performance that allows them to bask in the glory of other men's desire. This is evident in the way they display awareness of their own corporeal image, pampering, preparing and then parading their bodies in carefully orchestrated encounters. The power of this performance is not to be underestimated: even now, in his mid-50s, through the prism of memory, Faizal imagines the returnee's body being bathed, donned in carefully selected garments and embarking upon a kingly stroll around town.

There is, in all of this, a powerful sense of attraction. Whitening functions simultaneously and, paradoxically, as a transformative force that projects feminine qualities upon the returnee. It could thus be argued that it facilitates the displacement of sexual desire for women (who are absent) into an urge for the commodities of the returnee and his captivating corporeal image, which become the object of various sorts of libidinal investment. Queer? Perhaps. But the question misses the point. Indeed to classify in this way underestimates the difficulty in disentangling the origins, orientations and ultimate directions desire takes. Attraction for returnees and their gadgets, remember, could equally be read as displaced desire for an absent femininity – forbidden and less accessible than men who become de-facto recipients of sexual interest.

Indeed, the status of returnees who splash cash around is at the same time 'hyper-masculine' in that it effectively feminises (or rather castrates) men like Faizal who can only dream of someday matching their spending capacities (Osella and Osella 2000: 121). One respondent recalled his 'eyes ripping' (an Urdu expression for seething with covetous envy) as he witnessed a Mirpuri on a return visit from Britain spending more in a single shopping trip than most Punjabis from his village could hope to earn in month. Osella and Osella (Ibid) have argued convincingly that expenditure of this kind functions as a kind of fetish in the Bataillean sense – one that derives added significance from the distance migration splices between sites of consumption and production. Reading parallels between cash and sperm as symbols of male potency, they underline the intimate correspondences between sexuality and the excessive, deliberately public spending of money that get lost in utilitarian accounts of migrant behaviour.

My own research would support this argument, but as a corollary sketches in the labour process in destination countries, the significance of which creeps in at the edges of interview discourse as disavowed realities, mystified by this excessive expenditure and its corresponding mirages of potency. Absent (invisible) labour and present (visible) expenditure form two sides of a sexual–economic dialectic. Their entwinement is particularly evident in reminiscences of the sending context narrated retrospectively, with hindsight, in destination contexts, where immersion of the migrant's body in the labour process is the context in which memories are recounted.

Faizal laughed out loud when recalling the perceptions of returnees he had held as a young man growing up in a village in Gujrat in the 1970s and 1980s. Laughter, as noted in the previous chapter, signals irony. Here it connotes a sense of having been duped. He now understands first-hand why and how migrants wilfully underplay their lowly status in receiving countries to preserve their self-esteem upon return, accentuating what Marx observed as the innate tendency of commodities to obscure the labour process: 'Whether he's really got money or not, when he comes back, he's going to make sure he has money then – even if he's been cleaning toilets to make that money. No one knows that! But he'll wear white clothes, and be wearing a gold watch … '

Remittances and the introduction of commodities from abroad ushered in ever more pervasive market-based social relations, consumerist ideologies and individualistic desires. As the 1970s wore on, state sponsored capital-rich development in areas with high rates of emigration witnessed conspicuous patterns consumption develop to the point where Pakistan became one of the poorest countries on earth with a penchant for imported luxury goods. Leaving aside the ironies of this in a country with such appalling social indicators, there is a paradox here: desire for commodities as symbols of wealth acted as a spur for actions that in many cases led to proleterianisation; a life of toil and unimagined deferral of gratification. Having been seduced by the prospect of a life of leisure and glamour, men such as Faizal now work 12-hour days, seven days a week. How does one reconcile this perplexing contradiction at the heart of contemporary labour migration from Pakistan?

A partial explanation can be derived from the insights of Campbell (1987) in his analysis of the Romantic ethic and the spirit of modern consumerism in the West, where he highlights some of the apparent anomalies at the core of capitalist societies. Modern consumerism, defined by him as a kind of 'illusory hedonism' that emerged after the industrial revolution with the formation of a middle-class living above subsistence level, is distinct from 'traditional' hedonism in that 'the joys of longing rival those of actual gratification' (Ibid: 203). It is associated by Campbell with a 'dissatisfaction with real life and eagerness for new experiences' that have come to shape modern life, which is characterised by 'the ceaseless consumption of novelty' (Ibid: 205) and a tendency to 'create desire' (Ibid: 222).

Social scientists, Campbell points out, have long posited a false dichotomy between this modern illusory hedonism associated with Romanticism on the one hand, and the so-called Protestant work ethic on the other that supposedly came before it. A certain 'latent' romantic spirit, he points out, goes hand-in-hand with the 'daydreaming' that is involved in delayed gratification. Even within the contemporary middle-class lifecycle, these two supposed polar types are not so easily divisible (Bohemian youth is often followed by bourgeois middle-age). Delayed gratification creates a 'rich emotional inner life' of romantic imaginings. The existence of a Puritan character can thus, ironically, reinforce romantic personality traits whilst denying their legitimation. Given the strong association of the 'Protestant work ethic' with masculinity in a gendered public sphere, he goes on, it is often particularly pronounced in men (Ibid: 222-23, 225-26). A similar sort of paradox characterises the romantic attraction to western hedonism of immobile youth in 1970s rural Pakistan: taunted with glimpses of the pleasures that consumerism appeared to offer, they daydreamed of acquiring the riches necessary to purchase them through migration.

Freshies

Much of what the old timers recounted is present in the testimonies of Freshies. Psychological push factors that, although difficult to identify and quantify with any precision, play an important role in motivating individual migrants to up and leave. One thing, however, seems clear: curiosity 'to see' the West has intensified with the increase in restrictionism. The growth of a vast business in facilitation (Part III) has turned migration itself into a commodity that can and must be purchased – the ultimate product and status symbol in communities that now live above subsistence. This is reflected in the rising costs of smuggling, which went up by around £1,000 each year during the period of my conducting this research.

The mystique and romance surrounding emigration has been greatly intensified by the incremental increase in restrictionism instituted by the British government since the beginning of the 1960s. Only a relatively small proportion from South Asia had taken up the opportunity to migrate following the British Nationality Act of 1948, which left something of an Open Door for Commonwealth populations to enter the UK. The passing of the 1962 Commonwealth Immigration Act changed this instantaneously: by subjecting New Commonwealth labour migration to Britain to reduced strict quotas, the British state unwittingly stimulated immigration to hitherto unseen numbers, as thousands rushed to 'beat the ban', a number of whom may never have migrated had it not been introduced (Hiro 1973: 106-109; see also Shaw 2000: 15-20).

Several of the men I interviewed, by their own admission, were allured by the forbidden nature of migration, and cited wanting 'to see' that which lies behind the 'purdah' ['curtain']. Tanvir, a grocer from Jhelum was one of nine boys in his class of eleven who migrated in the 1980s. Though he did so by marriage and thus without taking on great financial and other kinds of risks, he insisted that migration is by no means a strictly rational calculation, and is given added appeal by virtue of its forbidden nature.

> *So why did you come?* Young blood. There's a *purdah*. You always want to know what's behind that: to see it for yourself. The next man will tell you there's nothing there but you will want to see for yourself.

Like many men I interviewed, he spoke of his own migration explicitly as a kind of irrational, impulsive and spontaneous endeavour – one which, with hindsight, could by his own admission, be regarded as ill-advised. Rubbing his bloodshot sleepy eyes, he told me his two class fellows who stayed put – one a solicitor and the other a head-teacher – enjoy a standard of living much higher than his own, and then reflected philosophically on the fact that whilst he works 12-hour days, they 'don't even get up to get themselves a glass of water' (domestic help in Pakistan is cheap and plentiful for the middle-classes).

Another man from Jhelum I met in East London, a 32-year-old market vendor (not listed in the table), explained his (illegal) migration from there in the late 1990s as part of a 'craze' amongst young men that was raging at the time. His life now, he added, in terms of personal hopes and aspirations, 'is finished', underlining the ongoing discrepancy between what is anticipated prior to migration and that which is ultimately experienced. This discrepancy plays an especially important role in driving migration that is irregular, given that its objective benefits are considerably less predictable than those enjoyed by previous migrants under Fordism. The costs of migration have spiralled to a point where they are difficult to calculate, as will be seen in Parts III and IV. Recollecting his sobering early weeks of job-hunting in dreary East London, Khan Sahab remembers:

I thought, 'London's not what I thought it would be.' I'd heard that in London, no one gets ill; that there's no tension, no worries. I heard there's snow but everyone has money and jobs. I heard everyone's happy, and that there are beautiful women. When I wasn't getting a job I felt bad – that my impression had been wrong.

The shock experienced at destination by immigrants whose heads are filled with rosy portraits of life in *Vilayat* prior to migration has long featured in classical accounts of migration. These accounts, however, do not unpack the precise symbolism in the language used by migrants to describe what exactly it is that they assumed they would experience, and as a consequence, miss an important element of what it was that built up their (now shattered) expectations and hopes. The reference to 'beautiful women' in Khan Sahab's above-cited testimony is particularly noteworthy in the context of remarks made by Shahid, the social worker I spoke with whilst doing fieldwork in Lahore. When I asked him about what it is that motivates migrants who head West in particular, instead of listing all the usual structural problems that characterise life in Pakistan, he explained that what appears to be a purely materially driven phenomenon is in fact linked in complex ways to the structure of gender relations and sexuality, especially for those young men of lower middle-class backgrounds that make up the bulk of Pakistan's international migration to the West. Whilst the pleasures of sex remain tauntingly visible in the lives of the country's elites and on television through advertising and the global media, they are firmly out of their grasp in what remains a conservative society. Nor can their frustrations be easily alleviated through marriage whilst they remain unemployed, unless they accept a match that brings downward social mobility. In short, as is often the case, competition within and among men, particularly in relation to access to women, is central to workings of the gender order (Ditz 2004: 1-35):

> *Shahid:* Another reason is that they have no access to women, to sex. No access to upper class women. They just play cricket and video games. Marriage is the only way for them to have sex. Because upward mobility for them is blocked, they feel a terrible frustration, especially those who want to see more of the world, experience what they see plastered on TVs.

The explosion of new media and mushrooming satellite television channels in Pakistan over the last decade is relevant here. The cultural production of sexual desire by consumerist ideologies in sending contexts is increasingly important in understanding the irrationality in risk-taking that human smuggling has normalised since the 1990s. If sexual liberalism is experienced by a small segment of the population, many millions more can press their noses up against the shop window by watching foreign television channels. No great analysis is needed to understand the kinds of promises consumerism now makes to the lower middle classes: the bizarre appearance, in recent years, of white women prancing around in Bollywood dance numbers sums up the entire argument of this book. In contexts of boredom and unemployment, images of this kind – astounding in their lack of subtlety – drive and effectively capitalise surplus masculine sexual energies, firing them across the surface of the planet in specific directions to ends which sometimes prove less useful to them than Europe's restricted economy (Parts III and IV).

I met 31-year-old Punjabi chef Chima in Florence. His decision to migrate in 1996 was taken at the age of just 21.

> I had a desire to go abroad from early on. There were friends, and others, men who were abroad. I thought I too wanted to live in a free setting. Be happy. Live in Europe.

> *AA: When did it begin, this desire?*
> I had a friend who was abroad. Before he left we would talk about going and we would say 'We'll go abroad'. 'If one of our friends' circle manages to go, even if our parents don't give money, we can put our money together and send one, and after he was gone then send another, and like that we would go. There was a desire to come.

> *AA: How does that desire come into existence?*
> It begins when a person says 'I want this thing. Even if it harms me.' We'll make our own money – good money and spend it whenever we feel like it. We'll do aiashi.

> *AA: Can't you do that in Pakistan?*
> You can but there are some restrictions. Parents say don't go here, don't go there, you have to do what they say. If you go out at night you have to tell them 'I'm going'. If you come back late they beat you.

The professed desire to experience 'freedom' here aligns migration with subversion and the assertion of one's youthful, generational identity. The decision to migrate is made, as with the old-timers, by and amongst a male community of friends, not by the household. The latter, if anything, is perceived as standing in the way of the individual's life designs, with parents represented as controlling killjoys from whom the young male migrant seeks economic autonomy ('we'll make our own money', 'spend it wherever we feel like it'). Paradoxically, given the patriarchal nature of the Pakistani migration system, 'making money', here, is about freedom from patriarchal control; to be 'happy' in a 'free setting'; to do *aiashi*, a word that suggests 'indulging in hedonistic pleasure' or 'getting one's kicks'.

This last vague but controversial remark expresses a set of sentiments associated with another term that was used by several of the respondents interviewed: '*ghumna*' – an infinitive verb that means literally, 'to roam'. The will to adventure and travel, which had featured in many of the accounts of the younger men I interviewed in London, resurfaced in Chima's narrative even after migration. Though his experiences in the aftermath of arrival were dominated by anxiety following extended sojourns of illegal residency and work in Germany and Italy, he casually mentioned leaving Italy to travel during a period of unemployment. When I pressed him about this inexplicable lapse into recreational mode, he responded with surprise that I would assume he or any other migrant worker should be any different to any other tourist or traveler in their desire and heterogeneity of interests:

> Nothing much was happening on the work front anyway. I went to roam around … I don't stress. I had a good roam. I stayed with Yasir in Belgium – that was good – then with a friend in Germany. Then I went to Austria, then to another one in Slovakia, and then I came back to Italy.

> *AA: What do you do when you roam, why do you enjoy it?*
> Why does anyone go to Italy from Germany and Britain? [Slightly annoyed].

> *Some people say Pakistanis only leave [migrate] to work, for money.*
> Some people leave just for money. Some are passionate about money. Some, like me, like to roam. Like to get their kicks. Some like to get their kicks with girls. They like to fuck around. Some like to see things, to see what things are like, to see different people and countries – they see that as getting their kicks. Some get their kicks from cooking and eating with friends. Everyone has their own way of getting their kicks … [NB Though in English it can signify 'mess around', the Urdu/Punjabi verb used by Chima ('chaudna') has only one meaning: to have sex.]

Sarfraz, a Punjabi who migrated to Italy at the age of 19 in 1994, had no hesitation in confirming that *aiashi* can indeed be factor in many young men's decision-making, pointing out that the oppressive regime of conservative control over individual behaviour in Pakistan makes it near impossible for young men in villages to experience in the kinds of pleasures that are routine in the West:

> *AA: Do men leave for reasons other than money – for aiashi?*
> Absolutely. Young men absolutely have it in mind. In Pakistan if you want to drink, you can get alcohol but it's not allowed. If the police catches you they'll put you in jail, the consequences are serious. Living with your family too is an issue … If a man likes to drink, even if he can afford to, what enjoyment will he get doing it when any moment he could get caught.

> *AA: And women?*
> Yes. If you do anything like that over there, the chance of getting beaten up is high. The risk is such that you could get shot if you … someone's sister or someone's daughter. That sort of thing happens all the time – you only need to read the newspapers. And so it's not easy to enjoy it.

Sarfarz's elliptical reference to the act ('you could get shot if you ...') is a reminder of the sensitivity of sexuality as a topic. He cannot bring himself to use the word (Chima's relative bluntness is a reflection of the fact that I had known him personally for over a year before interviewing him – and his unusually extroverted personality).

The notion of illegal labour migration as a form of youthful subversion is a counterintuitive argument, but one that has a basis in previous anthropologies of Pakistani migration. Werbner (1996: 88-91) has pointed to the fact that, despite its surface level solemnity and religious character, 'Pakistani culture' is in fact composed of diverse strands, its meaning contested by genders and generations. Positing a dialectical tension between the overt piety of elders who espouse high 'Islamic' ideals and a more subversive, sensuous South Asian youth sub-culture that seeks to carve out spaces of fun, celebrating the body and various sorts of transgression, Werbner cites the cult of cricket as a prime example of 'masculine glamour' that transgresses national boundaries (Ibid: 94). Irregular migration, in sending contexts, it is argued here, can be seen as another.

This is not to reduce migration to the outcome of a psychological game. These processes of establishing status are embedded in a material context and have real socio-sexual, material experiential consequences. Above all, as Shahid earlier quoted comment explained, it impacts upon inter-male competition for access to women within Pakistan itself, which is central to the gender-order. Within the sectors of rural middle-class society that these men occupy, marriage possibilities (the sole means of sexual and emotional development for single men) are rigidly structured by a man's social status. To be excluded from the ranks of the returnees restricts one's choice of bride and extends the wait for a suitable match, particularly in a district such as Gujrat where rates of emigration are high. For men in their early and mid-20s especially, this wait can be a passage of intense frustration.

Not all migrants are young, of course. Some are married at the time of emigration. The manifold factors that influence migration decisions are weighted differently for those depending on their household obligations. Indeed, given the diversity of ages, classes and marital backgrounds of migrants at the time of emigration, the arguments advanced in this chapter are unlikely to be uniformly applicable. Those relating to specifically youthful subversion and sexual adventure, for instance, do not affect married émigrés in their 30s and beyond in the same way; others, such as the appeal of travel and worldliness, also apply unevenly; others still, such as the pervasive reach of consumerism, apply universally. In view of this diversity, it is important to bear in mind that the youth cultural aspects under discussion are part of a general masculine ideology that sanctions pursuit of selfhood. It encompasses broad strata of men in different ways.

Married and elder men are less likely, of course, to openly confess to being drawn by the pull of transgressive forces. But this does not mean such factors do not figure in their thinking at all. Indeed, for Freud, the hold of the reality principle over the pleasure principle – 'not a very educable drive' – is only ever tenuous at best: acceptance of 'reality' is in fact never more than temporary toleration of un-pleasure on the 'long circuitous road to pleasure' (Freud 2003 [1920]: 45-8); and 'even where there is control of the drives, the aim of satisfaction is by no means abandoned' (Freud 2007 [1930]: 17). Susan Sontag, in her 1967 essay on Georges Bataille and the pornographic imagination, makes a similar point when she reminds us that whether or not people actually experience the full ecstatic pitch of their sexual capacities doesn't mean the existence of such possibilities 'doesn't haunt them anyway' (Sontag 2001: 104).

Moreover, even for the minority of migrants who were married when they set off – usually the most insistent that they did so with the intention of increasing household income – the association of migration with youth was quite possibly part of its appeal. Indeed for some of the older men, one gets the impression that migration offered the possibility of continuing, revitalising and reclaiming their youth at a moment in their lives when it was about to disappear. In this way, it promised to sooth the haunting many of us feel at a certain point in life when your twenties are gone forever and what was once the distant future (death) creeps nearer with each passing moment. Migration is a fetish indeed.

Conclusion to Part II

Part II analysed a distinct phase of the migration process we now leave behind: men of all ages and backgrounds in both London and Italy initially emphasised self-sacrificial and materialist motivations ('I am here to make money'; 'I am here for my family' etc.). But there is a sense in which such claims, reeled off automatically, began to unravel upon probing, underlining their inadequacy as an explanation of migration's causes. Classical accounts of migration have taken such claims for granted, underestimating personal ambition and selfhood as motivating forces of migration, which is driven as much by a felt need to impress one's community of men – male friends and associates, as well as kin – than by any desire to delight and support one's family.

Migrant testimonies were marked, for the most part, by a striking absence of any explicit search for romantic love or sexual fulfilment. But interview data point to sublimated and displaced sexual drives, energies and desires behind the impulse to migrate. These are particularly evident in illegal migration, which is increasingly expensive, perilous and (as will be discussed in the next chapter) sometimes disastrous for those individuals who decide to embark upon travel abroad. It involves risk-taking that does not always pay off in obvious ways, a fact that should compel us to scrutinise the rhetoric of materiality espoused in migrant discourse for deeper logics of desire and disavowal, and point us towards thinking more precisely about the local, gendered and generational contexts in which the decision to migrate is made.

The spectre of young men cajoling their households to finance their being smuggled must be seen against the absence of equivalent or even remotely comparable independent female primary migration from Pakistan. Women around the world are migrating independently more than ever before. Yet remittances from abroad have done little to challenge ideologies of masculinity in Pakistan and some studies have even demonstrated that they tend to reinforce purdah and the control of women (Gardezi 1995: 100; see also Ballard 2002). In some areas of rural Pakistan, masculinity and migration have come to be defined almost in relation to one another in a cycle of mutual reinforcement that normalises certain kinds of risk-taking by men – often against the instincts, wishes and/or interests of other members of the household, not least its women.

Some political context is needed here.

What made patriarchy so enduring in other male-breadwinner migration systems such as those in Europe, before the progressive changes which disrupted gendered migration patterns in Europe in the 1960s such as 'birth control' (Brettell 1987: 209), was state policy. Latin migration systems forbade independent female labour migration throughout the 19th century: Sarasúa's (2001) sketch of Spanish male and female temporary migration in the 18th and 19th centuries identifies the state's role in legally prohibiting women from partaking in the most dynamic spheres of the emerging market economy by denying them the right to seasonal migration (31-3). Irish women in the 1960s, in contrast, inherited a tradition of independent female labour migration; Brettell (1987: 136) points out that the role of the state, which did not outlaw independent female migration in Ireland despite the church's clamour, was the most important difference between Ireland and the Latin cases.

Similarly, the psychological processes discussed in Part II must be situated within the wider institutional, political-economic context of contemporary and historical Pakistan. As early as the late 1970s the Pakistani state began to adopt a policy of encouraging international emigration as a means of alleviating the country's intensifying economic woes. The Gulf boom, in the context of the country's ongoing poor macro-economic performance had fundamentally conservative effects in virtually all realms: politically, they undermined the ability of opposition movements to mobilise the support of urban workers against the military regime of Zia-ul-Haq (capital inflows in the form of remittances kept them docile [Noman 1988: 164-5]); economically, by facilitating lazy macro policies based on maintaining the economy afloat with external aid and remittance windfalls without bringing about structural, institutional and industrial change and development (the ability of the state to constantly make payouts to powerful factions and lobbies has been deeply harmful to the economic development of country as a whole, despite its misleadingly high growth rates in the 1980s [Sayeed 2002: 232-6]); and socially, by distorting patterns of consumption, which became decidedly conspicuous in districts like Gujrat, without changing substantially patterns of social and human development.

Without going into details of the country's disastrous recent political history – well documented by Tariq Ali and others – it is widely accepted Pakistan entered a downward spiral in the 1990s that shows no signs of abating. The social consequences of all this explain the competitive masculine ideology I have sketched in Part I: 'a social order unchecked and unregulated by public virtue'; a 'savage capitalism' that subordinates all public tasks to private aggrandisement via primitive accumulation' (Pasha 2001: 20). The state's predatory role has fostered a 'universal egotism'; the normalisation of violence, brutish and 'arbitrary behaviour' has accompanied a general situation in which 'social Darwinism has become the abiding principle of Pakistani society'. The persistent illegitimacy of government has led to the holding of citizenship in especially 'low esteem', creating a culture of 'self-seeking' (Ibid: 37-8) which, together with a market-logic, now permeates all aspects of society, including family and biraderi (Ibid: 41).

Manchuelle's (1997: 19-22) analysis of African societies as based on competition for power is relevant here. In such contexts, he explains, building clientele and 'holding one's rank' is crucial at all levels. Prestige becomes associated with honour, status and associating with the powerful rather than personal morality. All key stages of life become occasions for ostentatious displays of wealth (above all weddings, but also, return visits from trips abroad). Poverty, conversely, becomes castigated for its dishonourable status and lack of association with power. In societies where corruption, calamity, inequality and injustice are rife, this castigation of poverty as weakness and dishonour can be damaging upon the average individual, who experiences varying degrees of helplessness and powerlessness: an unhealthy, neurotic and compulsive desire for personal power is likely to develop (Kelman 1972 cited by Gilani [2001: 53]).

This is particularly pertinent in Pakistan, where the underlying sense of powerlessness of the individual manifests itself in the fact that 'people are keen to associate themselves with someone currently and/or ancestrally powerful' as a means of overcoming the daily feelings of marginalisation that are commonplace:

> Thus one witnesses … the social habit of name-dropping. Discourse is marked by belligerence and machismo. The rule seems to be that you are by definition weak and powerless, unless you can prove otherwise. Thus many positions are taken and postures adopted with the purpose of looking powerful. This is a complicated game and often results in adopting positions which make no sense whatsoever … such posturing has some very unfortunate consequences (Gilani 2001: 53).

It is against this structural backdrop, that the non-rational component of masculine migrant subjectivity – its penchant for aggrandisement and outrageous risk-taking – begins to make true sense. Illegal migration to the West is not the only example of this, but it is a good one, especially when we consider what has taken place at the other, lower end of the Pakistani migration system, and how it has affected groups that experience greater levels of vulnerability and marginalisation.

Integral to the consequences of appalling governance and endemic levels of corruption we have noted in recent decades has been the deteriorating position of women, helped along by the Hudood Ordinances – a series of 'Islamic' laws introduced in the 1980s under the military dictatorship of General Zia which effectively criminalised female rape victims and legitimised violence against the most vulnerable children of an already patriarchal society (Shaheed 2002: 344). A not insignificant number of those who suffer most are immigrants trafficked from neighbouring Asian countries such as Nepal, Bangladesh and Afghanistan, where catastrophic destruction has seen this country become the world's biggest sender of refugees, many of whom are smuggled and/or trafficked into and/or out of Pakistan. (The Zia years also fostered a context in which the smuggling (and trafficking) of goods, drugs, arms and people into and out of Pakistan flourished). By all accounts, irregularly resident women who are smuggled into Pakistan from Burma, Bangladesh and Nepal in particular are more likely to be harassed and detained than aided by the police, in whose hands a shockingly high number are routinely sexually assaulted (Jalalzai 2002; 2003).

They are not a uniquely oppressed group. Pakistan's own wretched 'indigenous' underclasses are not the subject of this book, but must be borne in mind: 50 per cent reside in semi-legal squatter dwellings within their own country, having migrated from rural areas themselves to build houses in informal shantytowns and work within the informal urban economy (Shahnaz 2004). So too the thousands of Pakistanis trafficked within their own country each year. For some reason, these receive even less media attention than women and children trafficked into servitude in the Gulf as domestic (and sexual) slaves or camel jockeys (Jalalzai 2002: 2003). Movement within the Pakistani migration system is thus deeply polarised at its two extremes, and powerfully segmented along various lines, one of which is social class. Another is gender, which determines global patterns of movement in 2011 (as it did in 1947) in such a manner that independent labour migration and international irregular migration from Pakistan are rare among women of any background.

PART III
Death

Introduction to Part III

The first part of this book established the relatively affluent and powerful position of many Pakistani emigrants to the West within their countries and communities of origin. Its remaining sections examine their plight in the migration process.

The following chapter presents a political-economic analysis of migrant networks from Pakistan, offering an alternative to the modes and units of analysis adopted in extant literatures. Discussion hinges on the way kinship ties, friendship and commercial connections and associations between smuggling agents – as structured by restrictive state policies – mediate, reflect and constitute relations between labour and capital. We draw inspiration from Bataille's refutation of any attempt to define human activity as dictated exclusively by rationalising interests ('balanced accounts' [1997: 169]): his 'notion of expenditure', which likens the economy to an organism that produces more energy than it needs; surplus must be spent wastefully, destroyed or expelled from the system as base matter. The *general* economy encompasses all; the *restrictive* economy expels excess from, and back into the former. Interplay between the two is a useful metaphor for thinking about the function of human smuggling in global capitalism, in particular the manner in which it conveniently funnels, filters, disciplines and facilitates the ingestion of immigrant labour as it passes through the bowels of Europe's productive system. Political borders and other prohibitions on migrant mobility – equivalent to taboos in matters of sexuality – define Europe's relationship with Afro-Eurasia, the restrictive economy's relation to the general.

Thinking of smuggling in this way allows us to see more clearly the interests it reflects, imbues and serves, which in turn renders visible the trouble with utilitarian economistic representations of migrant networks as inherently equilibrating and rationalising. It also helps to address the shortcomings of debate in media and policy circles, where smuggling appears exclusively as a narrowly conceived criminal problem: deracinated from the formal economy, mafia-run traffickers and thuggish agents become, in this narrative, an unfortunate byproduct of today's increasingly anarchic globalisation; their success signals a loss of state sovereignty (for a discussion see Ahmad, forthcoming 2012). Quite apart from obfuscating the historic role of the state in generating illegality through restrictive policies, this is a discourse which ignores contradictions and obvious conundrums: for all the talk of 'Fortress Europe's growing impenetrability, when, why and how is it that some borders get crossed illegally by migrants – sometimes with relative ease?' (Andrijasevic 2009: 396). Restrictionism, it will be seen, is less about outright exclusion than dispensing with, transferring and redirecting surplus energies in ways that prevent immigrant labour from rising above its status as usefully productive inputs within processes of accumulation that bind Afro-Eurasia to Europe in relations of domination.

The approach we adopt is historical: when and in relation to what structuring policies, material contexts and interests did human smuggling networks evolve? What, if any, are their antecedents? The chapter begins with a re-assessment of the available historical accounts of Pakistani migration, of which there are close to a dozen cited in this book. Despite the fact that their authors uncovered important material I draw upon myself, not a single one makes more than a passing reference or a throwaway paragraph to brokerage and illegality. None theorise or even contemplate its significance as evidence of migration's commodification. If this was once understandable given the political marginality of illegality as a migration issue, now that facilitation of migration is a multimillion-dollar global business, the murkier 'criminal' aspects of which regularly grab news headlines, the question of how and why human smuggling developed can surely no longer be ignored. As will be seen, the two decades following 1962 are far more important than is currently acknowledged. To understand these years and the contemporary state of affairs, however, it is also crucial to make some brief remarks on developments in the colonial period, when migration (and smuggling) from South Asia to Britain first began.

Human smuggling in the colonial era

Lascar migration networks in the 19th and early 20th centuries were commodified through the activities of intermediaries throughout the migration process: agents who facilitated the hurdling of bureaucratic obstacles and sometimes, the circumvention of migration controls through provision of false documentation. Commercial recruiters operated at the Bombay and Calcutta docks. They owned lodgings near the shipyard and helped peasants fill in their contracts with the British navy or company concerned: 'Initially loans were given on credit, and paid back when the newcomer was employed'. Kinship networks, from the outset, operated in parallel to commercial chains. The two were intertwined given that the same brokers would help kinsmen for free whilst profiteering from strangers (Gardner 1995: 41; Ansari 2004: 38 [citing Adams 1987]).

In Britain, new arrivals turned to owners of boarding-houses in East London, where ships docked, for advice and help with paperwork (Visram 2002: 199, 210-15, 224). Police records contain important evidence of individuals profiteering from brokerage in the interwar period, including a silk-merchant named Hasmatrai Rewchaud, believed by police to have paid fares of £16 to £18 per head for a large number of Indians to come to Britain so he could recruit them as peddlers (Ibid: 257, 262). A trade in passports and other documents necessary to secure residential rights developed following a series of prohibitive laws including the Coloured Seamen Act of 1919. Posters at seaports were put up to discourage the idea that Britain was a land of opportunity; the Home Office restricted the granting of peddler licences to Indian applicants within the UK (Ibid: 217-18; Ahmad [forthcoming 2012]).

Overall, however, the British state was ambiguous in its attitude towards the lascars, as it was more generally throughout the 19th and early 20th centuries in its immigration policy, which wavered between apparently politically motivated impulses (racist xenophobia) and perceived/actual economic necessity: asylum controls, for example, were often relaxed when it suited the short-term demands of the British economy (Panayi 1994: 39). If on the one hand, a series of bureaucratic obstacles established the British labour market as part of a restrictive economy, on the other, the encouragement of lascar desertion by private employers during periods of high demand for labour met with no or little rebuke. The Home Office even dropped its objections to the hiring of seamen when influential employers appealed to the Board of Trade and Industry on the basis that it needed the manpower (Visram 2002: 196-7). By mid-1942, it was estimated that 3,000 Indians were employed in British industries across the country, including Becton Gasworks in what is today Newham (Ibid: 268). Lascars, the point is, were never prevented from entering, residing and working in Britain altogether – controls merely served to funnel in a select few and shape the conditions under which they could access the labour market.

The same apparent dynamics were equally visible in France, where demand for labour among French employers often served to undermine the policies of the interior ministry. In 1905, when a law was instituted that allowed Algerians passage to France, labour recruiters in the coal, agriculture, chemicals and mining industries keenly used labourers from Kabyle to break strikes (MacMaster 1997: 51-2). When the interior ministry attempted to barrack off Algerian workers in specified living quarters (camps), workers travelled within France on forged identity cards, often with the complicity of employers. Four thousand were unaccounted for by the end of the First World War. They settled in enclaves near major factories where they were employed, concentrating around cafés, of which there were reported to be 54 in Paris alone by 1918, replicating the pattern in Marseilles (MacMaster 1997: 63, 68) where Sonike sailors from Dakar began stowing away and working without papers or using fraudulent documents in the 19th century. The Sonike too, had their cafés and hotels, which operated as 'mutual aid associations'. These 'remarkable institutions of solidarity', as Manchuelle describes them, provided new migrants with 'hospitality and contacts in the employment market' (1997: 197-9, 211).

Though neither MacMaster nor Manchuelle raise the issue of profiteering, the latter's data contain a reference to African hotel and café owners who 'acted as intermediaries for local factories when French enterprises started recruiting black Africans in Marseilles in the 1930s'. These individuals, some of his sources suggest, returned to Dakar and other sending context harbours to enlist prospective workers. The recruiters were African sailors who had contacts with members of the Marseilles underworld. The latter, in a revealing twist, were themselves intermediaries for Parisian enterprises (Ibid: 215-16).

As in Britain, trafficking in sailors' registration papers was common, and operated in parallel to kinship networks in both Dakar and Marseilles: sailors who were retired or went on leave passed them onto their relatives. Those without kinsmen who were sailors had to pay handsome sums to intermediaries in Dakar including both powerful and influential individuals as well low level profiteers. In 1926, the French Ministry of Colonies started an enquiry over its own representatives in Marseilles whom it suspected of selling provisional documents to undocumented African sailors: state officials have never been immune to involvement in profiteering from migration brokerage. Indeed, kinship networks operated in parallel to commercial ones, webbing together the interests of profiteering migrants-turned-agents, local industrialists, corrupt state officials and criminal underworld elements.

What can we learn from the past? The presence of an informal economy fed by smuggling networks that funnel labour into Europe through cities like London and Paris today is hardly unprecedented. Such channels have mediated the relationship between Europe's restrictive core and Afro-Eurasian labour since at least the colonial era. The apparent ambivalence of state policies towards labour from the periphery reflects the fact that states were never homogenous or unequivocal in their orientation: the tension between interior ministries and economic actors such as factory owners has always had the convenient function of pulling and squeezing labour simultaneously: borders and other kinds of restrictions ensured workers' energies were spent to suit the needs of 'useful' production in Europe.

Other kinds of expenditure – of sexual, erotic energies – were taboo for immigrants. Reproduction, with all its associations of normalcy in work-life balance and leisure was discouraged by laws that made settlement difficult; recreational sex was balked at: the ultimate symbol of threat to the restrictive priorities of Europe's colonial metropolitan economy was the non-white immigrant who dared rise above his station to sleep with a white woman, a phenomenon that triggered real concern among policy-makers when in 1944, a report on the perceived menace of miscegenation between 'coloured' men and working-class white women documented the presence of four hundred coloured people in Stepney alone, forty-nine per cent of whom are listed as Indian. Thirty-two were Indian men with white partners, fourteen of whom had married. Of the 136 'half-caste' children, 61 had Indian fathers (Visram 2002: 274). The authorities were deeply concerned about the erosion of racial barriers in pockets of London that such relationships appeared to be causing.

However, short-term economic demand appears to have trumped – or at least compelled the temporary suppression of Britain's deep-seated racial xenophobia. An Open Door policy operated in the 1950s until being slammed shut in 1962 with the infamous Commonwealth Immigration Act. The tap, in other words, was turned on and then abruptly off again – this time with far-reaching consequences for human smuggling.

Chapter 3

Fortress Europe, Afro-Eurasia: Human Smuggling and Restrictive Economy

The early post-colonial period saw the establishment of widespread travel agency in Pakistan. Khan (1977: 66) notes that at the end of the 1950s, 'the institutions of migration (travel agents, banks and airlines) were well established'. By 1961, according to Baba Saud, agents and their representatives had reached even medium-sized cities and towns such as Faislabad. Facilitation consisted of filling out forms necessary for the issue of passports, making travel arrangements and purchasing tickets:

> *Baba Rashid:* I had a passport made with great difficulty. I didn't have one. It was very difficult. First I had a passport made for the Middle East … So there I put my security – 800 rupees, and my passport was made. Then to come to England [with] the security [it] was 2,500 hundred rupees. So on top of the 800, I put 1,800 rupees down for 'security' and had my UK passport made. I got my UK passport. When I came here, at that time you didn't need a visa or work permit or anything, just a passport.

Aurora's (1967: 41-5) account of migration from South Asia during the 1950s suggests agents at that time continued to operate within the historical parameters of the colonial South Asian migration systems which operated under British rule in at least two important ways: (1) They tended not to cater for destinations in Europe other than Britain (2) Many specialised in sea-based travel premised on colonial circuits of travel. They were also probably already involved in smuggling. The Indian Workers' Association cited passports in its policy programme as 'a problem of great concern to all Indians in Great Britain', adding that 'so-called agents' had 'fully exploited the situation for their own selfish motives and obtained fantastically large sums of money' from the formation of 'passport rackets'.

After the Commonwealth Immigration Act of 1962, which saw the introduction of a voucher system that required prospective immigrants to have a sponsor already in Britain to arrange a job for them before they could enter, smuggling networks began to evolve into the highly developed and widespread business they are today. By placing South Asians already resident in Britain in considerable positions of power, the Act dramatically increased the scope for profiteering by immigrants themselves, most of whom had never previously been travel agents or brokers. The upshot was a sudden commercialisation of kin and friendship networks;

a different kind of organic freelance smuggling resulted from the augmentation in state restrictions:

> *Nadir:* It started initially on a friendly and help basis, and then they realised they could do it for money … The clever ones started up agencies and got established with contacts [in the UK]. They were ambitious – they spread the word to get groups together and brought them. Word would get around that 'they are doing this' – that 'he's done it successfully'. They would make them travel individually or with a group, create a sponsorship letter … They developed the technique – the art of doing it.

Considerable diversity in smuggling methods thus developed in the 1960s, some of which took place within the ostensible framework of the law: travelling on the passports of deceased migrants, for example. Declaring nephews and nieces as one's own children was not uncommon. Faizal, a middle-aged migrant from Gujrat now in Italy, said this practice was widespread:

> From my area, 60 per cent went to England. Mostly to Nelson, in Manchester. A few families went to London but Nelson is full. They're the old ones … A few men I knew went there. They called people from back home. They said here is good: 'It's all happening here!'.

> *AA: When?*
> Some went in '74.

> *AA: Why do you remember '74?*
> My cousin took my brother, declaring him as a son. That's how it happened in those days. Men with one son would write declare four or five sons and take them with them.

Even among kin, childrearing arrangements of this kind could involve financial compensation to the carer. Nadir cited examples of this kind of adoption being done for a fee: a family 'would go to Denmark and declare a few extra children of that age group and then *negotiate* … to bring them.' There was nothing unusual about this kind of transaction: the ancient practice of sending children away to work as a last resort has been known to involve payment to a broker. Fontaine (1996: 146-7) notes that when mountain societies packed children in the Alps off into apprenticeships, they made contractual arrangements with migrants who were paid to organise 'a capo' for the child in Italy.

The specificity of modern smuggling lies in the extent to which 'mutual-aid' in international migration has become subject to profiteering since the Act of 1962, which precipitated the gradual dissipation of the former, its displacement by the latter as it became increasingly clear just how lucrative brokerage could be. The inflationary effect on migration costs is hinted at by Shaw (2000: 30) and Kalra

(2000: 69) who quotes two interviews with different migrants, one of whom left Mirpur to migrate in 1960 by ordering a passport from Karachi and paying his fare without any protracted problems, and another who, *after* the Act was passed, had to pay an agent 5-6,000 rupees to get a ticket, passport and visa from Rawalpindi. He also had to wait for a voucher from the UK confirming he was registered with the labour ministry. Dahya's research led him to conclude that during the period 1960-65, agents' charges went up as much as 800 pounds (1974: 82; see also Aurora 1967: 41-5).

Data on both sending and receiving contexts in virtually every study of migration from South Asia since the 1960s suggest there was a sudden growth in human smuggling, brokerage and unequal relations of power within migration networks in the 1960s. Ballard and Ballard's study of Sikhs in Britain, for instance, reported that over time 'social' arrangements and networks became 'more structured' (Ballard and Ballard 1977: 30-31). Gardner's more recent account of migration from Sylhet (then East Pakistan) notes the role of 'key individuals' who mediated the whole network and were of 'central importance in promoting migration': 'some had boarding houses in London where newcomers could stay, and back home they acted as brokers, encouraging men to try their luck in Britain, lending them money, and giving them contacts for jobs.' These men replaced the 'earlier *sarengs* [labour recruiters at ports]' who 'had filled this role, helping men from their own areas and families gain work on the ships ...'.

Colonial recruitment systems were thus displaced in the early post-colonial decades by a transcontinental business in brokerage connecting East Pakistan to the UK, its protagonists being migrants who 'encouraged their kin and neighbours to take up vouchers and join them' (Gardner 1995: 45-6).

This changing sociology of smuggling was bound up with fundamental geographic restructuring of the relationship between core European restrictive and general Afro-Eurasian peripheral economies. New forms of facilitation – above all, small-scale overland journeys through Central Asia and the Mediterranean – led to the gradual erosion of colonial pathways tying South Asia to Britain. This spatial reconfiguration was part of a wider transformation in the Eurasian 'migration system' (Kritz et al. 1992): a geo-spatial formation formed over time, connecting 'movements of people to concomitant flows of goods, capital and information sustained and reinforced by social, political and institutional networks and relationships which make possible and encourage migration along certain paths and not others'. Human smuggling was just one of a number of economic activities UK returnees were involved in.

Nadir: They would bring consumables and gadgets, and on the way back take family members' in transit vans purchased in the UK. They'd make them wait in France and Holland, make a trip to the UK and return for them – a different route. Or they would brief them on how to get through to the UK, beat immigration laws, and they'd come independently.

Returnees, remittances and commodities flowed in one direction; migrants travelled illegally back in the other, whence these came, as a direct result of their penetration, often in vehicles not dissimilar to the vans used by hippies on their intrepid adventures along the GT road. That migrants sometimes stayed in the same hotels as western tourists in cities like Kabul suggests diverse kinds of travel and cultural exchange overlapped as they passed over Pakistan's Western border into Afghanistan, through Iran and then Turkey. Methods and routes of migrant and tourist travel were not dissimilar: Peshawar, Kabul and Istanbul by truck and bus – onwards by train, foot and car. Indeed the experiences of men who travelled through Central Asia in the 1970s to Greece or West Germany (via East Germany) from Lahore and other parts of Punjab underline the intersections of smuggling routes and overland tourism. Some felt safe and confident enough to depart without the advice of agents, leaving in small groups of friends and with small sums of money that covered the costs of accommodation and food in Kabul and Istanbul for up to several weeks. These included teenagers away from home for the first time such as Guyoor who arrived in Istanbul via Kabul and Peshawar in 1972 at the age of 19, and Riaz Ahmed who shaved for the first time in Kabul, where he stayed for six weeks at the age of 18 in 1977. The 9,000 rupees he paid his agent in advance covered the costs of his entire journey, during which he roamed around the city, ate well and even went to the cinema (his monthly salary as a teacher in Mandi had been 350 rupees). Kashif Bhutti was not so fortunate. He paid 20,000 in 1980 to make the same journey. Still, he too recalls shopping in Kabul, and staying in good hotels. Irfan Ghani, whose testimony is quoted at length below describes Kabul in terms that reflect a society and economy quite distinct from the situation associated with contemporary Afghanistan: 'It was very, very liberal under King Zahir, you couldn't wear traditional clothes. Girls were wearing skirts and men were wearing ties. In those days in Kabul you could get around with Urdu even Punjabi because most of the shopkeepers and money-traders were Sikhs'. All of which suggests Kabul was part of a flourishing Eurasian tourist economy in which travel was connected with youth and leisure – good, cheap hotels, affordable food and shopping.

Several of these men (none of whom are listed in the appendices for the reason that they were interviewed as part of a research update in 2010) remembered seeing hippies ('white people … smoking hash') in hotels 'everywhere' from Lahore to Peshawar, Kabul and Istanbul. Irfan Ghani was one of a tiny group of youngsters in Lahore with interests in pop and rock culture in the late 1960s. Though somewhat distinct from the other men I interviewed in terms of his background – urban, middle-class, educated in an English medium school run by missionaries – his recollections provide evidence of the extent to which western mobility and consumption in Asia shaped the context in which overland smuggling was taking place. He remembers, for instance, that tourists would frequently ask permission to park their vans and camp on the front lawn of his family home near Mall Road. Naturally he would get talking to them ('about Bob Dylan, Jimmy Hendrix, Janis Joplin….'). At 16, he and a friend boarded a bus to Peshawar in 1970. From there they hitchhiked to Kabul – at the time, 'just littered with hippies'. At the dormitory in which they stayed, they met a 'German guy':

> We got up in the morning and said 'Hi' and he said 'Hi'. There was this huge hall – we went there and sat there. He said, 'Guys, you gotta do this, really'. It was the first time I smoked hash. It was ten in the morning. After two cups of tea with lots of milk and sugar and eggs we smoked again. Me and my friend thought, 'This is something that could be done on a regular basis'.

German guy was clearly enjoying considerable spending power. He generously paid for them to visit Mazar-i-Sharif which, according to Ghani Sahab, boasts 'the best hash in the world'. In exchange for this kindness they were expected to do help him with a problem of his own.

> He had these two giant family sized toothpastes and a shaving cream packaged in plastic. He had unrolled them from the end and taken 90% of the cream out. I had to make tiny balls of hash. My friend had to put them on the tip of a pen and burn them, put a cap on them, dip them in liquid wax and put them in the tubes. We did this for 2-3 days. He left some cream on the front and we put hash at the back so it didn't smell. Mizar- i- Sharif's local toothpaste is very pungent. Then he asked, 'Do you guys wanna shave and brush?'. We squeezed it and shaved and brushed our teeth ... That was the end of it. I didn't see him after that.

The extent of mobility in people and produce is impressive. German guy may well have been a hippy; he was also a small-time drug smuggler profiteering from the ease with which some goods and bodies moved in virtually any direction during this period. It's worth comparing this liberal regime with the conditions of movement for ordinary Pakistanis trying to get back into their own country. At Quilla Saifullah, the first checkpoint for travellers from Iran, Ghani Sahab and his friend were among those in a long line of people harassed by border guards. The tourist economy in which hippies and hash moved was administered by states that subjected their own populations from provinces like Balochistan – Pakistan's most economically marginal and backward zones – to authoritarian regimes of control and informal taxation.

> There was this big bloke at the check-post. He was interrogating people. There were two men ahead of us and he asked the first what have you brought? He said, 'Ten dinner sets from Iran'. The guard kept one. The next man had brought something else and he showed those. Then it was our turn. He asked us what we had brought and we said nothing. So he asked what we had gone there for. We told him for leisure. He didn't believe us so he made us take our clothes off and he checked us and our rucksacks thoroughly. He even opened the seams of our rucksacks to see if we were hiding anything. Then he interviewed us for an hour to ask us what we had gone there for. Finally after more than an hour

of interviewing he let us board the bus. It took us a night and a day of travel to reach Quetta. This route was off the hippie trail. A glass of water cost you a lot in those days through that trail.

AA: Who were the other travellers?
Pakistanis who had brought in goods from other places to sell in the markets of Quetta.

Off the hippy trail, then, a Pakistani traveler could be strip-searched and made to jump through hoops just to get home. Along it, cheap hash could be transported to continental Europe with little fuss in tubes of toothpaste. The contrast contextualises human smuggling routes as historical formations webbed to broader East-West systems of exchange in which movement of bodies and goods was given momentum by tourists from countries as diverse as France and Germany.

The smuggling trail through continental Europe (France in particular in these early stages) resulted in the organic growth of a third phase between sending and receiving sites: transit. Its end destination was less clearly defined, and often reached spontaneously in a somewhat convoluted manner. Failed or aborted attempts to migrate were not uncommon amongst those who eventually reached their targets, a fact which is reflected in the following extract, in which Nadir recalls the experience of his elder brother, who set out for the UK from Dinga in the 1960s.

My elder brother left [the village] as a soldier in the 1960s. In 66 he spent two or three years there and got frustrated. He tried to improve his education. In the meantime, a UK friend said he would take him … They went by road. They got held up in France and Germany for a long time. The agent couldn't get though. We communicated through letters. They would find someone on the way, or stay in a hotel. They were B&Bs. We told him to come back. He did but this trip gave him awareness. He was restless when he came back. He found a way on his own.

Prior to the current phase of globalisation and the diffusion of new communications technology, an important alteration in the geography of the Pakistani migration system was taking place. If the 1970s and 1980s remained a period in which the bulk of migration in Western Europe was based on the old colonial systems (Colleyer 2005: 699-718), the Pakistan-UK bilateral international migration system was quietly developing into a multilateral organism that would soon develop a number of other centres spanning Western Europe. The UK remained the number one destination of choice but a number of other alternatives were established by (initially) illegally resident pioneers who began to set up businesses and communities, taking advantage of the absence of internal controls within states which, at that time, were slow to deport irregular entrants. The steady trickle of men held up in transit whilst on their way to the UK in the 1970s thus evolved into a patchwork of nascent communities across Western Europe. The British Nationality

Act of 1981 cemented this process by curtailing the possibilities of legal entry to the UK for migrants without connections abroad. In 1982, a convention held by a UK-based organisation called the Centre for Pakistan studies was presented with reports from France, Belgium, Holland, Denmark, Norway, each of which had already become home to between one and ten thousand Pakistanis, many in legally ambiguous positions (Ahmad forthcoming 2012). Men like Nadir's brother.

> In the mid and late seventies people started going to Scandinavia. Denmark and then Norway. In Denmark, they'd have been there 7-8 years illegally, and then got to stay. They'd apply for residency with the help of solicitors. Deportation was not there at that time. My brother found out you can go to Denmark without a visa if you have some money in hand. He did that, with a cousin. He took the chance: he flew to Denmark directly and settled there. At that time there were only 100-200 people. They worked in factories and services. My brother drove a taxi. His children are now doctors.

Reproduction and upward social mobility: hardly an existence Bataille would have celebrated from start to finish as the epitome of erotic perversion. Nonetheless, these are lives spent on more than 'useful' economic activity. Based on rootedness in a single North Western European destination, a stable existence, citizenship and marriage rights (not to mention welfare benefits and entitlements to certain minimum pay and working conditions), Nadir's testimony underlines the fact that despite the gradual geo-spatial reconfiguration of Europe's migration system that was occurring in the 1970s, outcomes for migrants did not drastically alter in this period: men who arrived in Scandinavia and Continental Europe in the 1970s and 1980s fared similarly to their East London predecessors. Afro-Eurasian labour was shifting around, but lifetime investments of expenditure in Europe's restrictive core could still be made in singular destinations with expectations that today – post-Schengen, post-9/11, post Iron Curtain – seem increasingly remote. The general economy still seeps into the core. But the terms of exchange have altered.

The smuggling business today: A global enterprise

Short. Fat. Bald. Dr Akram is a middle-aged man who wears spectacles. He doesn't smoke cigars. He bears no unsightly scars and does not possess (let alone carry around and menacingly stroke) a designer furry pet. He is, all in all, a far cry from media stereotypes of the evil, ruthless, criminal trafficker. The sheer lack of threat to my personal safety was, I must confess, a tad disappointing at our first meeting in 2003.

Akram is a travel agent. A co-ordinator of sorts, whose principle tasks include procurement of travel documents (at that time fraudulent passports and doctored visit visas); booking any necessary airline tickets from Pakistan; devising routes and journey plans; briefing travellers on what to do at all stages of travel, including transit, which can last weeks or even months. During these periods it is his and his overseas colleagues' responsibility to feed and house travellers, or supply them with enough cash to do so themselves. His competencies are numerous, and include detailed knowledge of immigration and asylum law (Akram showed me a pile of hardback law books on his desk). He is, I was told by several of his admirers, good at what he does (hence his title – "He has a PhD in smuggling"). Like many of the best in his line of work, he offers money-back guarantees to clients in the event they do not reach their intended destination.

On the surface, smugglers play cat-and-mouse with the authorities. In truth, the role of the Pakistani state is ambiguous in relation to human smuggling. Smugglers like Akram – 'big agents' – work with contacts in officialdom, elements of which, it should come as no surprise, have built up a considerable stake in the success of their activities. The involvement of port officials in the practice of smuggling has been widely reported within the media, and is common knowledge among journalists and policy-makers (not to mention migrants and smugglers). A Google search on 'corruption, FIA, human smuggling, Pakistan' will generate numerous links to news reports in reputable English language newspapers including *The Dawn* – more than can be usefully listed here. The alleged connivance of prominent politicians (in some cases ministers) will surprise no one in a country whose President's nickname is Mr Ten Percent.

Set up in 1974, the Federal Investigation Agency's duties initially included controlling the smuggling of drugs and goods. Historically, it had little incentive to stamp out illegal emigration; if anything, the logic of Pakistan's long-term policy of growth oriented, remittance-driven development made emigration of any kind a phenomenon to encourage until after the Cold War, when human smuggling moved up the political agenda in discussions between the West and Third World states. In 1996, the FIA's duties were officially changed so that it became an organisation devoted exclusively to combating human smuggling. Pressure from Western governments following the rise in asylum claims during the 1990s led to the introduction of fines for airlines proven to have failed to spot fraudulent documents. The establishment of a special PIA task force whose duties include examination of passports by experienced experts and interviews of suspected irregulars is just one example of an increasingly strict regime which, since 9/11, has been further buttressed through linkages with American concerns about terrorism (Ahmad forthcoming 2012).

None of which has halted illegal migration. Smuggling networks have always acted as an interface between migrant labour and the restrictive economy through corrupt elements in sending and receiving states. The former were drawn much more tightly into the latter's proliferating regime of surveillance machinery during the previous decade: technology sharing agreements and cooperation on development issues between the EU and countries as diverse as Pakistan, Libya and Morocco now routinely encompass discussions over migration control which is being 'sourced up and out' from previous national levels of policy-formation (Lavenex 2006). The stakes, as a result, are higher, and as politicians, port and FIA officials come under pressure from external forces, they expect higher sums from smugglers to facilitate exit from airports. Networks are thus even more deeply commodified and squeeze travelers at both ends of the migration process.

Just how much profit a given transaction generates and for whom is difficult to calculate. The price a smuggler such as Akram charges for a package covers ordinary transportation and administrative costs in addition to fees for the purchase of fraudulent documents and/or bribing officials. One thing is clear though: the impact and costs of this tightening restrictionism have been thus passed on to migrants themselves. The cost of a 'package' of the sort offered by Akram increased considerably in the decade from the mid-1990s as restrictionism tightened. Chima and Rafeeq, whom I met in Italy, paid between 1 and 1.5 *lakhs* in the mid-1990s to reach Italy from Pakistan (one *lakh* being roughly equal to a thousand pounds). By the late 1990s and into the new millennium, the price had gone up to between three and five *lakhs*, as Hamza, Waqas and Atif testified when I interviewed them in Italy 2006. Kamran paid seven and half *lakhs* to make the same journey a few months prior to when I interviewed him in London in 2003.

Smuggling networks today also encompass corrupt elements within an array of transitory countries, connecting agents in Pakistan to dozens of cities through which their clients must travel in order to reach destinations inside North Western Europe. As security at airports tightened in the 1990s, the organisation of clandestine sea and overland border crossings came to dominate the activities of smugglers – particularly through Eastern, Central and Southern Europe and the Mediterranean which, following the collapse of the Berlin Wall in 1989, have became increasingly integrated into the West European migration system. The global extent of organised co-operation displayed in 'Pakistani' smuggling networks is today unprecedented, and depends on locally stationed cultural translators: 'We have lawyers, informers abroad – settled Pakistanis, friends, contacts in the UK, the Czech Republic, Lithuania', Dr Akram explained. 'We have Pakistanis living in Poland who are married and have learned the language'. These friends are former 'travelers' (migrants turned mediators or 'agents') who co-operate not only with each other and agents in Pakistan, but also with outsiders in crucial 'bridging' ties with local operators, to whom aspects of the process have effectively been sourced out or sub-contracted (namely ensuring migrants are fed, housed and if necessary clothed, as well as transported on successfully to their next point of transit in the smuggling process):

> *Asad:* Peshawar was the start. I took a plane to Karachi where I met two friends from my area. (Not by chance – the agent had organised this). We went to Dubai (I was on a genuine Pakistani passport). Then we went to Moscow. We spent six days there. An Afghan guy was waiting for us at the airport. He took care of us. There were no problems getting through the airport, we had a visa. So we were three guys in a room in Moscow. Then an Afghan guy took us and gave us to a Russian guy who took us to the Ukraine border. We stayed at his place for two days. He gave us to a Ukrainian agent. Then we went by car for 16 hours.

We crossed the border and went to Kiev. He gave us to a Russian guy who took us to a border. We spent two weeks in a room there, and then he brought us to the Slovakia-Ukraine border. Then two guys from Slovakia took us across the border into a forest near Bratislava ... We left for Austria (the agent took us there). There some Afghan agent took us to Germany, where we spent two or three days. He gave us to a Punjabi (driver) and a Russian (who was with him). They took us to Germany in two or three days. They then drove us to Belgium, where an Afghan guy took us. We stayed in Belgium for 13 or 14 days as the routes were shut. In the end there was no route to the UK so we went to France (the Afghan sent us). We were in Paris for two to three weeks. A Kurd –an Iraqi agent took over from there. He put us in a truck container. I think it was carrying cotton: us three and three more Kurds from Paris. We slept. It was cold but okay. We got to the UK via Dover.

The remarkable succession of transfers involved here – 12, to be precise – reveals smuggling networks to be a part of a highly cosmopolitan transnational 'rainbow' economy in which many ethnic groups of diverse national origin are involved (Pieterse 2003: 29-58). The idea that these actors share any great degree of group-based 'particularised trust' (Uslaner 1999) seems dubious; they are not necessarily friends, relatives or even of common ethnic origin. If they collaborate with each other, it is in a highly organised and professional manner for the express purpose of providing a service that brings commercial gain to participants in the operation, each of whom receives a cut in the profits. Interactions between migrants and smugglers are generally fleeting, and of little social consequence. The former are effectively funnelled by sending agents from their various countries of origin into the hands of local networks that converge along the EU's various external borders, above all, with Eastern Europe, Turkey and the Mediterranean coast. Abdul, now in Italy, is one of those who sailed on a boat across the Mediterranean from Malta with men from Morocco, Sudan, Sri Lanka and Pakistan.

What determines smuggling routes? If smugglers relied on air travel between Turkey and Europe during the mid-1990s, restrictionism at airports led to increased use of sea routes from the late 1990s: between 1998 and September 2001, 45 ships sailing off Turkey's coast were caught in Italy and Greece carrying a total of 12,903 irregular migrants. In the first eight months of 2000 Greece received three ships carrying 707 undocumented migrants; during the same period of the following year the figure was 2,409 (Içduygu 2003: 51-4). Improved policing of the Western Mediterranean – Italy and the Canary Islands – which became a 'backdoor' into the EU for a period of several years after that has made its 18,400 kilometres of coastline Fortress Europe's 'weak link': by 2007, Greece was receiving an estimated 50,000 per year. By 2009, Mytilene, a tourist island just off the Turkish Izmir coast, was reported to be receiving 500 illegals per day (Smith 2007, 2009).

Pathways of illegal entry into Europe, the point is, vary over time. When I met Akram the most effective and reliable means of facilitating irregular migration from Pakistan was through Eastern Europe overland. As he explained, however, this route was never a singular artery through which migrants constantly flow, but a multiplicity of capillaries that, in conjunction with a number of contingent factors, opened and closed at irregular intervals.

> Land routes change due to the weather, when it snows. But also, for example, Poland-Germany can be done three ways. Or if the Czech route closes; if they get strict – that is, if a guy gets caught, we know about it within seconds. Old routes re-open within a week sometimes. Sometimes new ones open. Strictness changes by the day – these days it's Lithuania. Once you're into Western Europe, that's it.

This last reference to Western Europe as a kind of continuous and singular entity is an important one, and conveys the increase in intra-European mobility since the Schengen treaty agreement began to be implemented from the late 1990s. The erosion of border controls between EU member states (excluding Britain) is one of a number of factors that has allowed migrants to move – with and without the help of smugglers – between countries such as Germany, France, Spain and Italy in secondary illegal migrations that follow their initial entry into the Europe. It is reflected in Akram's pricing system: five to six *lakhs* for Europe, defined as the Schengen area; six to seven *lakhs* for travel to the UK. (Travel to the UK is somewhat more expensive than reaching the European continent given the added difficulties of crossing the Channel).

The cost of being smuggled across borders within the Europe varies considerably between those which cover relatively easy border-crossings in Eastern Europe such as Ukraine to Slovakia (as low as 100 dollars) and entry into the EU. Mushtaq's agent organised for him and seventeen other friends to travel to Iran and then Turkey in 1995, at which point they made their own arrangements for onward travel: 'From Turkey agents would take about 3,000 dollars at that time. Those who bring you from there to Italy, they would work out the right time'. Rafeeq came to Italy from Germany by truck: 'I paid the driver 3,000 Euros (it was lire at that time)'. Sarfraz, also living in Germany preferred to enter Italy via France:

> I got a map. From Munich I took a train to Belgium. I got off at the first stop – Hanover. From there I went to France. You couldn't go from Paris to Italy as they checked that train. So I went from Paris to Nice. I got off at Nice – from there Moroccans bring people to Italy. Local cars don't get checked that much. Where they checked I got into the boot. So I came to Milan.

The ease with which some migrants completed certain parts of their journey renders clear that some borders are easier to cross than others. Jameel traveled from Copenhagen to France in the boot of a car in 1992 with the help of his long-settled relatives in Oslo, who accompanied him there:

> I had a Scandinavian visa. My *mamu* and my chacha's brother, we got in a car. I hid under the seat. In 1992 it was four *lakhs* to make that trip. Now it is over seven! I paid nothing. We went from Germany to France. There was a police check on the ferry – we got through. I never had to go through any difficulty.

Pela made several clandestine border crossings in 1989-90 though forests by night on foot with friends, from Austria to Switzerland, and then to Italy and back again. 'There were paths through the forest. It was not that hard. There were even some lights, we could tell which way to go'. Apart from the first journey when they were accompanied by an agent, a Pakistani friend whom they paid for showing them the way across the Austro-Swiss border, they travelled independently:

> There were four of us. At around 7pm we got to a city. A friend dropped us off at the border and said, 'Enter from here'. We didn't know where we were going but we kept continuing. At eight or nine in the morning we came across a child. We asked him where he was going. He said he was coming from home and on his way to school! Poor kid got frightened! ... He spoke Italian and German, which we spoke a little of. First we spoke to him in English, but he didn't know it ... It was through him that we realised we were in Italy! We had entered the forest at 8 o'clock and we had walked all night in the forest without knowing where we were. We didn't know which country we were in but we kept on going! There was a man who worked in the forest, maintaining the trees. We told him we wanted to go to the town. He realised we had come from Switzerland, and told us, 'Go the station'. He ordered a taxi to get to the station for us. It cost a lot but we weren't bothered. From there we got a train to Milan, from there to Rome.

Having applied for documents in Italy, they felt confident enough to return to Switzerland by a different route: 'I tried a different way back from Varese, which is after Milan. We were allowed to reside in Switzerland but we couldn't enter legally, so we had to return some other way'. Astonishingly, they then came back to Italy yet again, nearer the time when their papers would be ready. This particular crossing is evidence of inter-continental mobility irrespective of Schengen's implementation: sheer geographical proximity can be enough. At the other end of the spectrum, passage across the Channel, perhaps the most difficult of clandestine crossings within the EU (reflected in higher fees demanded by smugglers) can, in some circumstances, also be made without the services of agents, as Wasim's journey from Belgium to London suggests:

> So I climbed into a lorry of foam mattresses – not a closed container. I had some chocolate, some drinks. I was alone. I slept but when the lorry started I woke up. The security guards (who checked the lorry) didn't see me. In England, after two hours or so, the lorry stopped at a petrol pump. I saw no one was around and climbed off.

The table 'Pakistanis in Italy' (Appendix IV) conveys the extent to which Pakistani immigrants residing and working illegally within continental Western Europe continue to move with relative frequency across national-state borders to neighbouring countries' labour markets and are less geographically centred in their economic activities than previous generations of migrants from Pakistan who settled in Britain, few of whom ever spent time working in countries other than the UK: no less than 14 of the 20 individuals interviewed in Italy had worked elsewhere in Western Europe before arriving there (another two had worked in the Middle East and North Africa).

This would appear to confirm the hypotheses associated with new theories of migration which emphasise the importance of migrant networks' all conquering agency under conditions of contemporary globalisation, an epoch of 'unprecedented global mobility': exchanges of information on labour market opportunities through cross-border networks; proliferating capital flows and the circulation of people across borders of states that are supposedly losing their control over who enters and exits the territories they delineate, etc. It would also appear to confirm the assertion that the European Union is a particularly favourable context for migrants who prosper due to greater tolerance of plurality and regional economic integration (Levitt 2001: 16, 26): the success of smuggling networks today suggest migrants move across borders more easily than previous generations, many of whom have remained anchored in the UK since arriving in the 1960s-1980s. States are losing the battle to 'control' and manage migration etc.

In truth, however, the key to understanding the successful operation of smuggling networks in facilitating secondary illegal migrations lies in the labour markets they nourish. Europe is carved up into distinct zonal constellations by state policies and macro-economic processes that are beyond the control of migrants. Most of the time networks (and the movement of migrants within them) are responding to economic and political changes – not shaping them.

Afro-Eurasian labour is absorbed by a hierarchically structured restrictive core: leaving aside the UK, migrants express a clear bias towards a West European (and largely Franco-German) centre of preferred destinations. Seven respondents had worked in Paris, painting and decorating, tiling, roofing and doing electrical work informally and/or using false documentation. All the while they lived and worked for other Pakistanis in these occupational 'niches'. Three worked in German cities, mostly in the service sector as cooks and kitchen helpers, where Pakistanis work within ethnic enterprises for South Asians/and or other settled minority groups in the restaurant sector such as Greeks. In Germany they worked both on and off the books but mostly using genuine documents as they had claimed asylum and were thus legally resident. Belgium, Austria and to a lesser extent Switzerland are all loosely connected to this Franco-German core.

Eastern Europe lies unambiguously at its peripheries, and figures in testimonies as a series of transit destinations where Pakistanis seldom seek or experience meaningful incorporation within the labour market. Dish washing, peddling and in one case petty criminality were resorted to by those who found themselves stuck in destinations like Russia, Ukraine and Slovakia for a protracted period of time (the London sample in particular reflected this). Wasim spoke of 'places you'd go if you want to do that stuff – it's easy to recruit people, and get into that. Just hang around train stations.' He financed his onward travel from Austria by recruiting Pashto, Dari and Farsi speakers with similar designs to form a group of customers for a local smuggler, charging a commission for his services:

> The agent was German. The cost per head was 450E from Austria to either Germany or Belgium … I got the guys together. I knew them from the camp [in Slovakia] … Some Afghani/Iranian guys who wanted to go to Germany. I gave him [the agent] around 450E and I kept the rest [about 900E]. We went by car to Cologne City. I went with the agent on to Belgium. I was using my Austrian phone chip to check on the guys. I was guaranteeing their passage. I kept all the money [and didn't pay the agent until they phoned and told me they arrived]. I got one of them a train ticket to Hamburg (he had a friend there). I gave him 20 Euros for food and water, and gave him my mobile number.

The same is true, to some extent of the Mediterranean fringes, from where migrants generally seek to make their way to mainland Europe. Malta, Libya and Turkey have become key transit points. An IOM survey of 53 irregular migrants in Istanbul and Van province near the Turkish-Iranian border confirmed Turkey's status as a Central Asian absorption point that filters migration into Western Europe from South and West Asia and Africa. Practically all those interviewed intended to continue westward; over half had already attempted to do so, mostly for Italy (Içduygu 2003: 38).

An emergent patchwork of Pakistani communities appears to have settled and attained a significant level of economic incorporation in the European Mediterranean: Portugal, Greece, Spain and Italy. If these countries have now become destinations, however, Pakistanis first settled there because immigration had become tighter in their preferred destinations of Western Europe, squeezing them Southwards to the Mediterranean in search of residential (and effectively marriage) rights which became available during the various regularisations that began in the 1990s. The European Mediterranean was not, therefore, for initial arrivals, a first choice destination. Italy was not the second or even the third preferred choice of destination for the men I interviewed: they arrived defeated by their initial goal of settling in Western Europe. And having already invested months (sometimes years) on failed attempts to settle elsewhere, they began in the red, with the costs of relocation (and illegal travel) to recoup. At the same time, Italy was not a transit zone in the East European sense. In opting to relocate there, many of the earliest arrivals had left well-compensated jobs they had held for several years in Germany, France and elsewhere, where the toughening of asylum systems made structural incorporation increasingly difficult for illegal entrants in the 1990s. Migrating to the Mediterranean was thus characterised by a kind of horizontal, *spatial mobility*: a desperate sideways move, rather than one which reflects any kind of meaningful upward *social mobility*.

Why did migrants with relatively steady, well-paid employment in Germany and France migrate to Italy illegally? Testimonies make clear that, faced with the prospect of a lifetime's confinement to the 'relational' sphere (Portes 1981), they fled in search of basic citizenship rights so that they could stabilise their position in Europe:

> *Jameel:* The work [in Paris] was good. I earned a lot of money. But there was this nagging feeling of fear of being discovered in my mind. Tension. We would go to work on the train and come straight home. We would not go the centre of Paris much. During the World Cup we stayed at home the whole time. The checks were tough at that time, especially when there were bomb threats. When Jacques Chirac came to power, again there were bomb threats. I didn't want to leave France, but I just came here for documents.

> *Pela:* I was working regularly at that time [in Switzerland] at a clothing dye factory. I was earning 3,300 francs a month, working eight and a half hours a day, five days a week. That's good money. Very good, but I wasn't able to make papers. Without documents, how can a man live? You can earn money but it comes into your thinking that your family back there have needs beyond money. Your relation with them can only be maintained if you go back- which you can only do if manage to make papers … I wanted to call for them.

These typical responses underlined the fact that Pakistani migrants in North Western Europe were facing the ultimate new migrant's dilemma: being unable to enjoy well-compensated employment *and* legal residential/employment rights at the same time in the same place. That dilemma has continued to haunt them in Italy (Part IV), where conversely, they have been able to regularise, but now complain of the opposite problem to the one they faced when they were in North Western Europe: they now experience great difficulty in finding well-compensated employment. Indeed, the fact that several men had, during the course of their time in Italy, left the country in difficult times of unemployment for either Germany or France underlines the perceived status of these economies as strong, stable sources of employment in which capital can be generated relatively quickly. Of Paris, Bilal told me:

> Some men who have documents here [in Italy] stay here, but will go there [Paris] by train in the evening. They know there's work there. They'll arrive there in the morning. They'll go to such and such road or building or address. They'll have been told there's a contact there that can sort them out with work. They'll do that until their [Italian] documents run out, and then come back here.

The strength of demand, and levels of compensation for labour in both France and Germany (and other North West European destinations), it seems, make Western Europe distinguishable from Italy, Portugal and Greece in the Mediterranean, where migrants have settled for second-best locations in which, as will be seen, many experience lengthy periods of unemployment and poor wages in a trade-off for legal residential status.

What does all this tell us? Borders and other restrictions on residency and employment (together with their intermittent lifting) in neighbouring countries and regions within the European restrictive core now operate in unison as valves, opening and closing in ways that may seem to be out of synch but in fact work together to ensure collective European sovereignty and domination over an Afro-Eurasian labour force whose productive, reproductive and erotic energies are utilised, extracted, siphoned off and wasted in accordance with the needs of contemporary, neo-racialised capitalism. Despite the far reaching spatial transformations in migration regimes and systems from countries like Pakistan to countries like Britain, the essential relationship between Europe and clandestine immigrants today remains remarkably similar to the one lascars experienced in colonial times: borders and other kinds of restrictions ensure that expenditure of their energies suits the needs of 'useful' production in the West.

The rich countries of Europe and their labour markets constitute a restrictive political-economic core. Pakistan is part of a global periphery. Its labour supply (with that of other poor countries) is part of a 'general' economy in the Bataillean sense, the energies of which are absorbed where necessary by the restrictive core into its bowls, ingested as needed and expelled when unwanted or deemed surplus to requirements as 'horribly excluded' base matter (expulsion is discussed in the greater detail in the chapter that follows).

So much for balanced accounts. Any review of the evidence makes clear that if migration is a 'business', it's always been a dirty one. Helweg (1979: 27-8), Aurora (1967: 41-5) and Hussein's (2000) novel indicate the system was open to abuse by individual agents bent on extortion, coercion and blackmail against migrants during their early months within the UK. Brokerage's commodification has never been directed by some invisible, efficient and rational logic of supply and demand operating in a political vacuum – rather, key measures taken by western governments to 'control' migratory flows have increased the commercial activity surrounding all aspects of migration brokerage. What has grown is the sheer intensity of commercial activity surrounding all aspects of human smuggling: the opportunity cost of helping a friend or family member without strings has increased incrementally with each act of restrictionism since the 1960s, so that now the profit motive trumps kinship ties and strong bonds in network relations. Various other transformations in scope, scale and spatial extent of smuggling networks from Pakistan have been dictated by British immigration policy 1962-82, above all the dispersal of Pakistani immigrant flows and stocks around continental Europe.

The imposition of borders (and other laws which control migrants within states) has always been a way of shaping the terms under which labour in restrictive cores is extracted from general peripheries. Smuggling networks facilitate this exchange. Agents operate in the wake of restrictive policy, responding to and even mediating the interests of states at any given moment. The most recent phase of 'globalisation' in Afro-Eurasia has witnessed increasingly supranational control of Europe's restrictive economy – not in the democratic, progressive sense invoked by the EU in its post-Schengen public relations rhetoric. The sort of sovereignty-pooling implied in my use of the term has more in common with Kautsky's notion of ultra-imperialism than the propaganda disseminated by technocrats in Brussels. It refers to the shared interests of core countries in perpetuating relations of domination over their Afro-Eurasian peripheries: the displacement of colonial, bi-national systems of migration by an increasingly cohesive European restrictive economy. Indeed, Balibar and Wallerstein's (1991) arguments about the way in which capitalism is generative of chauvanism, racism and ethnicity can be extended: supra-national EU imperialism today is a system that ascribes diverse immigrant populations distinct, gendered sexualities in segmented labour markets; differing roles and rights in productive and reproductive activity, all of which are subordinate to those of 'indigenous' populations with citizenship rights.

Chapter 4

Eroticism, History and Base Materiality: Migrant Experience in Travel and Transit

This chapter is about migrants – their strategies, their experiences. Human smuggling remains our object of study, but we shift perspective from the previous chapter's maco (political-economic) and meso (network) level analysis to the micro, individual, experiential aspects of travel and transit. These reflect a paradox that defines migrant mobility in Europe's restrictive economy: on the one hand, many of the men I interviewed had been apprehended, detained, imprisoned and subject to various kinds of state surveillance in the course of their travels. On the other, most spoke of these experiences with a distinctly casual air as minor delays of little consequence. Several of those I interviewed in London and Tuscany had been sent back in the course of failed and successful migrations. Detention rarely halted their resolve:

> *Pela*: [1990] We were six lads leaving for Switzerland from Vienna. When we got to the border near Switzerland we tried to cross the border. We got caught that first time. The Switzerland police kept us for two days and then sent us back to the Austrian police who put us in jail for 20 days. From there we appealed and they let us go. We stayed in Austria for another five or six months, and then we tried again … along the same route along which we got caught.

> *Chima* [1997]: From [the] Czech [Republic], I got caught twice at the German border. They sent us back. The German guards are very polite. They don't do anything … They [the agents] came and got us and sent us again.

Some of the other men were given letters – orders to leave the country in which they were caught entering (Abdul) or leaving (Asad). Needles to say, these were ignored:

> *Asad* [2003]: The police caught us in a container on a ship from France [en route to the UK]. They sent us to a jail for three days. They then gave us a document saying we should leave in two weeks. They asked us if we planned to stay. We said no … The police are tough there. They'd stop us in the street. We had nowhere to sleep but we had these documents, so they would let us go.

Abdul [1995]: The [Italian] police caught us directly [upon arrival by boat in Sicily]. They said nothing. They took our fingerprints, gave us a paper saying, 'leave our country', and released us.

'Fortress Europe' appears easily penetrable in these testimonies, its border restrictions tame, its policing tokenistic. Ostensibly impervious perimeter patrols and regulation of the state's internal territory seem ineffective in practice, even pathetic.

In other ways too, interview discourse reflects a multifaceted relation between migrants and European transit and receiving states. The latter, far from being experienced as uniformly oppressive, provide moments of respite from the overall difficulties of the journey. Being held up voluntarily in a 'camp' in Bratislava where intercepted migrants are housed caused Asad and Wasim no obvious anxiety. Both saw being arrested as a strategically sound option at a given point in their journeys, having run out of food and funds (the former was abandoned by agents in a forest outside town). Indeed, the police's initial refusal to arrest him is described by him as one of *the* worst moments in his difficult travels:

Asad: We went into Bratislava. The police arrested us on the road. We were put into a hostel where our agent found us. We were there for a week or two – we weren't worried. There were lots of Asians there, there was food and we knew we would get here [London] in the end. We were free [to come and go] in the hostel.

Wasim: A low point was in Bratislava when even the police wouldn't arrest me. It was raining and I was hungry. [Eventually] I was locked up. And thrown out again! Then I went to the jail again. I went in at night and the next day an Afghan interpreter interviewed me and they took my prints. They sent me to a camp. There you got food. It was great, a good place for a guy like me. You could play football, eat, meet with people. After two months I started getting bored though, so I left (I was there of my own free will) and went back to the city (Bratislava).

Several migrants announced their presence to the authorities upon arrival at their intended destinations, lodging asylum claims as a way to legalise their residency and obtaining shelter.

Chima: [1996] I said I want stay to there [in Germany]… they sent me by taxi to Germany, to Leipzig. I stayed there two days and then came to Frankfurt where I started a case.

Wasim: [2003] We got to the Austrian border where the police caught us. They asked me questions. I told them my name, where I'm from, etc. They took us to a checkpoint, then a police station. The next day an interpreter who knew English,

Farsi and Dutch came.. They asked basic questions. The Austrian government gave me a one bedroom flat and a visa that gave me stay for six months.

Chima remembers being detained in Moscow – an experience of imprisonment rather than voluntary detention – as surprisingly unobjectionable. 'Jail' is described as a place where he lived relatively comfortably, met and spoke freely with other migrants of his linguistic background. Notice the distinct absence of dread for the state and its oppressive apparatus:

It was okay. You got food and drink. They would change the bedclothes. It was fine … You would get breakfast in the morning, dinner in the evening at a set time: you eat and drink well. We would play cards, go out and play football. There were other men. They were mostly Indian guys.

AA: You describe it like it was a hotel!
It was like a hotel!

How to explain this nonchalance? For all the surveillance and discriminatory treatment meted out by Western (and some East European) states, migration regimes in advanced industrial democracies tend to be experienced as relatively tame in relation to the sorts of brutality Pakistanis face in their own country and region. The South-West Asian migration system has rightly been likened to a modern form of indenture (Gardezi 1995; *The News* 2004d; *The News* 2004e). Abdul had been severely tortured by the Libyan secret police before leaving for Italy. He regards everyday violence in Pakistan itself – a military dictatorship at the time I interviewed these men – in many ways more intimidating than anything that could be experienced in European detention centres, where minimal human rights obligations put some limits on the harshness of the conditions under which detainees are held.

Equally, however, the benign representation of Europe's restrictive economy by Abdul, Chima and others is a reflection of its contradictory workings (discussed in the previous chapter). Borders, remember, act not only to exclude but – together with internal controls and restrictions – function as valves, opening and closing, filtering and funnelling Afro-Eurasian labour into a constellation of neighbouring European economies, distributing it usefully in ways that impel the sorts of apparently lax controls we witness at particular moments in the smuggling process. There are good reasons why European states are not in the business of uniformly and systematically detaining and deporting *all* illegal migrants at every opportunity; feeding, clothing and tolerating their presence in limited ways is just as much a part of how their labour regimes work – now and historically (see previous chapter).

Furthermore, any suggestion that European migration controls are somehow flexible and humane is countered by oppressive contractions in spatial mobility in the build-up to, and actual crossing of borders within specific countries for given periods of time. Sizeable chunks of journeys are spent hiding and waiting in passive dependency for agents to organise the next phase – intervals that can last several months, during which migrants find themselves boxed in small rented rooms in obscure locations as diverse as Turkey and China. With no real indication of when they will be collected by the relevant agent to embark upon the next stage of their journey, they squat anxiously, bored and restless in difficult, overcrowded living conditions, unable to walk around freely due to their shadowy legal residential status and without any connection to the localities in which they are stationed due to their lack of familiarity with of the local language. Mushtaq spent a month in Turkey; Sarfraz several months in Africa; Salman, two months in China; Chima three months in Belarus 'watching TV'. Waiting of this sort, needless to say, is rarely experienced as travel in the recreational sense.

> *Rafeeq:* In Moscow we stayed in a hotel for a week. The Russian would come and bring food, lentils and bread to the flat we were in. We were ten men, two in each room. Then in Minsk we were 20 people in one room for a week. It was a bad situation. You can imagine how it would be – the toilet and all. Then we stayed in Poland for a week in order to enter Germany.

This is somewhat ironic given all the talk of 'speed-up' and hi-tech travel and communications that have supposedly transformed the experience of international migration in the current age of globalisation. Levitt herself points out that international travel 'was also relatively easy in the 1900s as bigger, faster, safer steam ships crossed the Atlantic in little more than two weeks. Tickets were reasonably priced and could be paid for in instalments' (Levitt 2001: 22). The journeys of the Freshies I interviewed were easily more difficult, expensive and lengthier than these trans-Atlantic travels of the early 1900s.

> *Sarfraz* [1994-5]: He [the agent] took his time – six months, but he got me here. He took us as part of a football team from Faislabad. First we went to Africa. All agents have a method. He would arrange football matches and say he was the manager for this team. He left us there, dropped us off in Africa. Then he organised visas for England, Holland and Luxembourg. From there I went to Holland.

Contemporary migration can also be more dangerous than it was at the turn of the previous century. Many travelers are surprised by the extent of the difficulties they encounter during specific parts of the journey. Some are clearly misled by smugglers. This runs counter to the assertion, advanced in some recent scholarly accounts of smuggling, that migrants have developed effective strategies of finding trustworthy agents who 'have to gain trust from migrants' (Liempt and Doomernik 2006: 176); that 'in the long run the systematic maltreatment of clients would seriously harm the smugglers' reputation' and that 'migrants are aware of the high risks they face prior to the journey' (Bilger et al. 2006: 80-81). Such accounts clearly wish to undermine the caricatured media representations of smuggling as organised criminality, and have adopted the notion of smuggling as a 'business' that must operate efficiently and reliably like any other (Neske 2006: 136).

The problem with this argument – as illustrated by tragedies like the horrific suffocation of 58 Chinese in a lorry that entered the UK from Dover in 2000 – is that regulation by the need to maintain a 'good reputation' is hardly an effective control in cases where smugglers operate as part of unaccountable, loosely formed networks which provide a one-off service to an individual they will never meet again. Linguistic barriers to communication compound systematic and deliberate withholding of information about the journey itself (Bilger et al. 2006: 75).

Nor is it simply the case that there exist a handful of 'cowboy' agents that give professionals a bad name. For almost every success story there is an equivalent tale of deception, fraud or failure. It is not unusual, for instance, for agents to simply abandon their clients for no apparent reason in the middle of an operation. A porter at Karachi airport told me how he and several friends were left to fend for themselves in Iran by an agent who took their money and disappeared in the midst of border crossing (they were soon caught by Iranian border guards and severely beaten, before being sent back). Jameel, a cook who migrated to London as a domestic servant, was called upon to wire several hundred dollars to his nephew who got stuck in Turkey, having been abandoned in a small room with several other migrants by their agent with no means of advancing and no means of returning of home. Many of those who eventually arrived suffered similar hiccups in the smuggling process, which is full of unexpected difficulties and let downs at the hands of agents and smugglers:

> *AA: What was the low point of your journey?*
> *Asad*: The worst was the three days of hunger in the forest [near Bratislava]. We stayed there for three days. They [the smugglers] said they'd come to get us but they didn't so we left. We were so hungry!

> *Bilal*: A man I know had come from Pakistan to Greece. He was trying to get from Greece to Italy in a little speedboat with three or four men [including the agent who] got out and returned on another boat. He said, 'Just keep going straight. Don't turn.' ... How were they supposed to know what's straight, left or right in the water! After a little while, the petrol ran out. They had no idea where the boat was going. They saw a mountain, and as the boat pulled up by it, they jumped onto the rocks. For three or four days they stayed there without anything to eat or drink ... This was in 1995. If they hadn't seen the mountain, that would have been it.

Such tales are too widespread to be exceptional. The treatment of migrants like cargo to be transported with little regard for their safety is an integral part of the smuggling process. Any suggestion that regulation by 'market forces' is a meaningful way of ensuring quality service-provision misunderstands and paints a rosy picture of the smuggling 'business' – a commercial network through which misinformation is channelled to migrants routinely even where there is 'accountability' and 'trust'. Local operators, to whom border crossings are sourced out by sending country co-ordinators such as Akram, or whom migrants themselves approach at 'hubs', frequently display levels of neglect and callous disregard for the lives of their customers that border on the outright murderous, as the following accounts make clear.

> *Mushtaq*: At 2am … or 4am, they put us in big trucks. We stayed in there about seven days. Seven days! That's about 160 hours! Fifteen men in about 20 metres!
>
> *AA: How did you go to the toilet?*
> They provided a gallon for that. Before we got in they said eat and drink very little to avoid needing to go to the toilet. So we ate and drank very little. It was very hot so we took off our clothes … They didn't tell us about these problems before. They said it would take 20 hours. They said we would get there within 20 hours. But it took around 100 hours.
>
> *AA: How did you feel during all this?*
> We wept, and said, 'What are we doing in here?' We couldn't leave the truck either, for fear of getting caught. Then when we got to Italy, they took us out of the truck. And then here too, they put us in trucks for two days. Then at 2am, they took us out on a big road. The city was Bologna. We got here around August 1995.

A materialism that takes seriously the experience of being smuggled – an affective materialism in the Bataillean sense – is a history of disgusting toilets; grotty passages with no access to hot water and weeks wearing the same malodorous clothes and underclothes; Afro-Eurasian bodies compressed in a process which creates intimacy with one's own and other people's shit. Illegal border-crossings, we noted earlier, can be the easiest thing in the world. Equally, they can be experienced as suffocating nightmares of extraction, and discipline – a kind of processing that separates the useful from that which must be expelled or transferred to another corner of Europe's restrictive economy.

> *Rafeeq:* I had the worst experience of my life. I was in truckload of people from Minsk to get to Poland, and it was very difficult to breathe. I think they were Russians who took us. It was organised through the agents in Pakistan. It was a difficult journey – one of life and death. Quite a few people passed out. Five were unconscious. I was able to make a hole above me in the ceiling of the truck with a penknife I had, and managed to breathe. They stopped at a certain point to let people breath. I think if they had stopped ten minutes later than they did several people would have died.

AA: Were you worried?
When you see death ahead of course you worry.

AA: But you didn't know it would be like that?
I had no idea it would be so difficult, that I would have to go hungry so often. I didn't eat for a whole month virtually.

Having survived the above-described incident from Minsk, Rafeeq had another close shave crossing a river along the border between Poland and Germany. A fellow traveller was not so fortunate: 'There was no bridge. The water was very cold. As we were crossing, he got pulled away by the current'. Almost all the men I interviewed in Italy knew someone (or of someone) who had died in trying to migrate. Some knew of individuals who had simply disappeared: men who never arrived at their intended destination. Bilal recounts below, the tragic story of an acquaintance of his in Prato, whose bother was one such case:

> In 1998, there was a boat coming from Morocco to Spain. No one knows what happened to it. The man driving it and the men in it – there were 18 men in it. There's a man in Prato whose brother was on it. The day he was supposed to arrive, he went to meet him. He came back after waiting. From where the boat left, they confirmed that the men got on the boat. But no one knows what happened to it.

He went on to explain:

> Agents don't care. They aren't bothered about anything except money. They don't care if people die. They might give the money back but that's it. They don't have any humanity. They don't think, 'This is someone's brother or someone's son.' Not at all; the men who send you don't tell you what it's like. They paint a different picture. They say you'll be there in a couple of hours.

If the strength of smuggling networks lies in their global spread, their diffuse nature is also the source of their principle weakness. Responsibility for organising crucial border crossings is delegated to individuals in obscure corners of the planet who may never meet the 'big' co-ordinating agent in Pakistan. It is simply not possible to guarantee safety in human smuggling: linguistic differences and the ruthlessly commodified nature of transactions ensure that information about the risks is not always communicated to migrants. As is now well known, when things go wrong, they can do so badly. Given the frequency with which the unexpected occurs and goes unpunished, co-ordination of this network cannot be fully explained in terms of 'enforceable trust', by which the punishment for failure to comply with one's side of the bargain is exclusion from economic networks of exchange (Portes 1994: 431).

Interestingly, however, many migrants who had experienced the unexpected did not generally condemn smugglers. This is partly because there is no single smuggler who can be held responsible for the activities of all the participants of the smuggling network. Failure is accepted as an inevitable problem in smuggling networks. Ulrich Beck's (2000) conceptualisation of global scale risks, which he discusses in relation to the new dangers that face us such as global warming (Ibid: 218) is useful here: applying its logic in reverse to the specific issues that face an illegal migrant negotiating travel and transit through the global risk economy is not without complication. For one thing, the migrant faces personal catastrophe (injury or even death) where Beck is concerned to discuss the collective risks faced by advanced capitalist societies. Nonetheless, it raises two important points that are applicable to all economic activity within the modern global risk economy, of which human smuggling is a good example: firstly, global risks are less legible and less controllable, since they are spread across a great many actors operating at different levels over large interconnected spaces. Secondly, when risk results in damages, these cannot always be insured against since responsibility is diffused and cannot easily be attributed to specific parties.

These observations seem especially pertinent when thinking about commercial human smuggling networks, above all those involving one-off 'spot transactions', in which the question of who exactly is to blame when things go wrong and a migrant suffocates in the back of a lorry is in fact far from straightforward. Many migrants accepted the impossibility of insuring themselves fully against catastrophe in travel and transit, underlining their own perception of human smuggling as a kind of global scale risk that is an inevitable part of modern life.

Agency and experience

The remainder of this chapter explores the question of migrant agency – its nature and extents in the smuggling process. The latter should not be exaggerated, as most of this book makes clear. They should not, however, be overly generalised. Successful travellers reported a diverse range of experiences and relations with smugglers. The stories of migrants who opted to mobilise independently – that is, without the services of an agent – exemplify just how much autonomy can be experienced in travel and transit. Setting off on the basis of information and advice on how this can be achieved from successful returnees, they begin by flying to a destination in Eastern Europe from the Middle East, from where they hope to find a way westward by air or overland, often using fraudulent documents purchased in Pakistan before departure.

Several observations can be made about this type of traveller – a small minority in my sample admittedly. First of all, they are likely to be of less affluent backgrounds than most of the migrants whose testimonies were discussed in Part II, and may well be better represented among travellers from Afghanistan. They simply cannot afford a 'package' deal from a high-level agent like Dr Akram and invest less capital in the smuggling process at the point of departure. Secondly, they adopt attritional and opportunistic tactics, making their way through the East European, Mediterranean or North African semi-periphery in spontaneously engineered, incremental phases. They may be apprehended at borders or arrested within countries, and sent back part of the way, before trying again, spending weeks if not months in the unlikeliest of places (e.g. Belarus, Malta). The finite amount of money they depart with might run out, in which case they will need to raise money for the next phase of their journey in transit countries where they reside for lengthy periods, forging social capital by making contacts and saving cash earned from work at the margins of the restrictive economy – often its informal underbelly – peddling, washing dishes or petty forms of survival criminality like shoplifting.

As research on Kurdish networks in Greece has shown, relationships with the 'indigenous' population become a question of individual efforts in the absence of long-settled communities of co-ethnics (Papadopoulou 2002). Independent mobilisers will almost certainly opt to pay for the services of smugglers at some point during the course of their journey, but being on the ground they approach local operators directly which gives them a certain autonomy and altogether more organic relationship with smuggling networks, in which they can end up playing active roles in recruitment and transport. Wasim, who set off for Russia after being issued with a visa from the Russian embassy in Karachi in 1999, spoke of 'places you'd go if you want to do that stuff. It's easy to recruit people, and get into that. Just hang around train stations'. He financed his onward travel from Austria by recruiting Pashto, Dari and Farsi speakers with similar designs to form a group of customers for a local smuggler charging a commission for his services. A glorious sovereignty characterises his wanderings as a down-and-out in Russia and Bratislava: one that acts insubordinately, consuming only with regard to the moment of consumption (Bataille 1997: 169). A distinct lack of method is evident in his journey, which he related as a series of remarkable episodes. It has a chaotic, peripatetic quality; an anarchic sense of adventure reflected in unexpected chance meetings, encounters and dealings with native agents in subterranean settings, together with women, who feature in ways that echo the earliest lascars' relations with white (mostly Irish) women in East London (Visram 2002: 263-5; 273-4). Sociologists call these bridging ties, historically a crucial dimension of the facilitation of illegal entry and incorporation within labour markets. I call them sexual relationships.

> On the plane to Moscow I met a Russian girl (I gave her my wine and we started talking like that – by the end, I put my head on her shoulder and fell asleep). The immigration officials at Moscow were going to deport me [after questioning] but she filled out a form for me and got me through. I stayed with her for six months in her flat in Moscow … My girlfriend had a friend. She was from Ukraine. She introduced me to an agent. It cost me 250 dollars to get to Ukraine. [The journey was] seven-eight hours by car to the Ukraine border. Then by horse until the

> train station [where we took] the train to Kiev. My girlfriend's friend picked
> me up – I stayed with her for three months in her flat … she became my friend.

There was too much talk, in the 1990s, about the 'subversive' nature of cultural hybridity in conversations and circles that were anything but (Ahmad 2001). Without lapsing into exaggerated, celebratory claims about the importance of sexual intercourse across 'races', it seems important to recognise erotic transgression as an important part of experience in migration and human smuggling from Pakistan to Europe. For the migrant without legal rights of residence, sex of almost any sort is rebellion against a racialised capitalism that makes family unification impossible, consigns him to infinitely deferred settlement in any single country and strips his body of all rights to care, pleasure and intimacy in the labour process (Part IV) – a spirited Bataillean defiance of 'the sexual prohibitions, the historically constructed borders between different sexes, genders, classes, races, cultures, ages and even personalities' (Direk 2007: 96).

Beyond actual genital sexual activity, however, the domain of eroticism is about transgression of taboo in acts connecting expenditure, death and sexuality – experience at its most intensely felt limits (Bataille 2001 [1962]: 256). Death is associated with the sensuous possibility of life and sexual excitement (2001 [1962]: 59), a point which dares us to confront the perplexing yet undeniable fact that in migrating illegally, some individuals appear willingly to place themselves in positions of life-threatening insecurity. Illegal migration to Europe, in this more general erotic sense, is a profoundly carnal process: a forbidden and life-endangering form of travel, it manifests anarchic agencies through which individuals attempt to break free of state oppression and prescribed regimes of useful productivity. Whether they succeed is immaterial. The point is risking everything.

> The thing we desire most ardently is likely to drag us into wild extravagance and
> to ruin us … Men seek out the greatest losses and the greatest dangers. Anyone
> with the strength and the means is continually endangering himself (Bataille
> 2001 [1962]: 86).

We have already noted Rafeeq, a 30-year-old Punjabi I met in Florence, nearly suffocated en route to Poland from Minsk in 1995; while crossing a river on the Polish–German border, he witnessed a fellow traveller being pulled away by the current and drowning. If illegal migration is a desperate search for security, as it is so often represented, why did he carry on undeterred? Riaz, a 24 year old from the Federally Administered Tribal Areas of Pakistan had no answer when I asked him why he chose to play this 'game of death' (his words). The question is particularly pertinent in cases where migrants understand and consciously take mortal risks (Riaz himself, who entered Britain by truck when he was just 19 in 2004, admits he was under no illusions). Are we to believe migrants who attempt to walk across minefields along Greece's Northern border with Turkey (Smith 2007) are making utilitarian calculations about future financial security?

Perhaps Bataille's infamous brothel visit can help us understand the moment of absolute risk that some migrants appear to take in terms other than desperate flight from political and economic misery (Bataille 1997: 229). Madame Edwarda (literally) opens up the possibilities of genuine communication between the One and the Other. Risking vulnerability becomes exhilarating, thrilling and unsettling. Might Europe's interiority be the epitome of erotic alterity for the young traveler from Pakistan? More than self-preservation, illegal migration can be about opening up possibilities beyond utility; overcoming separation and distance enshrined in worldly differences to experience genuine communication with the sacred, mystical and imminent oneness of the human, the divine, the animal (Direk 2007: 99, 103-5). Freud himself identified this possibility of losing oneself in love's recklessness; 'at the height of erotic passion' the very borderline between ego and object is in danger of becoming blurred – that is, when the person in love asserts that 'I' and 'you' are one and is ready to behave as if this were so (Freud 2007 [1930]: 5).

All very speculative. What, then, would the empirical coordinates of this speculation look like?

The intense and contradictory emotions mortal risk produces are evident in the build-up to travel, and underline the complexity of the forces that generate emigration and drive travellers directly into mortal danger. Chima recounts a heady mixture of fear and excitement the night before he undertook his second attempt to enter Europe:

> I didn't want to go through with it. I felt worried in my heart. I lost the will to go … I wanted to go but then I didn't as well. I was worried. I thought, 'It's such a tough journey ahead. All that walking and the rest of it … What's the point of going abroad? Forget it'. Then I thought, 'No. I'll go. It will be okay. I'll be free from the family'.

Multiple intersecting and mutually reinforcing transgressions are at play here: youthful desire for freedom from patriarchal control above all (Part II). Notice too, the reference to a 'tough journey ahead': something spurs him on into danger's direction; thinking of the kind 'that does not fall apart in the face of horror' (Bataille 1997: 238). If the desire to migrate is generated by mythologies of capitalism and masculine ideology, migration is simultaneously a quarrel with political boundaries imposed by an international regime of travel; spatial taboos defined by the borders of Fortress Europe's restrictive economy. This risky, erotic component is lived and experienced in basely material ways in subterranean border crossings that entail intimate acquaintance with Europe's geographical terrain and geo-political formation – the restrictive-economy's every hidden orifice and remotest points of entry. Once inside the belly of the best, days, weeks, months are spent deep in the bowels of Europe's service-sector in restaurant kitchens preparing food for its tourists and citizens, or in Mediterranean fields picking fruit that passes through their digestive systems (Part IV).

Pakistani immigrants are represented in Britain as a stubborn and backward block of culturally homogenous trouble-makers refusing to 'integrate', but most of the Pakistanis I met in Florence were culturally European in ways that made Anglo-Saxon tourists look foreign. Quite apart from having travelled so widely to so many peripheral and metropolitan parts of the Eurasian continent, many had learnt European languages, some three or four. Immersion in the symbolic orders of the peoples that speak them – French, Italian, Dutch, German and Spanish – had acquainted them with the respective projections, fantasies and ways of imagining the Real that each of these systems of signs represents; each structure of feeling. They drank coffee standing up, knew decent from mediocre Chianti, swore like locals and gestured with their hands. The list could go on. Suffice to say, from the migrant's perspective, human smuggling and its aftermath constitute a profound and intense effort to communicate and connect intimately with alterity.

Death, history and base materiality

There's no guarantee, of course, of reaching intended destinations. Excretion and abjection of surplus labour from restrictive economies involves subjection of migrants to coercion and tends to mean incurring further temporal and financial losses. Chima's narrative of deportation is a case in point:

> *Chima:* We stayed there for three months. We were *very* worried. There was a small room. They put me and another boy in it. They would let us out for an hour. I was *very* worried … Until then I had never seen a jail … I grew up being free. I wanted freedom. I thought, 'When am I getting out?'

Upon being released, bribes were exacted from him and his friends by the Russian officials responsible for returning their papers. Keen to cover up the fact of their deportation to avoid the clutches of the FIA upon return, they were more than willing to pay a sweetener that would no doubt be considerably less than what the FIA would seek to extort from them.

> *Chima:* We told the immigration people to please give us our passports. He said, 'No, I'll give it to the airplane officials. They'll organise your return to Karachi.' He said, 'Give me 10 dollars.' We said, 'We have no money!'. [In the end] we gave the ten dollars and took the passports – he accepted the bribes.

What happens when surplus labour is returned to the general economy? In December 2003 I visited the Lahore 'Passport Circle', where deportees are sent from airports and held before being sent to an actual prison or deported back to their countries of origin. Around a dozen miserable migrants and small-time agents were seated uncomfortably in the dark on a cold hard stone floor of a cell down the corridor from the office in which I was sitting. An hour later, one of them was removed from this cage to be quizzed by the senior official I was interviewing: a seventeen-year-old Iranian boy who spoke neither Urdu nor English. His appearance was dishevelled, his cheeks red with dehydration and distress. (Had he been beaten?). As he entered the room, a vile smell, identical to the one I had earlier breathed in as I walked pass the cell, filled the air. He pleaded for a glass of water.

The officials told me it was not unusual for the odd Afghan or Iranian to be apprehended in Pakistan, though most detainees are Pakistani Punjabis. This particular individual was on his way to London, where his father, whom I met just a few minutes later, was living and working as a legally resident asylum claimant. As they met under emotional circumstances for the first time in several years, both struggled (and failed) to avoid breaking down into tears. The father, who had come all the way from London upon being informed of his son's apprehension in Pakistan, had almost certainly financed his attempt to join him. Now it had failed, he was in considerable distress, and desperate to prevent his deportation to Iran. A respectable sort, he wore a suit and gave me a business card I promptly lost ('Something something minicabs, somewhere in Shepherd's Bush'). A journalist I met at the Passport Circle told me not to worry, 'He'll get his son back. It'll cost him though.'

Deportation leads to yet another round of extortion by the sending state. A client I met in Akram's office had been threatened and intimidated by the FIA after being deported from Paris to Karachi – warned that if he did not pay a bribe of 10,000 rupees, he would be jailed on a fake charge of drug-trafficking. Ilyas, whom I interviewed in London, recounted the following story of a friend, an 18-year-old boy from Lahore who contacted him for help after he was apprehended in France by the authorities who

> deported him back to Pakistan where the FIA locked him up in disgusting conditions. They tortured him, and asked him for a bribe. I went to get him in Karachi. There were lots of deportees from everywhere, crying, begging to be let out. I paid two *lakhs* to get him out.

Another young migrant I interviewed in Italy ended up spending three months in a Karachi jail following deportation to the Karachi FIA. Unable or unwilling to pay the requisite bribe to be released upon arrest, he endured a harrowingly unpleasant experience:

> *Kamran:* At the airport we were offered a way out if we paid a bribe. I refused to do so. In 2002 I spent three weeks in detention with other migrants, then two and half months in jail. They make you work but we paid 3,000 rupees each to avoid work, and to eat. Sleeping is very uncomfortable – it's so cramped that you can't lie on your back. You have to be on one side all the time.

Further contraction of spatial mobility; bodies compressed and heaped together in small, squalid cells; harassment and blackmail by sending state officials – the punishing aftermath of deportation can continue for months after expulsion from the restrictive economy. Where do these mounting losses fit into the balancing of accounts described by theorists of the smuggling business? The household and sending community which originally financed the risk (Part II) absorbs a good deal of the financial pain, not to mention anxiety over the safety of the son, husband and/or brother in the clutches of the FIA. The remainder gnaws away at the increasingly tormented mind and body of the migrant himself, effectively back to square one. Many thousands of stories end thus, abruptly and involuntarily.

And yet, these are, in some ways, the lucky ones.

Excess must be spent if it cannot be absorbed in growth – 'gloriously or catastrophically' (Direk 2007: 97-8). The sight of young Asian and African men's bodies – dead and alive – being retrieved from capsized boats and offloaded from trucks has become depressingly familiar within the media. The growing number injured and/or killed in failed attempts to cross EU borders is now well documented. In 2006 alone, about 6,000 migrants are thought to have gone missing or died on the journey from Africa to the Canary Islands (BBC 2006). Precise figures are unobtainable because so many literally disappear, their corpses washed away at sea or left to decompose in mountainous terrain, far from home or intended destinations. Of those that are recovered, many are never identified: 'We try to give them dignified funerals but frequently it is nameless plaques, not head stones they are buried under', said the deputy prefect of the Greek Island Samos in 2007 in an interview, before adding that other bones often 'end up being destroyed' if uncollected by family members (Smith 2007).

How to conceptualise migrant sexuality and agency when the abrupt and brutishly violent invasion of structure results in its permanent obliteration? What kind of 'eroticism' is it that turns living, breathing bodies into anonymous corpses? Bataille's thinking, despite its seemingly bizarre glorification of massive destructive acts, remains useful: for all his apparent fascination with sex's relation to death and humanity's proness to anarchic waste, he understood perfectly well that 'the anguish of death, and death itself are the antipodes of pleasure' (Bataille 2001 [1962]: 102). His 'strangely ethical' vision understood the human need to defy the logic of utilitarianism – to engage in costly and often ruinous risks. But he would never have valorised tragic waste and social suffering of any kind, let alone that which is so obviously rooted in global inequity (Stoekl 2007).

Base materialism's refusal to accept the separation of economic and sexual spheres demands historicisation of expenditure. To exclude these corpses from an analysis of Europe's productive economy in a study of human smuggling would be tantamount to sampling on the variable; airbrushing waste from history in a way that reifies the restrictive economy's disavowal of the general. Attentiveness to the 'horribly excluded' and its expulsion from the productive system compels extended reflection on the meaning of these corpses which, in an age of unbounded recreational sexual freedom for those who reside in the metropolitan West, remain woefully untheorised in migration scholarship.

What happens, we ought to ask, when we place death of at the centre of debates about migration and sexuality? What do these corpses signify in an age where both at home (as a citizen) and abroad (as a tourist) positionality and passport bestows the Western subject with unprecedented opportunities to engage in travel that frequently involves exploring, experimenting and indulging in personal journeys of sensual and sexual discoveries of Self and Other? Thinking of corpses as once erotic, sexual and profoundly alive human beings driven by more than just money and hunger compels us to compare and contrast the constraints they faced with the freedoms that young people from Britain of similar age routinely enjoy when they embark upon 'gap years', study programmes and casual work. It also allows us to interpret their deaths in terms that go beyond victimhood, as a protest to the politically drawn borders of a world system that structures the mobility of capital and bodies to and from the global South in profoundly unequal ways.

The French historian Fernand Braudel, who pioneered the study of seas as historical units of analysis, did not live to see human smuggling's morbid consequences in the Mediterranean, but we can be sure they would have interested him. They signal, in dramatic fashion, many of the most important and vexed issues of time and space, structure and agency in historical analysis he sought to emphasise in his writings, above all, 'the question of boundaries, from which all others flow'. In the opening pages to his seminal history of the Mediterranean, he writes: 'to draw a boundary around anything is to define, analyse, and ... adopt a philosophy of history' (Braudel 1992 [1949]: x-xi). His own inclusive conception of the Mediterranean as an uninterrupted space within vast and diverse empires and civilisations that dwarf contemporary 'Europe' in age and territorial span refers to the African desert as its 'southern face'; it bears little resemblance to Fortress Europe's restrictive demarcations, encompassing the general economy and indeed the world beyond.

> The Mediterranean is not a single sea; it is a complex of seas, broken up by islands, interrupted by peninsulas, ringed by intricate coastlines. Its life is linked to the land ... its history can no more be separated from the land surrounding it than the clay be separated from the hands of the porter who shapes it. It is not an autonomous world, nor is it the preserve of any one power. Woe betide the historian who thinks...that the Mediterranean ... has long been clearly defined ... How could one write any history of the sea, even over a period of only 50 years, if one stopped at one end of the pillars of Hercules and at the other with the straits at whose entrance ancient Ilium once stood guard? (Braudel 1992 [1949]: x-xi).

Contemporary imperialist mythmaking portrays the EU as heir to some ancient and medieval lineage expunged of Asian, African and Islamic origins and connections; textbooks and mainstream histories of Europe confirm this narrative by reproducing the obligatory sequence of chapters on Greeks, Romans, Christendom and the Italian Renaissance (e.g. Davies 1997). The thinking that underpins this kind of 'European' history is unlikely to interest the student of Braudel, for whom the bloated black or brown corpse, swirling off shore from Italy, Greece or Spain, is simultaneously emblematic of an event, a social process and part of the physical environment that constitute history in the Mediterranean. Having come into existence inside Europe's waters, it connects the restrictive economy perpetually to its peripheries in a powerful symbol of domination and exclusion – of Afro-Eurasia's disavowed oneness.

Braudel's ability to conceive of the Mediterranean as a unified space was premised on his sensitivity to the totality of human history in all its organic and intimate connections with the physical environment. It was conceived against a tripartite division of temporality into three speeds, ranging from the rapidly ephemeral (e.g. political) event to the medium term social processes examined in this book and then, finally, to the imperceptibly slow unfolding of change in man's relationship to his environment (xiv, 1-2). Every individual migrant corpse, in this framework, is a product of movement across these different temporal speeds in European history. Death in migration is a one-way trip through the symbolic into the Real signified materiality of a sign ('Europe'). It occurs in a single, horrific event, after which national, ethnic and other classifications lose much of their relevance. The corpse, that is to say, becomes part of the physical environment – the sea, which is itself 'the greatest document of its past existence' (Braudel 1992 [1949]: x-xi). As long periods of time pass, its anonymity doesn't really matter. Nor indeed does the precise moment when it came into existence: 'No simple biography beginning with a date of birth can be written of the sea' (Braudel 1992 [1949]: x-xi).

If the only way a migrant can secure a place in European history is to travel by means of single event (death) to the longue durée it seems churlish to speak of agency or even individual freedom of action. Braudel, a convinced structuralist, dismissively compared 'so-called freedom' of this kind to a 'tiny island, almost a prison' that merely underlines the ways in which 'all efforts against the prevailing tide of history – which is not always obvious – are doomed to failure'. The individual, in his reckoning, is

> imprisoned within a destiny in which he himself has little hand, fixed in a landscape in which the infinite perspectives of the long-term … [stretch] into the distance both behind him and before. In historical analysis … the long run always wins in the end. Annihilating innumerable events – all those which cannot be accommodated in the main ongoing current and are therefore ruthlessly swept to one side (Ibid: 662-4).

As a final word on illegal travel in human smuggling, this will not suffice. For whilst I learned of many tragic stories in which the long term ruthlessly swept aside pathetic attempts to swim against the overwhelming power of its irresistible currents, there are thousands of instances every year in which dogged perseverance across Europe's Mediterranean fronts – overland and sea – can be read as a remarkable moment of victory for the individual – rather than death and defeat by structure. In travel and transit, migrants act as decision-makers and risk-takers, displaying levels of endurance and apparent fearlessness in the face of annihilation that are barely comprehensible. Border-police checkpoints, hi-technology surveillance and in some cases, live ammunition are negotiated as surmountable obstacles; extreme weather conditions, hunger, thirst, exhaustion and severe cold are shrugged off in single-minded pursuit of desire's target.

> *Chima:* You couldn't get water on the way. I was *really* thirsty. Hungry. It was really distressing. I was exhausted. It was cold, really cold. There was snow. It was really difficult to walk. For some people it's harder – those who aren't strong. But people help them.

Border crossings like these are reminiscent of Xenophon's epic Iron Age Eurasian march from Persia which for centuries has occupied a somewhat ambiguous place in the canons of ancient classical Greek literature for its stirring yet strangely inarticulate account of ten thousand stranded Greek mercenary soldiers' return through the Armenian highlands and modern Turkey to Greece. The *Anabasis* contains numerous passages that lend themselves to appropriation by atavistic, modern Western imperialist identities (confrontations with exotic [Kurdish] 'barbarian' foes, for example). Its most important message, however, is surely the impossibility of return. Less imaginative than grittily real, Xenophon's descriptions of a remarkable campaign across impassable rivers and treacherous mountains in the harshest weather is a tale of endurance and life lived fearlessly at the point of death: a thousand mile trek that resonates powerfully with contemporary narratives of human smuggling. His army's relentless onward trudge into a seemingly endless series of mortal confrontations is remarkably resonant with the testimonies of migrants today who are exposed to some of the same elements on the same geographical terrain.

Shahid, whom I interviewed in Lahore in 2010, successfully made the Mediterranean crossing from Libya to Italy in 2003 at the age of 25. His testimony reads like an agonising delivery; a gruelling and violent birth, in which he and over a hundred other men veer vertiginously close to drowning – both literally and affectively (death is the psychoanalytic equivalent of infinite submergence in the 'oceanic feeling' we spend our lives seeking to recuperate). The narrative bleeds eroticism. Nauseating extremes of inner experience, the physical symptoms of which include actual vomiting; anarchic resistance to prohibitions on movement; equality within a 'headless community' of Xenophonic, sovereign risk-takers. Even the realm of the mystical enters the story at various points (at the brink of catastrophe, travelers pray in communal preparation for a horrified encounter with the divine).

That every single one of them is a Muslim invader of sorts makes it impossible not to think of Tariq's landing at Gibraltar in 711 – his stirring speech of no return made, it is thought, after burning the ships on which he and his men crossed the Mediterranean ('Oh my warriors, whither would you flee? Behind you is the sea …'). War too, of course, can constitute a form of carnal communication between two sets of risk-taking armies locked in deadly embrace (Direk 2007: 96). Like the seven centuries of Muslim settlement in medieval Spain that followed Tariq's defeat of the Visigoths, migrants today are perceived as invaders long after their arrival on European shores. The absolute risk they take in communicating with alterity is met with indifference (Part IV); their history is regarded as external to that of the EU and its constituent nations.

The narrative that follows is worth reproducing at length. If nothing else, it provides evidence that for all the inevitability of structure's ultimate victory over individual attempts to swim against the direction of its most terrifyingly imperious and unforgiving tides, the long term doesn't always have the last laugh.

> An agent was there to pick us up from the airport in a big car. We drove a while, and then stopped at a place called Sabha… There was a big house the agent had rented. It had a big room and a cook. We stayed there for seven days. Then we were driven to Tarablas [Tripoli] – a rented flat with four rooms on the 2nd floor. There were already four guys and with our party the count became 10. We were told to stay in that flat, that we shouldn't go out. They filled the refrigerator with lots of food … They came to pick us after 14 days. We drove for two hours into a forest; in the middle of it was a big house with a huge gate. We were taken inside. Around 70 people were already there. All of them had rough long hair and beards, all were Pakistani … There were arrangements for ablutions and prayers but we weren't allowed to wash. There was barely enough space to lie down at night, and the place was full of mosquitoes. Some had been there for the last 20 days, some for 25. They were complaining about the conditions and the food. People working for agents used to come to deliver food supplies. They used to come in cars with packets of bread, potatoes and onion and leave immediately. The same evening two cars entered the house and told us that it was time to go. We were told cars would take us in shifts. We were told to be silent. I managed to hop into the first shift. We were taken through a forest to two isolated rooms. They were lit with lanterns. There were already 50 people in there from Tunisia, Egypt, Iraq. At night the main agent came. He said get ready – follow them through the forest. Leading us was a black African whom, we were told, we had to follow. We were not allowed to keep any of our luggage; no clothes other than what we were wearing. It was the start of winter; October. We started walking at midnight. We walked in the desert and stopped before a road. Soon we stopped at a place where we could hear the sound of the sea nearby. We were then told that from there we will move in groups of 10 towards the shore. We were told there would be a big ferry, a ship. Turned out it was more like a small boat used by fishermen. It wasn't easy to get on – we had to

go into water. We were scared when water level was touching our necks. Our clothes got soaked. The boat would come and take people ten at a time and leave without stopping; we only had seconds to get in. The driver didn't care whether people have jumped successfully. Eventually all 120 – the 70 Pakistanis from the big house and 50 others who we joined later on were jam-packed in the boat. The agent flashed the light to signal that we were good to go. The driver set the compass at 30 degrees, for this would take us to the Italian shore. We were told that it would take 18 to 20 hours to reach there. We were given loafs of bread, cubes of butter and many gallons of petrol … Even though we had a big supply of food, we ate very little, for the atmosphere at sea is such that nobody really likes to eat. Our clothes were wet and some of us were vomiting … We sailed into a big storm. Waves were blocking our path – they weren't allowing us to go in our direction of 30 degrees. This continued for about an hour. Water was coming on the boat. The driver came out of his cabin and started to cry. He said we should all recite the *Kalma* since we had no chance of survival. He said he had been on many ships to Europe but had never seen the sea in this much trouble. He was Libyan. His brother was also in the ship. He spoke Arabic. There were some men on board who had been living in Libya for some time; they translated his message in Punjabi… We all recited *Kalma* and it was clear that we were about to drown. The driver's brother, an 18 year old went to the front of the boat every now and then to set it in the right direction. The elder brother was crying continuously. The younger brother took over the driving. He started the stand-by engine and increased the speed while setting the compass at 40 degrees. He pierced through the water for an hour or so. The boat balanced a little. He kept on manoeuvring for some time and after six hours of hard work and fear we were out of the storm … After 26-27 hours into the journey – the whole day had passed and it was now midnight again – we saw some lights. That gave us hope we might survive. We were all exhausted. We were scared, and sick of the water. Nobody said a word. Nobody was in any mood to talk. The threat of drowning stopped us from doing anything … One guy, a Pakistani, was so faint he was about to fall into the ocean, but we saved him. We saw some big fish of the size of our boat. Sometimes they were moving parallel to our boat. I don't know what they were. But if they were sharks, they could have done us harm by jerking and tossing our boat. They were really big compared to humans … After three hours, we approached the lights. It was an Italian Island, Lampedusa. The agents had told us to turn the red light of the ship on when we got close to lights. As soon as we did, five big ships rushed towards us flashing blue lights. We were surrounded by five ferries. They made announcements using loud speakers, and flashed searchlights on us … They told us to follow them. One ferry was ahead of us, one was either side and one was behind us. They also had guns … After half an hour we reached the shore. There were many people – media people with cameras, doctors etc. – awaiting us. Many of us needed immediate medical attention. Some were faint, and had no sense of what was going on. The doctors checked us out in hospital. Then we had to take our clothes off – they were checking if we had anything hidden. Then they gave us new clothes, trousers and t-shirts along with towels and soap. We took showers. The facilities were good. Then we were allotted rooms. The bedding and everything in the room was new. They gave us things to eat, coffee, bread and milk, fruit; whatever we wanted. They treated us like guests. We slept like babies that night.

Conclusion to Part III

If migration from Pakistani Punjab was once virtually synonymous with heading for the UK, it increasingly means setting out for North America, Australia or dozens of cities in Europe and, of course, the Gulf. A gradual erosion of colonial migration systems tying Britain to South Asia occurred in stages following tightening British restrictionism in the post-war decades. Initial legislation in 1962 diverted Pakistani migration towards Scandinavia (particularly Denmark and Norway) and parts of continental Europe – flows which began as trickles of irregular male entrants who resided without legal permission and worked informally until being regularised, after which time they called for wives and dependents. All this was part of a wider Afro-Eurasian process replicated in France's relationship with the Maghreb and francophone Africa; Germany's ties with Turkey; Britain's links to the Caribbean. European countries that had historically received immigrants primarily from their historical spheres of influence began, in the 1990s, to become destinations and transit points for a new geography of immigration into Europe from the global South. Irregular migration has established Pakistani settlements in Paris, and their Algerian equivalents in North London (Colleyer 2005: 701).

These developments have had important implications for the gendered geography of migration from Pakistan to the West which, having begun to even itself out in terms of male to female ratios for a brief period in the 1970s and early 1980s, is now perhaps as uneven as it ever was, with men dominating primary irregular flows to international destinations across the globe. Family reunification has gone some way towards evening up the ratio of men to women amongst regularised and settled populations in countries such as Britain and Denmark, but flows to newer destinations such as Italy, Portugal and Spain remain predominantly male. The latest regimes of migration control, which make it harder for men to regularise their residency and marry, are accentuating the spatial, material and symbolic distance between the sexes by cementing the male migrant into a role of the lone, bread-winning male.

States – not the Russian mafia – have orchestrated these changes. Human smuggling networks and Europe's much maligned asylum systems work together as a mediating funnel ensuring a steady supply of cheap pliant labour to private commercial actors, much as they did in the colonial era when the Home Office's determination to curb migratory flows from India came up against private employers hiring lascars during periods of high demand for labour (the latter appealed to friends in the Board of Trade and Industry). Today, bouts of door-slamming operate dialectically with *laissez-faire* policies that legitimise the presence of 'unwanted' immigrants: periodic regularisations within Italy and

Spain, for example, have been effectively staggered to ensure the distribution of Afro-Eurasian labour around Europe in useful ways. Control of Afro-Eurasian labour through colonial migration systems, that is to say, has been replaced by a new imperialism conducted at the supranational level.

The idea of a 'Fortress' surrounded by a moat is thus unhelpful. Think instead of a bull charging at a matador. With each attempt to pierce the fabric of his cape, a colossal expenditure of energy is wasted on a moving target; labour – the beast being baited – is ultimately subordinate to an order of capital. Taunted, shaken up and shifted around, chewed up and spat out. The best it can hope for is ingestion into Europe's restrictive economy. The reality of the migration process as Pakistani labour migrants experience it unfolding over time is one in which constraints and structures play an increasingly prominent role, eclipsing, in many ways, the romantic and imaginative forces that drive decision-making in sending contexts. In illegal travel and transit, the migrant's body is subjected to severe exhaustion, hunger, draconian regimes of state surveillance, technologies of discipline and punishment as soon as it enters Western space (and in many cases before, for instance, en route to the West in the Middle East).

On the other hand, the notion of hapless passives being led astray by agents in decisions they have no say in underestimates the extent of agency and volitional risk-taking in illegal travel. For one thing, sociological realities make it inappropriate to differentiate categorically between migrants and smugglers: some migrants turn to facilitation as a kind 'side-line' once abroad. Others go on to specialise in it. The difficulty in stating what constitutes an agent is thus acute, and compounded by the fact that facilitation takes a great many forms, ranging from the highly organised network co-ordinator within the sending context to the local, indigenous groups that specialise in facilitating particular border-crossings in transit.

These last peregrinations are akin to Xenophon's westward march and ultimate victory over an endless array of Eurasian foes, mountains and elements. That illegal travel can have more in common with the ancient world's most dangerous military expeditions than the sorts of recreational and professional mobility to which many European citizens are today accustomed says a good deal about the unevenness of contemporary 'globalisation'. It's also a reminder of the resilience and stubbornness of the human spirit. Afro-Eurasia's mobile armies of labour exemplify this agency in a war they are losing. History will remember their brushes with death in the vivid and sensuous narratives of survivors, spliced as they are with sexual encounters and the sampling of various forbidden pleasures.

What of those who perish? History must find a place for these too. The Mediterranean's status as a watery grave is at one level, a mark of total exclusion, the corpse a dreadful materialisation of permanent absence and obliteration.

And yet, a world of starkly racialised political geographies – in which our changing relationship with the physical environment is increasingly likely to raise more and more difficult questions about human solidarity and its limits – impels a more historically conscious, empathetic kind of thinking about Europe's relationship with its peripheries than this last tragic and frankly incomplete statement seems to accord. I have tried to argue in Part III that migrant corpses don't need our pity (pity is, after all, a synonym for indifference). They were once bodies that housed desirous, concupiscent and youthful beings. Their deaths are a protest against the inequality of a world system which says some bodies matter more than others.

PART IV
Loss

Introduction to Part IV

East London's textile trade in and around Aldgate had been an immigrant-dominated industry since at least the 18th and 19th centuries when the arrival and incorporation of the Huguenots transformed Spitalfields into a dynamic centre of the silk-weaving industry which was gradually replaced and reinvigorated by Jewish tailoring towards the end of the 1800s. The latter was in turn succeeded by Pakistani (and Bangladeshi) leather-making and textile production from the late 1960s (Kershen, 1997: 74-5), as it was in Manchester (Werbner, 2002) and elsewhere.

It would be some time before Jewish 'middle men' (in Portes' sense) vacated the leather and rag-trade altogether; for the most part South Asians were inserting themselves as machinists, overlockers and cutters into existing Jewish businesses in this period, during which the relationship between employer and employee can be classed as 'paternalistic' (Burawoy, 1985: 94-8; 111-16). Workers, that is to say, were dependent upon a single employer, and entering into a neo-feudal bargain that gave their bosses benevolent responsibilities in exchange for 'loyalty'. Imran spoke of his father's boss as a 'master', 'father', 'landlord' and 'friend', suggesting a personalised relationship that involved close supervision and control.

As immigrant settlement spread further East to Newham and Walthamstow, factories as diverse as steel and rubber production plants, engineering firms and flour mills began to absorb the labour power of subsequent arrivals. Most of these were more ostensibly 'modern' than those in and around E1, with migrants less attached to a single employer, moving from job to job, forming less personalised relationships with colleagues and bosses than earlier cohorts and their sons had done in the family-run Jewish enterprises. The composition of the workforce led to the formation of more identifiable South Asian 'ethnic' constellations; as such, migrants began to be stratified more clearly in terms of ethnicity and racialised under a more antagonistic regime that, following Burawoy (1985: 40) is referred to here as 'despotic' – that is, one that entailed the arbitrary and wilful imposition of discipline and control over workers by capitalists, in this context, with the complicity of hostile indigenous workers. The position of South Asians at the bottom of the racial ladder ensured their designation to the most unpleasant, physically taxing jobs like heavy lifting. Hardships in labour were compounded by poor housing arrangements; Baba Anwar remembers: 'The living situation was horrible, to be honest … In each room there were four people sleeping. And in some cases … one bed was used in shifts as well'.

In 1974, however, the current principle British statute governing the conduct and management of occupational health and safety was introduced (Robinson and

Smallman 2006: 87). It was around this time across the Western world, and in Britain specifically, that an impressive series of victories by labour over capital at the national level ensured that, at the local level, the sorts of despotic accumulation regimes that were prevalent in East London factories in the 1960s gave way to new Fordist technologies of production, along with the social relations that accompanied them. In small increments, the Ford plant at Dagenham established itself as the largest single employer for Asians in the East London area. The better wages it offered signalled a new era of stability, security and prosperity together with an improvement in working and living conditions for migrant workers. This, the relatively protected epoch of the Fordist worker, is remembered fondly. The recollections of Rashid Sahab, who started working at Ford in 1972 and stayed there up until his retirement, are fairly typical: 'It was good working at Ford'; 'Ford's wages were the best of all'. Karim Sahab is similarly positive: 'I think that was a time when we all had a difficult time getting decent jobs, decent wages. Ford was a safe haven for Asians.'It was, he explained, seen as something of a privilege and much preferable to working for 'apne' ('our own' [Asian employers]).

At the exact moment at which the Babas began to experience better working conditions at the Dagenham Ford plant, they forged a new set of connections with the leather and textile businesses in E1.

Thirteen thousand women and almost 30,000 children migrated from Pakistan to the UK between 1962 and 1967 following the implementation of the Commonwealth Immigration Act, beginning the trend of family reunification. A community that was almost exclusively male in 1961 was rapidly transformed into one that, by 1974, was 35 per cent female. By 1982, the predominance of men dropped to just 58 per cent and by 1991 it had virtually disappeared altogether (Ansari 2004: 253-4). Rather than trigger the adoption of a more balanced life-style and relaxed approach to work for all Pakistani immigrants, women's migration ushered in an intensification and diversification of economic activity within households. If the latter had previously been a place of respite where migrants slept in between shifts, they were now absorbed into the textile industry with the family itself becoming integrated into the production process. Imported brides and their children who migrated as young dependents were put to work by the Babas, who facilitated their incorporation within the sectors they were leaving, thereby ensuring that Aldgate's enduring appetite for 'sweated' labour was met by the newcomers.

The transformation of some 'homes' into factory or work/sweat shops ensured factory production continued to operate beyond official hours of production on weekends, holidays and during evenings. Asian women workers thus played an important role in meeting the needs of demand for cheap labour in an industry that boomed for much of the 1970s and 1980s. Their labour contributed to the transformation of East London's economy from industrial to small enterprise. Paid by the piece at unfixed rates of compensation and hours of work, homework reflected the structure of demand for flexible cheap labour in manufacturing following de-industrialisation (Phizacklea 1988: 22). Its invisibility allowed migrant men to draw on their wives' labour without conceding their status as patriarchal breadwinners (Ansari 2004: 271-2). Having sourced the work for them from elsewhere, men such as Baba Rashid were their wives' direct employers, raising the key question long posed by feminist scholars, of whether men and women within the same household might have different class positions (Oakley and Oakley 1979: 178).

This is not to suggest women suffered more than men in all respects: for one thing, they did not experience the cramped living conditions that the Babas had to endure in the 1960s before they owned their own houses. The privileged position retained by Pakistani men (and to some extent, boys) as guardians of public space was not without its responsibilities and risks, as is clear when contextualised within the well-known history of racial terror that culminated in series of brutal attacks and murders across East London in the 1980s, including, perhaps most famously, that of Altab Ali, after whom a park in Aldgate is commemoratively named. It should also be remembered that women did not endure quite the unsanitary living conditions and overcrowding that were typical of male migration during the 1960s. Nor were they at risk from industrial accidents and ill health associated with despotic labour regimes in this last period.

The point, rather, is that women's labour played a crucial role in launching and maintaining creative and dynamic development of many of the most successful enterprises (added labour power, intellectual and creative resources).The same is likely true of children. Testimonies reveal it was not uncommon for the burdens of household labour – both waged and unwaged, to fall upon eldest daughters in particular. The latter bore some of the brunt of the high volumes of work their mothers were expected to do. Saida explains the division of domestic tasks between her and her sisters:

> Before going to school, my younger sister had to clean half of the house, and I would have to clean half. Getting up at seven o'clock. That's how we shared our work, and in the evening we'd have to help mum – when you would come back from school you'd have to do your schoolwork and help her.

Nobody regarded factory work in this period as a picnic. The 1960s especially are recalled as a period of extremely hard graft. Malik Sahib feels a fierce sense of entitlement to the material gains he made in this period ('we gave our blood to this country'); the physical toll of the 1960s and psychological impact of unemployment in the 1980s are not to be underestimated. Moreover, the Fordist golden age was short-lived; British industry was rapidly dismantled in the early 1980s. Reduced to a 'redundant colonial/racialised labour' force' (Grosfugel and Georas 2000: 108) in what proved to be a global economic downturn, the Babas were effectively left stranded. Thousands lost jobs and unemployment became widespread.

And yet, most of them appear to have coped well on a combination of savings, welfare benefits and pensions. They may have begun as a subordinate and vulnerable workforce, but as citizens, they were entitled to a degree of protection from the unpredictabilities of the labour market. Some had already benefited from having arrived when house prices were cheap and, having purchased property, continue to enjoy rental incomes that supplement their pensions. This partly explains why they refuse to see themselves as victims, and why many remember the period as one in which they were properly rewarded for their toil. More generally, their status of respected elders within the community is derived from engagement in public life. The Babas I met included former Union activists, religious leaders and councillors who enjoy a considerable degree of institutional 'structural incorporation'. Their extensive involvement within a local public sphere appears to have allowed them to recover much of the dignity and self-esteem that may have been lost in the early years. Their sense of achievement allows them to narrate their life stories with pride and enthusiasm.

Much of their confidence too, no doubt stems from their identities as husbands, fathers and household heads – roles that imply sovereignty and expenditure beyond useful production in a restrictive economy. Being able to marry and have children transformed their status from individuals into persons: reproductive, sexually active human beings. This essential component of masculine (or indeed feminine) identity cannot be taken for granted in migration today. Human smuggling and illegality have become increasingly prevalent and pronounced, citizenship harder to come by. In this regard, migrant experiences of life and the labour process during the early decades of post-war Britain and Europe compare favourably with those of migrants today. This is especially but not exclusively true of those who struggle to regularise their residential status and work illegally, as will be illustrated in the chapters that follow.

Chapter 5
Myths and Realities of Return and Arrival: Gender and Generation in Pakistani Migration

A series of restrictive state policies including the Immigration Act of 1971 and the British Nationality Act a decade later substantially reduced migratory flows from Pakistan to the UK up until the mid-1980s, prompting the social scientist Muhammad Anwar to conclude that 'large-scale immigration from the colonies is now over and that the unification of undivided families is the main source of immigration' (1995: 275). Less than two decades after this pronouncement a glance at the statistics in would suggest that Anwar's assertion needs re-evaluation: figures in the new millennium reveal a number of what are increasingly acknowledged as 'new' migratory flows. The augmentation in volume and proportion of Pakistani immigration (as compared the share of other countries that supply labour) to Britain since the 1990s is unmistakable: total international immigration from Pakistan to the UK from 1995 to 2004 was 29,100 (ONS: table 2.3, p. 6), up considerably from the figure of 17,600 over the previous corresponding period of 1992-2001 (ONS: table 2.3, p. 6).

The vast majority of this latest wave of arrivals is made up of single men. Independent female international migration from Pakistan is almost non-existent, and although 7,590 of the 212,000 Pakistani nationals admitted into the UK in 2004 were Mangeters (spouses), a greater number (12,600) were students and around half were visitors (Home Office 2004: table 2.2, p. 34-5). Where family reunification became an option for 'old' migrants within a few years of their incorporation, immigration law today makes it far more complicated for those who enter as students and visitors to marry and virtually impossible for those who enter illegally without regularising. The defining characteristics of the new generation of migrants in Britain are thus its predominantly male and single makeup, along with its increasingly precarious legal status; even many of those who enter the country legally find themselves compelled to work in violation of their visas within the informal sector (see below), or to use fraudulent documents within the mainstream (Ahmad 2008a).

The same is true of Italy where Pakistanis remain a predominantly male community; statistics for Prato in 2004 registered a gendered imbalance of 877 men to 358 women (Stefani 2004: 48-9). Fifteen of the 20 men I interviewed are married, but only four were living with their wives and children in Italy (the remaining eleven spouses were in Pakistan). This had as much to do with the relative weakness of their economic position as legal constraints. Jameel explains why most men cannot afford to call for their families even after their status has been regularised:

> Those who are satisfied are 10-12 per cent, maximum. The rest of us – we buy our shirts and trousers from Pakistan. We buy shoes from there. Because it's so expensive here that if you buy here you won't save any money to send back. Why do you think people don't call for their families? Why do they send them back when they come even when they have papers? They can't afford the rent. Those who were making 1,800-1,900E are now making 1,100-1,200E. And that for twelve hours of work daily. So it's 800E for accommodation. You've spent 200-250E on food for the family. It's a hundred or two for bills (electricity, gas, water etc). God forbid you or your kids get sick, or you need to buy clothes, or you have people staying with you. What are you going to do? That's why people get a place for 800-900E, live with six or seven guys and get 150E together each to cover the rent. Then you try to reduce your food costs, and then your spending on coffee and cigarettes to 100E, so that you can save 800E. And then you try to have 200E spare in case of an emergency, if you get a call or something happens. You send the rest back so that your family can eat. If you buy someone a coffee you lie awake at night in bed and think 'I just spent 1.50E unnecessarily, so I'd better reduce my cigarettes for two days' ... You cook once and make it last for three days ... This is the life here. It's truly difficult...

Even the most 'settled' are highly uncertain about the possibility of building futures with their families in Italy.

> *Mushtaq:* It's very difficult to get by here.

> *Waqas:* For anyone who has a wife and kids, there's house and car, gas, electricity and other bills to pay ... and the government is not interested [in helping] ... The kids are crying ... you need to put petrol in the car.

> *Bilal:* My family have come here quite a few times, for two or three months at a time. You can't settle down here though, with a family. It's just not possible to afford it. To cover the costs of the house, to pay the bills, to feed the family, to have a car – it just isn't affordable. What people do is, two families get together. Then they can just about manage.

Zia, the second longest settled of the men I interviewed is a homeowner who lives with his wife and children. Despite holding onto his job through the shocks that rocked Prato's textile industry in the early 2000s, he remains pessimistic:

> There's no real future in Italy, it's a matter of living in the present. If you manage to start a business it's good.

AA: What's the matter with what you're doing?
There's a lot of unemployment. You have no idea when the factory will shut. It could happen anytime and if it does, there's no future here without work. There's no security.

Worries about their own plight are compounded by fears for the future of their children who will one day be expected to find work in a labour market struggling to absorb Italian graduates; children who, unlike British-born Pakistanis, will not benefit from speaking English as a first language. Some Pakistanis in Italy continue to harbour hopes of transferring to an English speaking country for this reason alone. Others want their children to remain in Pakistan, where they can complete their education in Urdu and English.

> *Jaldi:* But my children's future is not better in Italy because the language is Italian, which is useless. I want to shift from here. I have a brother and a sister in America, so I'm trying there.

> *Chima:* My younger brother – it will be good for him if he studies in England.

> *Atif:* I'm thinking it's better for my children to be educated there [Pakistan]. The Italian children here work in the evenings to make ends meet. There aren't many opportunities.

Virtually every man I asked said the realities of migration are not what they expected. Some expressed doubts as to the merits of the lives they had chosen, though explicit regret was rare, partly because risks which lead to lateral moves are difficult to evaluate; partly, perhaps, because there is little to be gained from lamenting grave mistakes that cannot be reversed. When asked why it is that they do not simply return to Pakistan, part of the answer lies, they explained, in the simple fact that, having been away from Pakistan for a period of several years, many have little choice but to make the most of their circumstances in Europe. International migration is a process with opportunity costs: businesses are sold, jobs vacated and employment networks dissipated following departure, ruling out the possibility of return:

> *Jaldi:* It's like when something's stuck in your throat. We can't go back to Pakistan, nor can we stay here happily. I can't go back there now – I won't get work. My networks are finished. I'm 38. At the time I left I was a graduate – there were very few people with Masters [degrees]. Now the whole country is full of unemployed graduates with Masters and postgraduate education. What job would I get? In nine years in Europe, none of the men I've seen who talk about going back actually do.

Waqas: It didn't take long [after coming here] before worry set in – I realised there's nothing here either. Slowly, my options had finished. I'd wasted the time I'd spent there too, by shutting down my business.

Much of this will sound familiar to students of Abdel-Malek Sayad who decades ago observed the difficulties in return migration experienced by Algerians in France, men whose struggle to reconcile their newly socialised 'work bodies' in the peasant context from which they originated was only half the trouble: 'Quite apart from [these] changes they themselves undergo as a consequence of emigration', noted Sayad, the 'very range of possible positions they might occupy within the social context of the community [they once lived in] has been altered in their absence' (Sayad 1999: 284, 303). The prospect of confronting this transformed emigration context, in which return to one's exact circumstances at the point of departure is impossible, is even less attractive in view of the increased costs incurred in the migration process today. Those who experienced the most difficulties since arriving in Italy were among the most adamant about having no intention of returning to Pakistan precisely because they had invested so much time and money in migrating, and were now incorporated into (and trained for) work in European labour markets:

AA: Why don't you then go back to Pakistan?
Chima: Things change … When you get in a car and go somewhere, every so often you have to pay for petrol; the car breaks down. That hurts but it is part of life.

Several were flirting with the idea of yet another sideways move. Jaldi was among the most bitterly disappointed with his life in Prato of all the men I interviewed. He drew explicit comparisons with the superior existence he led in Germany as an asylum claimant whose long hours of low paid work were made worthwhile by state benefits, and lamented the difference in overall quality of life in Italy and strong North West European economies with welfare protection and good public services:

Jaldi: My wife and I have been here for three and half years, we still don't like Italy. There's nothing here. Just work. In Germany, if I can't get work, I know I'm not going to go hungry. The government will give me money. They gave me some. And medical treatment was free. Even when I was working I was getting some money for my wife and kids. Here, I've worked for four years at the same factory. I still don't have permanent work, they could sack me today and what would I do? I don't have a house – I'm sharing accommodation with another family. Here rent is 800-900E. How can a man earning 1,200E or 1000E or 900E pay that? Most men [with families] live in house shares. One man can't afford it…

… I was a kitchen hand in a restaurant in Hamburg. In the beginning the money was 1,500 Deutschmarks, by the end I was getting 2,500. There was no problem there. The government was providing accommodation, medical treatment was free, transport was cheap there – you could get a travel card for 30 marks that lasted 24 hours. I never needed a car there in five years there. I'd always get the train or bus. Here, immediately I had to get a car. Insurance is very expensive, 1,600E a year, for a man earning 1,200E! Plus petrol and maintenance. I haven't enjoyed Italy. I'm stuck here though. If you want to buy a house in England or America, you can buy a house. I've been here for four years – I've paid 20,000 in taxes without any benefit.

The subjective nature of 'economic' decision-making, the subject of Part II of this book, is highly apparent in this passage. Without denying the difficulties of life in Italy, many of these migrants have a distorted view of life in Britain, where it is certainly not the case that 'you can buy a house if you want'. His pessimism about the future is matched by that of Jameel, who paints a depressing portrait of Pakistani life in Italy, this time, contrasting it with an equally rosy portrait of that which he has seen in Scandinavia, where his brother lives:

My cousins in Norway, they're settled. Their children lived and studied there. They grew up there. So and so is working in a bank, so and so is in the post office. Someone else has made a shop, and some other guy is driving a taxi. This is the Pakistani community in Oslo. They look so fresh when they're back from work that you'd think they were back from holiday. Well dressed and in good condition. Look at the men here, everyone is stressed, spent. Haggard. Hard up.

The association of Northern Europe with security, prosperity and welfare benefits is somewhat ironic given that one of the most significant groups of new Pakistani migrants working in Britain is composed of those migrants smuggled into the UK without legal permission; these include men without documents, without the right to reside and work – men in a similar position to their Italian counterparts. (Of the estimated 430,000 illegally resident migrants that populate the UK (Woodbridge 2005), Pakistanis, being one of several nationalities that figure prominently in Home Office asylum and immigration statistics, are likely to be well represented. In 2004, the year in which this research was conducted, 1,710 Pakistanis applied for asylum. The vast majority were men (Home Office 2004: table 3.2, p. 43).

Why then, does the grass in North Western Europe (from which many of these men fled) appear so green? By increasing the costs of successful migration and incorporation within destination countries, human smuggling and ongoing problems of illegality have added a perverse twist to the impossibility of return identified by Sayad (1999) and Muhammad Anwar (1979). The more time, cash and labour pumped into the project of settlement in Europe, the harder it becomes to confront the possibility of migration's unprofitability as an enterprise. The practical difficulties associated with return on the one hand, and the futility of ploughing forward in the same direction on the other, leave only one option: another hopeful gamble that requires yet more cash and more importantly perhaps, a renewed belief that somehow things would be easier elsewhere. This last state of mind entails a romantic leap of considerable proportions now that the promise of glamour and pleasure in some far away European future (discussed in Part II) has been corrected by years of experience.

Thankfully (or not), human beings are good at being foolish. Forgetting, as Mark Edmondson (2003 viii) writes in his preface to the Penguin edition of *Beyond the Pleasure Principle* and other writings, is integral to 'erotic repetition' – the basis of the 'conservative nature of the drives' (2007 [1930]: 54-5) noted by Freud in *Civilisation and its Discontents*. We are doomed, psychoanalysis explains, to learn near nothing from experience. Loss in the wake of love's desolating aftermath is a hangover soon misrecollected. The morning after, we sober up and head straight back to the bar for another pint of intoxication and seek out some new unattainable object to pursue 'the way a starving man pursues bread'. How else to explain the longing of Pakistanis in Italy for a new life in London?

Anti-social networks

The impact of increasing restrictionism at the European and national level on the 'social networks' of Pakistani migrants in Italy, where a flourishing business in regularisation has developed, is striking. Newcomers pay settled migrants for helping them with the acquisition of legal residency by providing documentation that is necessary to make a successful application, including (if necessary fraudulent) work contracts, proofs of address and other related papers, together with correctly filling out, in Italian, the complicated bureaucratic forms required by the Italian state to process paperwork. The spiralling cost of regularisation is indicative of the pace at which the regularisation business has grown: Azum paid 5,000 Euros in 2002 to a Pakistani agent for a procedure for which, in 1990, Pela paid virtually nothing.

The word 'agenti', which means something like, 'the act of profiteering from facilitation', is a practice or action, and appears far more frequently in the Italian testimonies than the term 'agent', which connotes a person (Ahmad forthcoming 2012). This underlines that few individuals can be categorised as such by virtue of their full-time occupation. Agenti is conducted by migrants themselves – individuals who engage in facilitation of regularisation in a manner that is opportunist, and normally supplements their other income-generating activities. Such activity, as Chima explains, is hardly a closed industry or the preserve of criminals and mafias:

> *Chima:* An agent isn't born an agent. Anyone can become one. A guy who is working in factory can become one. Agent means 'getting something done, and taking money for it'... They know the language. You get them to get house

contracts done, and contracts with employers. You give them money to get a domicile. They'll pay 4,000E to get in done, charge you 6,000E and then pocket 2,000E. Or another example is you can go to these Doner Kebab shop owners and say: 'Give me an [employment] contract for 400E.'…. Some give fake contracts.

Most of this activity involves settled migrants profiteering at the expense of freshly landed countrymen and co-ethnics. Some appear to have acted with the aid of native Italians who took payments for issuing housing and employment documents. Agenti, the point is, cannot be pinned on the actions of a small number of greedy, unscrupulous criminal gangs. Few people admit to having profited from it, but most acknowledge it has become integrated into the very social fabric of the migration and settlement process. It is a cause and consequence of the growing commodification of social networks, and has brought about a corrosion of solidarity within communities of labour migrants, who find themselves increasingly squeezed by the growing cost of circumventing state migration controls – costs effectively recovered by ripping off the next man. 'Many people made a lot of money', according to Jaldi, in the regularisation of 2000. Jameel gives us an indication of how much his facilitator made in the regularisation of 1998 alone:

AA: Do they make a lot of money?
Jameel: Definitely! Mine had at least fifty to sixty customers. (I did some research into where one could get documents made most cheaply. At that time in 1998 it was Brescia.) He was doing it cheaply but for lots of men – others were asking for more but doing only eight, ten, 12 or 14 cases.

Agenti appears to have proliferated rapidly after the initial regularisation, so that by the time Sarfraz arrived in 1998, he and others were already being greeted upon arrival in the central train stations of Italian cities by agents touting for customers. Some offered shelter as part of the package. All extracted handsome profits:

A few Pakistanis I met, they said, 'Come with us.' They would take people in at that time for rent.

AA: How did you find Pakistani people?
Whenever there's a regularisation you'll find people roaming around trying to explain what you need to do to get documents made, how to do it. Some are helpful, some aren't. Some take advantage. Some harm you. I stayed in a place near Milan in the beginning. I applied for papers and stayed there for a year. He [the agent] was asking for six million [lire] to get it done as an urgent case. He didn't manage to get it done urgently so he took five million in the end. Five million each (we were two guys). He didn't do such a good job but we got our papers done after a year and a bit.

Agenti is not specific to Italy, but part of a wider process in the EU. Conversations with migrants about what they had witnessed and experienced in other countries revealed that new 'chains' of migration to continental Europe are part of a migration business that is far more endemic, systematic and profitable than anything witnessed previously in European history. Large-scale regularisation programmes in various new immigrant-receiving countries, particularly in the Mediterranean region have created a particularly extensive migration business in which newly arrived migrants get involved even before they are incorporated into the labour market. For some, it is likely to be considered a more lucrative and attractive option than working. Several of Faizal's friends in Greece were making a pretty penny from smuggling migrants into Greece and then helping regularise their status as part of an expensive package provided by a highly organised operation:

> They all had a good scene there. They had good jobs. My two friends who brought me there, they were doing *agenti*: getting people's papers made. The settled ones, the ones who have learned the language – they get together with Greeks and have men brought in on ships. Greek shipping companies are always coming and going from Turkey. They'd bring ten to 15 men like that at a time – smuggle them. These friends of mine – they had good houses on rent. They were eating well in restaurants. (The [only] reason they didn't keep cars is that they didn't have driving licenses.)

Across Europe state controls with respect to immigration are likely to become even more restrictive. There is a growing consensus among even Britain's liberal intelligentsia that migrant families are a costly burden on the welfare state (Dench et al. 2006) and the perceived 'problems' surrounding illegal work and trafficking (together with a general atmosphere of dismay with 'multiculturalism'). If the Dutch experience is anything to go by (Leun et al. 2006), these are likely to include sterner measures to restrict welfare benefits, laws that make it more difficult for irregular entrants to legalise their status and crackdowns on illegal work.

All of which makes the importance of profiteering from regularisation certain to increase with or without large scale-regularisation programmes of the kind witnessed in the Mediterranean in recent years. Anecdotal evidence suggests extortion, profiteering, blackmail and an extensive regularisation business has already taken hold in Britain. A 'gang' of Indian Punjabis was famously jailed for five years after making 'millions' from having brought up to 400 clients to the UK from Punjab via the Balkans or Russia and Paris, and then across the Channel in people carriers through Dover for 8,000 pounds sterling each (Morris 2004). *The Times* reported the discovery by police of a workshop producing fake passports worth one million pounds in the home of a 27-year-old Nigerian failed asylum seeker in 2004. The haul included 50 UK passports, passports from other countries and replica 'permission to stay' stamps that police believed had been made in India or Pakistan. It also included blank and fake identity kits: birth certificates and driving licences – all forms of documentation that could allow an illegally resident foreigner to live and work under a false identity in the formal economy and thus effectively regularise their presence in the UK (Tendler 2004).

Equally important is the way in which state policies create power relations between successive generations of migrants. Most new migrants in London live in rooms in rental homes of settled Pakistanis, since they prefer to remain near to residential areas populated heavily by co-ethnics for the apparent material, practical and psychological advantages that familiarity brings: above all jobs in South Asian businesses; cheap and informal accommodation arrangements; anonymity if they are 'illegal'. Often, they work for and pay rents to 'old' families, living in dwellings that once housed the Babas during their early years at Ford or other East London factories. Virtually all the new migrants I interviewed had Pakistani landlords and employers. This proximity throws into stark relief the difference between the lived experiences of these respective constellations of migrants, ensuring at the same time, their lives are interconnected in relations of unequal power.

Indeed, a vast power discrepancy exists between the old migrant family and the new, lone, male 'breadwinning' migrant individual, reflected above all in capital assets such as property and businesses. Newcomers are unlikely to be able to afford property even in the medium and long-term given the rise in prices over the last two decades. Few ever manage to raise the start-up capital to launch their own businesses and having been educated in Pakistan, suffer disadvantage within the mainstream labour market when compared with their British-born counterparts, who are conspicuous by their absence within the Pakistani 'ethnic' service sector. Despite the existence of discrimination within the British labour market (Blackaby et al. 2005), British men and women of Pakistani origin rarely show interest in the jobs newly arrived cohorts of Pakistani men will be restricted to for the duration of their working lives. Where they do appear, it is more often as employers of new migrants, which merely reinforces the class distinction between the respective groups.

In Italy, social divisions between migrants are not so obviously segmented by class and generation since all migrants arrived within a relatively short space of time since the 1990s. However, the immigrant economy is similarly fraught by imbalances in power. These are determined by 'network position': the migrant's relative strength or weakness within the immigrant economy, a status which can almost always be traced to correspond with the precise moment they arrived – that is, the particular migratory wave that swept them into the Italian labour market.

Take, for instance, employment opportunities in Prato's textile industry. These were filled through the functioning of networks which mediated the interface between supply and demand, funnelling jobseekers into the many vacancies that existed in the early 1990s. 'Italian employers', Bilal said, 'would recruit through men who worked for them – [they would ask and you'd say] 'I'll bring someone tomorrow morning'. Bridging networks between employers and individual workers thus allowed information to circulate throughout the Pakistani population in Italy (and even beyond) along the weak and strong network ties that connect its nodal population settlements. The knowledge that rates of pay, overtime and working conditions were favourable in Prato soon spread to the other industrial districts:

> *Jameel:* At that time in Prato there was loads of work. You could leave a job and get four more in one day. This was 1990 to 1996 ... The monthly salary too was higher here than anywhere in Italy. The reason was that there were three shifts. In the morning 6am until 2pm; 2pm until 10pm at night. The third shift was at 10pm at night until 6 in the morning. The pay rate was higher at night. Then, the pattern was three days work, one day off, so Saturday was part of the working week, and the pay rate for that was double. The ones from Milan [Brescia] or Bologna or Rome were making 700-900E, here people were making 1,800-1,900E. So if for instance, I went to Bologna, they would ask me how much I was making. I'd tell them and they'd think, 'We don't make that much in two months!'. They'd leave and come here.

The supply of labour funnelled through networks such as the ones which connect Pakistani Punjab to Western labour markets can continue irrespective of demand drying up or ceasing (Arango 2004; Knights 1996; Light 2000). In such cases, it is not unusual for supply to outstrip demand, leading to recession and unemployment. Migrants had their own terminology for the bust following the boom: 'Crazy'. (The choice of word, hardly coincidental, tells us just how irrational migrants themselves perceive the routine operation of social networks to be).

> *Jameel:* So everyone from outside came here, it got congested. People like me who are older stopped getting work as the young blood arrived. Unemployment started in Prato. This started in 1998.

The situation in terms of employment prospects and prosperity has changed considerably following the *Crazy* that developed in Prato, where its effects have been compounded by a more general economic downturn that happened to hit textile production at around the same time. The employment experiences of those who arrived since are thus markedly different to those who arrived earlier and managed to obtain factory contracts. They have experienced far higher levels of job instability and precarity. By the time Faizal finally started looking for work in 2002, the *Crazy* was in full swing. One of six men unemployed men I interviewed, he was under considerable pressure due to the cost of his being in Italy without employment. It was with some distress that he (and then Bilal) explained:

> *Faizal:* In 2002 I came to Prato. I made papers from there. And then I went to Pakistan. I stayed there for 8 months ... When I came back to Italy I was unemployed for two or three months. I came straight to Prato from Rome airport. Every man was working but I couldn't find anything. They said work is in short supply at the moment. Wait a while. So like that I stayed for three months.

Bilal: It's pretty bad now. Before they couldn't get enough people to fill vacancies … But now there are quite a few men unemployed. The last four or five years now, they'd give men permanent contracts after just a month, having confirmed that they do good work. Now they do that less. They say we've got work for you till July, there's but nothing in August. They'll hire again in September. My work is fixed, thank God. For those who have to keep looking for work every other month, sporadically, they face constant difficulty. Those who have permanent contracts, they can't be fired without six months notice.

Increasingly, new arrivals have struggled to obtain work in factories at all. Several of the (unemployed) men I encountered in Prato were there because they had failed to find work in Brescia and Carpi (the *Crazy* extends to all of the principal sights of settlement in Italy):

Farhad: So I got papers but I couldn't get work. When regularisations happen people turn up from everywhere and there's no work. There was a *Crazy*. I went from Paris to Milan and from there to Carpi. When my papers came through, I worked as a fruit picker – pears and things off trees, in Carpi. I was getting paid five Euros per hour … And after that I came here. Since then, sometimes I get work, sometimes I don't.

This was all taking place within the context of a wider economic downturn and general malaise that gripped Italy in the closing years of the then Berlusconi administration's government. Migrants reported that, intertwined with this decline of the industrial sector, a gradual contraction of the service industry, their other main employer, also took place. It suddenly became more difficult to get jobs in native businesses, which were suffering as a consequence of falling consumer spending. Sarfraz was one of those working at an Italian restaurant in Prato 'when the *Crazy* happened' in 2001. Within a short space of time he was made redundant.

Many who were able to resorted to self-employment, entering an ethnic economy which now absorbs most surplus Pakistani labour in Italy, but supplies the wider native populace as well as co-ethnics and other immigrants. Communications and the service-sector have emerged as the principal two routes that Pakistanis have opted to take in starting their own businesses. Dozens of telephone and internet centres ('PCs', as they are known) and takeaways ('Doners') have appeared in Italian cities following another wave of internal migration triggered by dispersal from saturated labour markets. A handful of migrants own grocery stores, but the vast majority prefer not to deviate from the tried and tested formula, emulating the few existing successful businesses that first appeared in a risk-averse pattern by which being an 'entrepreneur' means opening identical businesses to existent establishments in a bid to appropriate their custom (Knights 1996). The result: abject failure – the unthinkable – is avoided. But profits for everyone get reduced.

In Prato and Florence in particular, a growing number of such Pakistani businesses appeared in 2006 in the *San Lorenzo* area, near the central market, alongside Bangladeshi, Nigerian, Turkish-Kurdish and Arabic grocers and takeaways. Most of their proprietors say they prospered initially, but that an atmosphere of desperation rapidly began to pervade a local economy flooded with shops and establishments offering the same goods and services, eroding any dynamic aspects of entrepreneurship that once may have existed. The intensity of competition has made price-cutting rife; so too self-exploitation by employers who work all hours themselves and intra-ethnic exploitation within the group by employers of their staff. Men work appallingly long hours for ever lower rates of pay in order to survive. Jameel, who helps out in the PC of a friend, explains the process, and its consequences for immigrant business:

> *Jameel:* You've probably seen in Florence, there's Pakistani owned Doners and telephone centres everywhere. Why? Because people can't work and they need to live – to do *something*. There used to be just three or four telephone centres in Prato. The takings were good. Bilal was the first to invest – this was 1994-5. They were taking 1,500-1,600E a day. Now things are such that a good day is one when you take – we all say this – 500E-600E on average. The average is 450E. It's 600E on the weekends, 300E on weekdays. Everyone tells us we're lucky – others are taking 200E, 250E. What we've done is start to do other lines… We sell phone cards, make a bit here, there. It's a hand to mouth system.

As employment opportunities contracted, state policies too began to bite harder. Internal controls of migration have intensified with the 2002 Bossi-Fini law, which attaches residential rights to employment status. Agenti, unsurprisingly, has become an increasingly important means of supplementing business income: offering work contracts (and in some cases, housing) to newcomers, 'helping' them navigate Italy's highly complicated and impenetrable system of bureaucracy etc.

The network, as a result, has started to eat itself, reducing the value of 'ethnicity' as a resource, and raising the spectre of internal strife as each wave of migrants bleeds the next dry. Apparent acts of solidarity such as hiring a friend or cousin are distorted by an ever present will to survive and profit off those to whom one is bonded most strongly: employers squeeze their co-ethnic workers (to whom they may even be related by blood) with ever greater ferocity. And yet, paradoxically, as this intra-group exploitation intensifies, migrants appear to become more, not less dependent upon the networks that have come to constrain them. The prospect of bridging out and taking entrepreneurial risks appears ever more remote, and network dynamism fades.

Boom-bust: Cycles of recession and prosperity in migration networks

How to explain the limits and failures of social capital and ethnic solidarity in what researchers generally agree is one of Italy's most internally cohesive, transnationally networked and newly arrived immigrant populations?

It seems fairly clear that networks, transnational or otherwise can only be as fruitful a source of social (or any other sort) of capital as the context in which they are fostered and develop allows. The deteriorating fortunes of Pakistanis in Italy is, at bottom, a consequence of fluctuations in the demand for migrant labour, falling consumer spending, and an increasingly harsh institutional climate based on immigration policies. Migrants showed impressive degrees of solidarity in the very earliest stages of settlement by pooling resources in difficult times, but bonded solidarity always thrived most when ethnic networks were linked by bridges to the mainstream economy. 'Pull factors' – above all, demand for labour – were the structural force that oriented network flows toward places such as Prato through bridging ties between Pakistanis and employers. Just as the need for labour had been plugged and the housing crisis resolved, the market went into a sharp decline due to the changing international situation in the world economy after 9/11, and the intensification of competition in textile production which started to be outsourced to production sites beyond Italy's shores. Suddenly, Jameel recounts, 'the work reduced. The night shift stopped – it was just two shifts. Then 35 per cent of the textile industry closed down.'

As unemployment set in, a profound feeling of insecurity weighed down on the community, which immediately felt the lack of welfare protection from unemployment that characterises migrant life in Italy. The amount of social capital yielded by networks and ties began to diminish. Many migrants I spoke to scoffed bitterly at the idea of group solidarity ('Your own kind rips you off'). This situation is rooted partly in Italy's general social and economic environment; jobs are scarce, wages are low and welfare protection minimal. Institutional constraints with regard to legal residency and discrimination within the labour market is part of a fundamental tension between the host society's adoption of a programme of economic development based on immigrant labour, on the one hand, and its refusal, on the other, to accept the social consequences of that reality (Rastrelli 2003: 101).

However, 'place' and national-state specificities are not the sole determinants of economic conditions. The rosy portrait these men have of life in Northern Europe is based on the experience of old Pakistani migrants who arrived at a different time, under different conditions. Many of these respondents are mistaking that experience as universal. They would do better to compare themselves with Freshies in London and across Europe, where the current historical moment is producing an experience of immigration that is starkly distinct from that of the 'old' fordist migrants who left Mirpur and Punjab for Britain up until the 1970s. The Babas enjoyed relatively decent labour regimes under Fordism in the 1970s, which represented an improvement over the paternalism of E1 and the despotism that reigned in smaller and medium sized factories where simple control is exerted in highly personalised settings. Moreover, first generation migrant families and households in Britain were economically incorporated in the 1970s and 1980s along segmented lines of gender and generation that allowed primary migrants to share (and in some cases pass on) the brunt of the collective labour burden to their families whilst maintaining patriarchal dominance.

Hardening immigration policies and altered labour regimes in destination societies have eroded the material base of the patriarchal migrant family as a resource for male migrants seeking economic incorporation within host countries. This last development has reconfigured gender relations within the context of 'new' migration since the 1990s, rendering many recently migrated men particularly vulnerable in ways that their predecessors were not. The existence they know is that of a lone, single (uninvited) guest worker which entails few of the powers and privileges that were once associated with Pakistani masculinity in East London. Settlement could take many more years than it did previous generations.

Fordist migrations took place at a time when housing was affordable; contemporary migration occurs at a time when house prices across Europe have soared to the point where they are out of reach for many natives. In the 1960s migrants in East London often purchased properties within a short space of time of their incorporation into the local economy. Their dreams of return in the 1970s and 1980s (Anwar 1979) appear something of a luxury when viewed within the context of contemporary migration. Pakistanis in Italy can only fantasise about a time when they will be able to manage even a joint purchase. They have few qualms admitting their intentions of being 'here to stay'. The irony is that, where previous generations migrated in search of quick commercial gain but left with an unfulfilled will to return, the current wave are spending inordinate amounts of money in a desperate bid to never have to return. The myth for them, it seems, is the idea that they will some day be fortunate enough to experience a meaningful arrival.

There is nothing romantic about migrant discourse on 'return' under the precarious conditions of late capitalist globalisation. The 'goal of return', which permeated old migrant discourse, must be contrasted with the probable 'fact of return' that awaits many new migrants without documents, an important conceptual distinction (Brettell 1986: 84). Even for the settled and regularised population, for whom return is not an inevitable reality, it remains a distinct possibility. At the very least, all sorts of questions surround theirs and their children's futures in Italy, and Europe more generally. The dominant myth that imbues the rhetoric of their discourse now appears to be one of 'arrival'. Migrants now effectively fantasise about the possibilities of settlement and stability in Europe, despite the fact that their testimonies suggest these have now become elusive. Their decision to migrate and invest ever-greater sums in paying smugglers and regularising their legal statuses (together with the money they are compelled to invest in businesses in order to create employment for themselves) underline the dream-like nature of their project.

Their status as lone breadwinners in a vastly transformed context of reception, together with their relations to previous waves of migrant families which are often characterised by relations of power and economic exploitation reveal the highly contingent, variable nature of masculinity and masculine power in different times and places. Many have worked and lived in several European states. But for all their internationality, there is little in their frantic cross-border activity that constitutes transnationalism as it is conceptualised by Portes and Vertovec et al. Neither circular, nor sustained, nor a meaningful expression of agency, much of their migratory energy is spent on internal moves within Italy's borders and on building bridges with Italian society, rather than with their relatives in Pakistan.

For all of their sacrifices, the Babas imported brides, headed families, set up mosques and formed transnational communities spanning Britain and Pakistan: lives of sexually reproductive and spiritually active expenditure beyond work. Though we cannot rule out the Freshies establishing themselves in ways that allow them to emulate some of these achievements, it seems clear the rules of the game have changed. Migrants today feel uncertain about the future, and with good reason. For some, the dream of economic prosperity, family reunification and permanent settlement they are chasing is being partially realised, though seldom without great difficulty and always at considerable cost. For others, it is likely to remain elusive.

Chapter 6
Time, Space and Illegality in the New Migrant Economy

The assembly line, it is well documented, produced miseries to which few would call for a return. Individuals who recount having experienced them frequently emphasise its brutally anaesthetising effects: 'routine' and 'continuous movements' (Linhart 1985: 117) which produce a monotony so dreary that a car factory becomes the site of 'a war of attrition', 'life verses death'. The latter, induced by the 'repetition of identical gestures' (Ibid: 120) must be contended with against a backdrop of maddening sights and sounds: 'drills, the roaring of blow torches, the hammer strokes of metal. In mindless factory work, 'time stands still' to produce the alienation Marx identified as central to the technology of industrialism (Ibid: 117-18). The effect of the production process, he argued in *Capital*, is to 'mutilate the labourer into a fragment of a man, degrade him to the level of an appendage of a machine', destroying 'every remnant of charm in his work', thus turning it into 'hated toil' (cited by Sayers 1988: 725).

But migrants who worked in London's factories were at least rewarded for their hated toil. Temporal structure and planning for the future are not in themselves destructive. In one sense, workers under Fordism were no different to all modern individuals and groups who sacrifice short-term pain for long-term gain, accepting spatial constraints in order to secure their own and their families' material well being and future: a key feature of modern societies, as George Simmel observed, is that they encourage this sort of calculation: 'under modern conditions money allows the construction of longer and longer means/goals chains, in which more and more of the apparent goals do not have any ultimate significance but matter purely as means, as way stations to further goals (Poggi 1993: 177).

Max Weber, of course, described the centrality of these values in the 'Protestant Spirit' of modern capitalism, an ethos which Richard Sennet argues is fast disappearing under late capitalism, the result of an assault on the routines and bureaucratic structure that characterised the industrial labour process. The latter is making planning for the long term impossible (Sennet 1998: 32). Indifference and lack of attachment, according to Sennet, more than alienation, characterise 'flexible specialisation', which he labels the 'antithesis of the system of production embodied in Fordism' (1998: 51). Migrants' working hours are 'flexible' only to the extent that they must comply with inhumane routines and working conditions. These are often fixed in ways that resemble industrial patterns: tasks are often intensely physical, repetitive and monotonous, and in many ways represent an intensification of Fordism. The latter, as Sennet himself points out, at least offered a 'legible' arena in which workers could assert demands. It existed, moreover, in the context of the boom years of reconstruction, when the purchase of property through mortgages was a realistic possibility (Sennet 1998: 43).

Migrants today suffer from an imbalance by which their sacrifices, in terms of time, are far greater than those endured by the rest of society, their rewards less. The deferral of benefits they accept is particularly profound, their 'means/ goals chains' so long that they loose great chunks of their lives working in order to secure futures that may never arrive. In the case of irregular migrants, the burden of living off borrowed time intensifies their compulsion to sacrifice and defer. At the same time, the impossibility of a future in the host country – of a meaningful life and having a family of their own, creates a curious temporal paradox: they cannot leave the country and return to their past lives in Pakistan, which over time, become as far from their everyday lives as their elusive futures. If the commonly used phrase, 'time is money', underlines the general fact of economic value's temporal co-ordinates in capitalist societies, it takes on a particularly dramatic relevance in the lives of migrant workers, who work excessively long hours for low rates of pay.

To a considerable extent, this is true of all new migrant workers, regardless of their prior trajectories. A glance at Appendix 2, which displays the range of employment outcomes for most of the new migrants I spoke with in London suggests legal status does not determine in any mechanistic way their prospects of finding work within the migrant-worker economy into which most new comers get inserted. Indeed the diversity in legal status and migratory histories that co-exist within the low-paid, manual, low-skilled service sector into which many new Pakistani migrants are absorbed is striking; so too the range in age, educational qualifications and length of time spent in the UK. The only unifying social feature of these men is the cheap labour they provide British society.

Testimonies of those who enter the country illegally are marked by certain specificities. Saud and Hasan were doing two jobs when I met them in London, and so worked seven days a week for a minimum of 12-hours per day. Khan Sahab and Aloo worked six days out seven for around half of the minimum wage. Hamid, meanwhile, was toiling away for as long as the weather would permit (there are no fixed hours in construction work). His only distress, he said, was on those days when the weather prevented him and his co-workers from getting on with a job. It took weeks to arrange a meeting because he was so busy.

Students like Nobil, in contrast, had more free time on their hands, and were more particular about what they regarded as acceptable employment, even in the short-term. Halim, who entered the UK on a visit visa, was amongst the very few migrants I met who had been sent by his family to find work specifically because they were in a difficult situation. Yet he appeared to be under less pressure than Khan Sahab, and was adamant about not doing the kind of hard physical jobs Khan Sahab had been doing for many months. Of the four months that had passed whilst he was here on his visit, he had worked for just 10 days, blaming his own 'laziness'. Although he did eventually go up to Leeds to work in a chicken shop, he remained orientated toward a long-term solution. Like Nobil, much of his time, as far as I could see, was spent getting bored – either at home (listening to music and watching DVDs) or in the local library. Despite the frustration, tedium and despondency at being unemployed these men suffered, there was relatively little urgency in their job-hunting and little willingness to do the worst kinds of work available. Neither Nobil nor Halim had accumulated any savings and were living off 'reverse-remittances'.

The probable reasons for these differences relate to the costs of migration for smugglees (smuggled migrants), which are generally higher than legal entrants. Their debt, it should be noted, need not be an actual sum of money owed to an agent – the latter will more than likely have been paid in advance. Nor is it necessarily an outstanding sum of cash owed to a family member for financing the migration – none of the men I met spoke in terms of repaying a loan to, or on behalf of their family. It is, rather, a kind of psychological burden the smuggled migrant *feels*. A sense that one's *time* in the UK has been paid for, can end at any moment, and ought to be used productively.

Students too must finance their college fees. But like visitors, their migration costs are less, particularly given the kinds of colleges they attend (seldom first-rate universities) and there is less uncertainty of how long they will be here. Over time, moreover, some students are able to take advantage of their legal right to work in the regulated economic sphere, earning the minimum wage. Their visas are for fixed periods of time that can be extended. Smuggled migrants, on the other hand, cannot afford to be picky. Even those who are legally resident and awaiting an asylum application can receive orders to leave the country without much notice, and know they will have difficulty returning. For those who are illegally resident, like Hasan and Saud, the pressure on them is to utilise every minute they have on western soil. They live a kind of ontological insecurity, with the constant possibility of being discovered and deported. This was suggested by employer, Asif, in an interview, in which he told me about the illegally resident individuals he had employed in the past:

> I know someone who worked twelve-hour shifts *over-time*! He worked 100 hours a week. Seventy hours was normal [for a migrant] – but he'd push up to 100 hours.

> *AA: What motivated him?* Money. And the fact that you're illegal: you can be deported at any time – you've got to work.

None of this is unique, of course. Commodification occurs in all forms of labour migration, as Sayad (1999: 289-90) observed when he identified the brutal effects of individuation that occur in everyday life when a person once intimately connected to family, household and community is plunged into a world where his body becomes nothing other than a 'tool for work'. The painful discovery of 'mathematical time – measurable and quantifiable, convertible into monetary value' – is reflected as much in 'leisure' as it is in labour, the former becoming mere padding for the latter when even the most basic acts of social communion like having meal are stripped of all meaning beyond survival (use-value) and reduced to a hurried, lonely affair in which nutrients are purchased, prepared and absorbed by a single worker making individual budgetary calculations, shopping, cooking and eating alone (Ibid: 289-90).

The specificity of smuggling's aftermath lies in the particular intensity with which this individuation is experienced. Take the routine of Saud, who wakes up at 4:30 am to start his main job (he works weekends at the newsagents where I met him). The total centrality of work to the exclusion of virtually all else is unmistakable:

> When I finish work, it's 3:30pm. I get home by 5:30pm. It takes an hour to prepare food. You need to eat properly to work like this, so you need to take your time over preparing food (people like me can't eat out). So by 8pm, I've eaten. I pray, and then by 9.00pm, it's time to get ready for bed, as I have to get up by 4.45am …

If restrictions on spatial mobility apply to all labour migrants for lack of time and money, they are especially pertinent in the lives of London's irregular Afro-Eurasian workforce, for whom international travel is inconceivable. Theoretically they are free to move around in anonymity amidst the vastness of the city. In practice, their enslavement to the clock ensures that they travel only between work and home, apart from periods in which they search for employment. Harvey's 'time space comparison' (2001), if anything, captures the antithesis of their experience: if capital now moves across the globe instantaneously, labour's mobility is deeply reduced, not only in its freedom to cross borders (Sutcliffe 2004: 261-80) but also upon destination, in the labour process itself.

In Part III it was shown that migrants in Italy had moved frequently across borders within the EU before settling in Florence-Prato. Patterns of mobility within Italy itself were similarly characterised by sporadic bursts of motion: no less than ten of the men I interviewed had worked in more than one town or city, including diverse and obscure destinations in Reggio-Emilia and near the Northern tourist resort, Lake Maggiore. Others I spoke with were headed for, or had contacts in other places still, such as Arezzo, Genoa and even Calabria in the South. In a country where internal migration of the native population has diminished in recent decades (Bonifazi and Heins 2000: 129; Faini et al. 1997: 571-9), the unsettled nature of Pakistani migrants is a striking reflection of their unstable position within the Italian labour market, which is identical to that of illegally resident Pakistanis in the UK who often move up and down the country between London and the Northern Pakistani settlements in search of employment and ways to legalise their status.

Movement of this sort, it should be remembered, takes place in periods of unemployment or during regularisations which promise legal status: it is not a sign of empowerment but a reflection of insecurity in the form of pressure to adapt to constantly changing circumstances. Though experienced by all of those who work within ethnic enclaves, it is felt particularly acutely by smuggled migrants due to the earlier cited burden of higher migration costs and the constant fear of being discovered and deported, as well as the fact that they do not qualify for welfare benefits. During workless periods, they therefore feel compelled to mobilise rapidly and make frantic enquiries in search of employment, leaving their dwellings if they have to. This is, of course, somewhat paradoxical given the static nature of their experience during periods of employment; their movement in space thus moves from one extreme to the other as they oscillate between spatial imprisonment and frenzied circulation within the ethnic economy in search of work.

Much of the time, changing jobs amounts to little other than a kind of horizontal (rather than upwardly mobile) sort of movement that seldom brings tangible long-term improvement in circumstances. Khan Sahab had left a previous job in a 'cash & carry' where his ex-boss had treated him tyrannically to work in Nasir's halal butcher's. It folded in the course of my research, leaving him, so to speak, back at square one, or not far from it. In some periods of unemployment, smuggled migrants can experience deteriorations in their situations. Their costs mount. Movement itself entails paying for transport, expensive temporary accommodation arrangements and covering other hidden expenses. It is not uncommon for men to request remittances from their households in Pakistan to cover these, reversing the stereotypical portrait of the breadwinning Third World migrant keeping 'his' family afloat with Western currency.

Melancholia

There was near complete unanimity in the testimonies of the migrants on the issue of life in Italy and the lack of satisfaction migration had brought them. 'Leaving money aside', Bilal explained, 'even if you saved half your pay here, Pakistan is still better than this to live. It's *our* country. We have *our* own land. *Our* family is there'. Indeed a deep sense of dispossession – loss at the emotional cost that comes with devoting one's life to securing a better material future, pervades the discourse of Pakistanis in Italy. Even migrants who have been relatively successful materially mourn the denuded social existence they lead – in his case, away from wife and children as well as parents and siblings.

Many of the men I encountered in Florence literally spent most of their waking hours drenched in sweat and grease, stood by an oven, carving up doner kebab in the summer months. Great chunks of their lives were (and still are) still being spent away from their families. Working hours leave little time or energy for maintaining telephone contact with their friends; building new intimate relationships and friendships is virtually impossible.

> *Arif:* The kind of life you live in your own country, with your own children
> or with your family in happiness – that ends here. If you are in Pakistan, you
> can give and take – you can share happiness and sadness. Here, you can't have
> that… There's no family here, no love – just work […] Men look after each other
> but…no one really has time for anyone. Men don't talk to each other about their
> family problems. No one has time to discuss these things – there's just always
> work to do. You have to work early in the morning until late at night. You get
> home late and have to leave early the next day …

The migrant's quotidian life is one from which love and even meaningful social
contact disappears. For those men who cannot afford to return home for years at a
time, migration suspends their sexual development for long intervals during their
twenties and thirties, in some cases before they have ever had sexual intercourse,
effectively blocking their progression to sexual maturity and adulthood. Faiz, for
instance, migrated to the Middle East and then Florence after marrying a cousin
to whom he proposed at the tender of age of 15: 'I've been engaged for six years.
To this day I haven't spoken to her … Never stood in front of her'. Married men
go years without sharing a bed with their wives. Most men with families in Prato
share small flats with another family in order to cut costs, reducing privacy –
hardly conducive to a thriving romantic life. In any case, 'even if you have a wife
here', Zubair told me, 'that in itself, and providing for your children becomes a
source of tension as it makes a man even busier.'

Then there is the labour process itself, hardly a source of hedonistic pleasure
and free sexual expression imagined in sending contexts. Migrants in Italy arrive
home after midnight, shattered with exhaustion to sleep in rooms shared with at
least one other man, usually three or four. Some suffered uncomfortable rashes
from the heat and the chemicals in cleaning products. Others burned themselves
regularly whilst cooking. Others still suffered deep cuts whilst chopping vegetables
(sometimes they would need to need to go to hospital and have their wounds
stitched up). Worse than any of these corporeal punishments is the ideology that
denies immigrant men the status of gendered, sexual beings. London, Florence and
many other metropolitan contexts of reception that absorb migrant labour from
Pakistan are ones in which Afro-Eurasian bodies aren't constituted heterosexually
(Butler 1993: 2). This is because the way in which materialisation occurs (or
rather, does not) within the labour process is conditioned by the mutually
reinforcing consequences of class position and racialisation which effectively
deny migrants the status and lived experiences that 'normal' heterosexual men
in advanced capitalist societies take for granted (Ahmad 2009b). If the latter is
'materialised' in a process that produces identity by severing the heterosexual
subject from its potential to experience same-sex love leaving the heterosexual
doomed to experience melancholia for the loss of queer desire (Butler 1993: 10),
sexual oppression for the migrant lies precisely in being condemned to a spatio-
temporal universe outside of the whole sphere of normative sexuality.

   This gulf between indigenous members of society and new migrants can be thought of as a sexual–economic structural inequality that operates at multiple levels through the maintenance of various legal, social and symbolic borders that work with and through class to reproduce the restrictive economy's domination over the general. Within the service sector, consumers do not view the bottom half of a male migrant's body; only the hands with which he works. Most of the men I encountered in Italy spent most of their waking hours in kitchens or behind a counter, their sexual anatomies cordoned off from vision to the rest of the world by a physical barrier that acts as a powerful symbol of their asexuality. The same was true in fashionable inner-city East London boroughs like Hackney, where I met young Pakistani men in 24-hour grocery stores selling condoms and alcohol to young couples their own age, often on their way home from nights out in the early hours of the morning to continue the fun. In Italy, of those South Asian migrants whose bodies do circulate within society, it is not unusual for them to peddle. Pakistanis and Bangladeshis can be seen selling flowers, targeting couples enjoying romantic dinners in restaurants or strolling, hand-in-hand, in piazzas. In Barcelona, they wander Las Ramblas, vending cans of beer for one euro each to bar-hopping night-clubbers. In all these situations, their position in the labour process fixes and reproduces their status as members of an asexual race-class, providers of services that enhance and facilitate the hedonism, romantic and sexual enjoyment of others. Unsurprisingly, it is rare that they are able to develop friendships with women in the local contexts they dwell in; even less common is intimacy of the kind that leads to sexual contact. If conventional societal and academic wisdom holds that these are pious, conservative men who have no interest in sex, and therefore feel only disgust at the decadence of sexually liberated Western youngsters, testimonies suggest that the reality is far more complex. Being confined to a sexless subject position is by no means easy to take, particularly as it occurs in the context of exposure, often for the first time, to liberal sexual norms in 'open' societies where the very intimacies and pleasures denied to the migrant are so ubiquitous, and so obviously experienced in surplus by much of the rest of society, which takes them for granted. Zubair again, this time upon being probed:

> It's very, very hard. You feel very bad. If you don't know something exists, it will never bother you. But when you see here that everything is open, when you see it with your own eyes, it's different. In Pakistan you don't see anything so you don't feel anything. But when you see girls talking to guys here, and dressed as they are, you feel really bad. You wonder, 'Why can't I have that?' But you're helpless … you don't have time to pursue that stuff. Still, you feel really bad that you can't have it.

In contrast to the desires and imaginings that spur social action examined in Part II, deprivation marks a point at which the inability of desire to be fulfilled is no longer a pleasurable force and motivational driver. Losing its 'normal' function, it becomes a source of inward torment, disillusionment, suffering and sadness.

Deprivation is brought about by curtailment of sexual expression and intimacy by external, political constraints and socio-economic structures. Seldom discussed by migrants, it remains mostly unconscious. When it surfaced in interviews, men were often articulating their feelings for the first time:

> *Faiz:* I'm going to tell you something about myself that until this day, I've never told anyone…In college I had a friend. I never had sex with her. We just talked, and spent time together. It's not that we never had time to do anything. There were opportunities. Sometimes – often, we were alone in my house. Sometimes we would be alone at her place. But in my head, I was thinking, 'I don't want to make myself impure'. I thought we would feel bad getting married to other people someday, having lost our virginities to each other. (I was already engaged). Maybe she wanted to do it, but it never crossed my mind. Then I lived in Saudi for two years, and it still never crossed my mind. But since I got here, I started ringing her. She's married now but I still speak to her on the phone … Now I spend my time regretting the fact that I spent three years with her and never had sex. We could have both made each other feel happy. I missed my chance. I've been here eight months. Nothing's happened yet. But it's not that I don't feel the desire. You watch [my italics]. You want it badly. It drives you mad … In eight months I've not had any contact with any girl, but I know I couldn't stop myself if the opportunity arose. You live according to the atmosphere of the society you live in.

Faiz is reduced to desperate, nostalgic regret of missed opportunities in a different time and place: daydreaming of an altogether different sort to the desirous, romantic kind that triggers migration in sending contexts. Freud called these symptoms of 'melancholia' – a loss that cannot be mourned, since it remains unknown to the individual sufferer (Freud 2005 [1917]). The principle loss experienced by many new Pakistani immigrants in Italy, I would argue, is that of the feminine to their worlds. It is, however, a loss quite unlike that associated with the psychic split which occurs in the formation of male heterosexuality, referred to by Lacan as a driver of the subsequent search for completion through desire for sexual alterity that characterises heterosexuality (Rose 2000: 53). It is a much deeper sense of loss since desire for the feminine has become a source of torment and deprivation rather than a pleasurable source of motivation that spurs action. A profound sense of alienation threatens to erode the very existence of 'desire' in the Self, which is insidiously corroded through the dehumanising impact of work regimes and racialisation in the labour process that de-materialise immigrant workers' bodies on a daily basis.

Narratives of loss: The costs and casualties of risk

It's as fashionable these days to insist on the importance of migrants' agency as it was, in the 1980s, to emphasise their helplessness in the face of structures. Certainly, the dehumanising terms of racialised capitalism in West European societies are negotiated: labour regimes don't obliterate migrants' sexualities, which are expressed in all kinds small and immeasurable but significant ways that remind us of their resilience as human subjects. Most of the younger single men I encountered were doing their best to enjoy what precious little free time they had and managed to fit in small doses of fun doing things they might not have been able to at home. Whatever difficulties they faced, they were at a stage in their lives when being away from the supervision of elders couldn't but be an adventure of sorts.

They muttered disapproval of loudmouthed, assertive young (British) Asian girls marching up and down the high street in groups or arm-in-arm with boyfriends, but most wanted nothing more than to share in the pleasures of their company and tried desperately to attract their attention. Some approached women directly, usually to have their advances rejected. All gazed longingly. It wouldn't take long for a simple walk down the high street to degenerate into *Pundi* (a Punjabi word for 'ogling', or checking out attractive members of the opposite sex). East London's vast, highly complex Asian diaspora with its own highly syncretic culture was in and of itself a source of considerable sensuous pleasure: watching Hindi films meant pining over Bollywood heroines; lyrics to the film songs playing whilst men worked or relaxed at home were invariably about passionate love and various kinds of desire; 'surfing the net' was a euphemism for devouring images of scantily clad Indian actresses and models and scouring marriage websites and chat rooms for cyber contact (occasionally it led to actual encounters). Even if the vast majority of their social interactions were with other men, then, a deep longing for women, sex and romance were seldom far below the surface.

In Italy the migrants I knew walked around town after closing their shops at midnight to break up the monotony of their working lives. Barred from entry into most nightclubs and bars by racist door policies, they would 'roam' around the piazzas, eat ice creams and stare at attractive women walk by. Occasionally, *pundi* would degenerate into a certain lechery that I found embarrassing. Someone from within the group would blurt out a lewd remark at an unfortunate female passer-by. Though these never went beyond a sleezy 'ciao' ('vuoi mangare un gelato?'), the rapidity with which the recipient would turn their head and accelerate off reflected its lack of charm. Over time, I became less judgemental of their actions as I came to understand that for men who have little or no access to women (other than when they serve them) being snubbed is better than being ignored. A negative response to a romantic overture has at least the benefit of reminding an individual in a low status job that he exists as a person; that he has a gender. That he is a man, albeit a reject, and not just a worker.

Some of the more extroverted individuals with a stronger command of Italian and less obligation to their households (and thus more time for recreation) occasionally went on dates with the (mostly Rumanian) waitresses they worked alongside in restaurants. This reflected, to some extent, the situation in East London too, where I saw several young Polish and Lithuanian women working for Pakistani employers in small restaurants within the ethnic enclave in a bid to add an element of 'glamour' to their establishments. By virtue of their proximity – both in terms of social class and daily contact in the work place, new female East European migrant workers were often the most likely candidates for romance.

In practice, however, most men spent their free time, as they did their working hours, in extremely close quarters with other men with whom they lived, ate and shared sleeping quarters. The maleness of their social world was frequently reflected in the transcribed interview texts of their discourse, which are generally marked by the total absence of women. From the emigration context to the long journey through transit and illegal entry to arrival and insertion in local labour and housing markets, the protagonists within their narratives are brothers, male cousins and uncles, male friends, male smugglers, male agents facilitating regularisation, male employers and male housemates.

Spatial and emotional proximity produced interdependency between men living and working together. Sometimes it fostered profound forms of tenderness. They cooked and cared for, mothered and fathered one another in the absence of friends, relatives and loved ones. The sorts of physical contact amongst men that is routine in many non-occidental cultures (and distinct from the distance that western men maintain between themselves and others of their sex) was intensified: the holding of hands, embracing and massaging of one another's tired and aching limbs took new meaning in the context of the obvious need for tenderness they each felt as a consequence of the brutishness of their lives.

And yet, compared to the inter-male friendship circles in Pakistan that drive migration in the first place, male communities in migration itself seemed joyless. The sheer lack of personal space forcing exhausted and anxious bodies into intense, relentless contact with one another subordinated individual expression. A stifling and claustrophobic lack of privacy gnawed away at the domain in which Selves might breathe. Commodification of ethnic and social networks (discussed in the previous chapter) precipitated competitiveness, bickering, jealousy and bitterness that manifested itself in countless aggressions that underline once more the interconnectedness of the material and emotional economies of migration. Dramatic arguments over money and loans that were not repaid were rife, as were ostensibly petty domestic squabbles over household chores. Both were particularly common in houses where migrants felt under greatest financial pressure, underlining the strain that economic hardship due to structural constraints puts on trust and solidarity.

None of these ostensibly material tensions are detachable from the deep sense of gendered melancholia that darkened the universe in which these men were condemned to live. This was reflected in the way individuals who sought to break out of the all-male environment by making contact with women outside the social networks of Pakistani migrants would immediately be subjected to criticism for their supposed lack of piety by their friends and acquaintances. I witnessed this myself in the lives of Zubair and Faiz, both of whom used their dealings with female customers in their shops to strike up conversations and initiate flirtation. The former explains below how this inter-male policing of sexual behaviour through the instrumentalisation of 'religious' discourses typically rears its head in everyday situations:

> If there's a girl paying at the counter and speaking to me for two minutes after paying, all of them, their ears will prick up. They will make up some reason for me to come over to them to disturb us. And then when she goes they will talk about how wrong it is in religious terms to talk to women in that way. They will try to talk to her themselves, or get in between us, or think up some reason to call me over … They're jealous. They want to end our interaction.

Melancholia tends to be accompanied by a deep and morose self-loathing, self-recrimination and impoverishment of the ego (Freud 2005 [1917]: 203-205). The migrant appears to lament his own choices as the source of his suffering; he somehow comes to believe he is being punished for his worthlessness and morally reprehensible choices. Typically, Faiz blames the materialism of Pakistani labour migrants as being the root of the problem. He laments their tendency to privilege the pursuit of capital accumulation over love (and by implication sex), putting it down to emptiness within their hearts: 'There's no love in our men. If there were they couldn't spend ten years here at a time'. He goes on to explain why he thinks they have such little luck with women as a product of their own unwillingness to commit time and resources towards pursuit. His reference to 'our' failure to perform material expenditure – closely connected with masculine potency through erotic associations of ejaculated sperm – is worth noting:

> It doesn't happen so much for our guys because they're unwilling to spend money. They'll spend 80 cents on buying a girl a coffee and then expect that she will spend the whole year with them. You don't get anything like that … They try. They want to [get women] but it comes down to not spending money … You can't get women spending that little.

Such bouts of self-loathing, in which the migrant blames himself for circumstances he could never have predicted, were surprisingly common amongst the men I interviewed. They run counter to the initial discourse of nobility and sacrifice many espouse in the first instance, and are contradictory to the claims they often made about being in Europe unwillingly ('I'm here for my family etc.'). Here, the migrant does indeed take personal responsibility for having made the choice to migrate through an admission that migration was driven by an irrational prioritisation of accumulation; pursuit of a chimera that has failed to deliver happiness. As Freud predicts, the melancholic subject loses all sympathy with himself rather than count himself unlucky or a victim of circumstance – he levels insults against himself and expects ostracism and punishment. Unacknowledged loss is particularly clear in the following passage, in which Faiz relates Pakistani immigrants to the contemptuous image of a dog. The depth of his bitterness was such he practically spat the word 'dog' ('qutta') not once or twice, but thrice in quick succession, following it closely with three repetitions of the word 'nothing' to capture the meaning of his current existence in Florence.

> The life of a man here is like that of dog. A dog's! You know the way dogs run, with their tongues hanging out. And then turn around to see there's nothing behind them. They were chasing nothing: nothing at all.

The analogy of the canine chase, evocative of a mindless, salivating, animalistic and bestial impulse, hints at the sexual dimensions of the fetish that drew the migrant towards the void he now inhabits. But that which is lost cannot be fully mourned; it remains, to a large extent, at a subconscious level. There is no explicit reference to women or sex. Indeed the following passage, which turns to the subject of religion, associates migration with a loss of spirituality:

> At least there was religion. Here we joke sometimes, that if we ever went back to Data Darbar [a famous Sufi shrine in Lahore], who knows if we'd remember how to say our prayers. In eight months here, I've been to Friday prayers once. During Ramadan I didn't manage to pray once. And what did I do? Work, work, work. What do I ever do? Work, work, work. Since leaving religion behind, I've lost all peace of mind. I keep thinking, 'I left religion in pursuit of the world. But the world keeps escaping my grasp. And at the same time – bit by bit, – religion is slowly disappearing from my life.

Such lamentations for a loss of the spiritual are hardly unique, of course. They invoke a nostalgic rhetoric of return long identified with migrants from the global South (see, for instance, Anwar 1979). Previous scholarship, however, reads such sentiments of loss narrowly and literally at face value. Faiz's above-cited lamentation for the loss of religion was sandwiched in between two earlier-cited passages in which he hinted at experiencing sexual misery and sadness at having missed the opportunity to make love to an old female friend from his college days. Sexuality, intimacy and religion are thus bound up in important ways that invoke Freud's key writings on the lack of satisfaction man finds in work and pursuit of worldly property, and speak to a consciously articulated sense of disenchantment that modernist and secularist thinkers as diverse as Durkheim, Weber, Mauss and Bataille all expressed in one way or another as they assessed the transition from 'traditional' to modern society in the West. Gendered melancholia and sexual deprivation in contemporary Pakistani migration should therefore be seen within the context of an older and broader spiritual malaise relating to disillusionment with the excessive commodification of life brought by advancements in capitalism.

The specificity of loss in 'new' migration lies precisely in its emphatically sexual dimensions. For all the sacrifices made by previous generations of Pakistani immigrants to the West under Fordism, those generations of men eventually imported brides, purchased properties, headed families, set up mosques and formed transnational communities spanning Britain and Pakistan. Few such communities (or their prospect) yet exist in destinations such as Italy, where the socially and spiritually corrosive effects of migrating internationally entail the complete abandonment of a socially embedded life – of spiritual fulfilment and work–life balance. The latter are forgone for a brutishly commodified existence at the margins of Western society, as Farhad, another migrant I met in Italy, explained:

> Here, we don't know how to act. We've lost our manners. We are like donkeys. All we think about is how many hours we've worked. How much money we make ... There's no place in our lives for Islam. We don't think about Islam, but for our employers whom we fear, we do anything. We don't fear God ... We abandon our work there, our families. And what do we get in exchange for working here? Cash. Does that bring peace of mind? Not a bit...that money we spend on good cars and houses ... But when was the last time we addressed our mothers with respect? When was the last time we addressed our fathers with respect? When was the last time we massaged their feet? When was the last time we brought them a glass of water? When was the last time we helped an old man? When was the last time we gave food to a poor man? In Pakistan, even if we don't pray we hear the azan five times and at least we recited the Kalma. What do we see and hear here? Nothing but the clock, hour after hour. And that is all we will hear ...

The cost of migration, Farhad suggests, is nothing less than the loss of one's soul. He speaks in drastic terms of a gradual descent into barbarism, chosen willingly but unwittingly (and thus unconsciously) by the migrant. The lowly figure of the donkey, a variation on the dog, conveys a similar sense of idiocy and ignorant culpability. Migration, by this reckoning, has come to entail the adoption of a deep-seated materialism that gnaws away at the values of hospitality, generosity, kindness to others, respect and religious devotion, along with love for one's family and fellow human beings. All of these were once integral to an existence in the sending context that has been abandoned. With it, a loss of the feminine, of love and of sexual intimacy (or its potential) extinguish the romantic sentiments behind the desire that drove migration in the first place. Though desire itself can never disappear, it has become a source of torment, the body a site of sexual deprivation. That these last sources of melancholia remain unarticulated by Farhad is reflective of his inability to mourn fully that which he has lost.

It is tempting to conflate these kinds of experiences and sentiments with the kind of nostalgia that Anwar wrote about in the 1970s. What distinguishes them from those the Babas may have once expressed at a similar point in their lives is the extent of alienation, a product of the extent of commodification in the contemporary migration process. Its higher economic stakes; its unprecedented costs; the more corrosive toll it takes on what Sennet calls 'character' and basic human values like trust. And like any game of high stakes, there are losers. Sennet points out that within the new capitalism, the less powerful individuals are, the greater the dangers inherent in their risk-taking. Often the weak are the ones who wind up 'feeling exiles' or losing their way (Sennet 1998: 85). In the aftermath of the unsuccessful act of risk, realisation of the 'impossibility of reward for effort' causes time to seem 'to grind to a halt' (Ibid: 91).

Faizal was unemployed at the time I interviewed him in Florence, and had been for several months. As was the case with several of the middle-aged men working in the new economy I encountered in both London and Italy, his age was something of handicap. Physically less fit and less able to cope with the stress of work than younger men, he would scold them when they tried to have small doses of fun by flirting with female customers and occasionally getting drunk or stoned after work to break up the monotony of their lives. They came to resent his killjoy attitude, and a gulf descended between him and his colleagues. He missed his wife and children immensely. He would return to Pakistan at intervals beyond his financial means; out of frustration he would loose his temper with co-workers and on one occasion was short with a customer. Three months after being sacked by his employer, who had come to see him as a liability, he began to despair. Time, for him, had indeed ground to a halt as he waited and waited for another opportunity to begin chipping away at the costs of migration. Without a salary, these costs, of course, began to mount once more: every mouthful of food he ate indebted him further to his former employers who, in the perverse logic of the migration business, had remained his landlords (most of his expenses during this period were covered by his last month's pay, which typically, had been withheld from him). A deep and dark depression came to pervade his thinking, as is reflected in the following evaluation of his own life, which he had come to see, after over two decades in the diaspora, in terms of total and complete failure:

> *Faizal*: I'm 43. Most of my life I've spent abroad. Twenty-four years I've spent, but I've got nothing from it. It's not benefited me at all. It's cost me dearly [pause].... I feel now that everything I've done has been a waste. I've not made anything out of my life. I've finished myself. I can't live in Pakistan now. And here, I have to stay here and just get by ... Maybe this is my fate ... Now I feel, I've lived my life ...

He went on:

> ... My brother is well set, because he stayed where he is. Unlike me, he didn't move around backwards and forwards, trying to get to Europe ... His family still lives in Pakistan. One thinks you'll have a better future here. But you don't

realise you'll come here and the future looks even more bleak. Now I think about it, I reckon the man who stays in Pakistan is better off. Even if he has less money, he's living a life of honour. Because he's living in his country, he earns money, feeds and educates his children in his country. He does everything there.

Jameel, another middle-aged man, made a similar assessment:

My grandfather did well in Pakistan. My father did well in Pakistan. They lived in Pakistan and put us through good schools and colleges. If only we would stop doing this … The truth is, by God, it is better to work there than here, when you think of the way we live here.

Men more advanced in their years were the most bitter, perhaps because they felt themselves less and less involved in family-life despite being deep into their forties and fifties. The working man's paradoxical ethic of sacrifice which dictates that 'the good home' can only be supported by longer hours of labour and the provider's physical absence (Sennet and Cobb 1993: 123) is powerfully resonant in their stories. For the new migrant, and especially the 'illegal' worker, to be the good son, the good brother or good father, Abdel-Malek Sayad's (1999: 303) oft cited notion of the 'double-absence' is tragically pertinent: the better they are at providing, the more absent they must from the lives of those for whom they provide.

What, though, happens when the migrant proves himself to be the antithesis of these expectations? When he becomes an increasingly expensive burden to his estranged family – an absent body but a real, material ongoing cost? Migrants, after all, like the rest of us, get sick. Old. Weak. Unemployable. The question is of particular importance in new migration, where the costs and risks, the failures and adverse consequences of unsuccessful gambles proliferate. Sayad's work on the factory era remains insightful. Illness and unemployment, he observed, can precipitate a deep psychological crisis and even a 'negation' of sorts given the migrant's very existence has come to be premised upon a delicate equilibrium (Ibid: 260).

I met Jameel in Prato in 2006, where he was on dialysis after kidney failure some two years after his arrival in Italy. He had worked in Paris for several years without any documentation before abandoning it, like so many others, with the intention of regularising his residency and settling permanently. This he had achieved, before calamity struck. At the time I interviewed him, he found himself out of work and unable to claim any health benefits. Refused the right to import his family by the state, which (probably correctly) deemed him unable to support them, he was living off reverse-remittances sent by his family in Pakistan and the Scandinavian diaspora. Return to Pakistan, where the cost of dialysis would have been unaffordable, was not an option. Nor was paying the airfare for his family to visit. Stuck more firmly in a state of limbo than he had been as an illegally resident migrant in France, effectively severed from kith and kin, his situation led him to question daily the very purpose of his life:

My father died when I was on dialysis – I wasn't able to see his body. And when my boy was married, I couldn't attend. Friends give me encouragement and help me out, but I feel, this life is no life. The truth is, it's a struggle. I've gone through as much someone can take. I will live my life to its end, but ... When I speak to my mother on the phone she weeps, and says 'who knows if we shall ever meet again?'.

Some time in 2009, I rang my gatekeeper in Florence, now an old friend of sorts. We began to speak of mutual contacts. 'What ever happened to Jameel, that bloke with the kidney problem?' I asked. Silence.

'Who?'
'The one with the kidney problem,' I repeated.
'Oh you mean Jameel?'
'Yes, Jameel.'
'Him, he's dead. Died some time ago'.

For a moment, I considered contacting the family to offer my condolences; perhaps sharing in their grief and offering to send them a copy of my interview with him. Then I wondered whether it would in fact bring them any comfort to hear him reflecting on his life towards its end. He'd scratched his head and gazed into the middle distance after speaking the above. Then laughed with macabre irony, shrugging in bafflement at the extent of God's apparent cruelty. His remarkable courage and resilience couldn't hide the immensity of his torment. 'Allah must be keeping me alive for a reason,' he kept saying, unconvinced. 'This is a great interview,' I recall thinking at some point after he had been speaking for some 40 minutes, before pushing him greedily to carry on with more questions, the way researchers and journalists sometimes do when we start to hear something which will go into an article or book published in our name. By the end, his lips and mouth had become dry, his throat parched. I ought really, to have paused and offered him a glass of water sooner.

Conclusion to Part IV

The opening of Aristotle's *Metaphysics* (quoted at the beginning of this book) assigns a special importance to seeing in human experience. Looking sensuously at the world around us is about accumulating a kind of knowledge; a way of apprehending difference, in which the visual is lived, contemplated and assimilated as a form of wisdom. As a metaphor for the desirous nature of emigration, Aristotle's notion of man's impulse to see is useful for thinking about migrant-sending contexts like Pakistan as the starting point of a journey that mirrors life.

Part II was about that naive moment in the migrant's life that affords a kind of innocent theoretical, speculation and hope about what living in Europe might entail.

It doesn't last long.

The act of seeing implies a certain distance that disappears once the journey gets underway and we enter the realm of experience. As the subject draws nearer to its object – like any held too closely to the eye – it cannot be imagined, contemplated, desired, theorised in the same manner. Voyeurism ends. Fantasy evaporates. If being smuggled to Europe from Pakistan is an index of masculine privilege, Parts III and IV make clear that masculine privilege is drunk from a poisoned chalice. Whatever its intentions, aspirations and fantasies at the point of departure, the gritty materialities of travel include perilous sea and overland border-crossings, transiting for weeks and months in unsanitary conditions, subjection to surveillance by states and being squeezed financially by agents, corrupt officials, employers and other migrants in numerous countries. Those who arrive safely and manage to insert themselves into local labour markets are compelled to endure working conditions and pay that leave precious little time and energy for activity beyond the work place.

Few on the Left would have seen it as such in the 1970s, but Fordism now appears a brief interlude of relative dignity for foreign workers in Europe. Migration is returning to its historically precarious roots: physical harm and death, pain, loss and disappointment were well known in the 19th century, the first modern age of mass international labour flows. The Brasilieros, travelers to the New World from Northern Portugal, were described by essayists as 'deceived compatriots' – hapless dupes who failed to consider the 'disadvantageous expenditures' (monetary, emotional and physical) 'necessary in order to get to Brazil'. These, it was documented, 'outweigh all the advantages'. A government inquiry called upon local priests to inform their parishes of the negative aspects of emigration (Brettell 1986: 79-80). One contemporary writer emphasised the 'foolishness of emigration', which 'brings more trouble than it is worth'; another made a series of financial calculations to show its lack of profitability empirically;

regional newspapers published lists of Portuguese nationals who died in Brazil of Tuberculosis and Yellow Fever (Ibid: 83).

Italian migrants in the Americas lived frugally, going without meat, decent food, the care of their families and sexual contact with spouses for long periods of time. Their sense of loss was compounded by the precarity of life in a pre-Keynesian world where the fear of unemployment was acute: citing La Sorte (1985: 61), Gabaccia (2001: 196, 203) quotes the revealing words of one individual who spoke of his job as 'this blood-sucking thing', 'my misery, my hatred ... and yet I [he] lived in continuous fear of losing the bloody thing'. Fontaine's study of emigraton from the Alps refers to the Barcelonettes of the Ubaye valley who invested heavily in reaching Mexico; emigration frequently held the promise of an illusory improvement in living standards: many of those who left in search of becoming rich ended up languishing in poverty, never to return for fear of the shame of returning in defeat; they remained single and failed to set up businesses of their own (1996: 158-60).

Like these historical studies, the research presented in this book underlines the folly of assuming that strong bonds necessarily generate social capital. The fate of any given migration network is shaped by political and economic structural conditions. There is nothing inevitable about their thriving or even their survival. Networks can get locked into terminal downward spirals from which recovery is impossible. Fontaine's above-cited history of European peddler migration networks from the Swiss Alps, which spans early modern times up until the 19th and early 20th centuries, shows how a once burgeoning process of migration centred primarily on kinship chains of credit and commerce dissolved when 'enforced solidarities collapsed in the face of business difficulties', making it 'increasingly difficult to make business associations work' (1996: 137-9). A number of insurmountable structural obstacles led to the gradual evaporation of the solidarities upon which network ties had been based: partnerships were retained as it was impossible to do otherwise, but suspicions mounted with economic stagnation and the resulting inability of migrants to pool resources and honour debt commitments: by the end, 'it was each man for himself' (Ibid: 155).

If these emigrations from Europe took place in vastly different historical contexts, my research suggests they speak to the contemporary world, in which there is plenty of room for exploration of the themes of loss and failure – taboos among theorists of migration and their subjects. The reticence with which migrants speak of the gap between their expectations prior to migrating and the realities they face as these unfold is striking; the embarrassing truths of downward social mobility are seldom explicitly discussed, but their testimonies – if you look hard enough – reveal failures and anxieties, disappointments and hidden injuries.

Further research might consider the psychological links between material and sexual vulnerability. There is anecdotal evidence that deterioration of material wellbeing results in actual psychosomatic physical symptoms: a recent study of Pakistanis in Spain found migrants literally reported fears that they were losing sperm in their urine (Valenzuela García 2007). Many of my own interviewees in Italy frequently complained of bodily deterioration in ways that seemed to be bound up with feelings of anxiety and loss of masculine potency. This is not to deny that they experienced actual deteriorations in their health – poor diet, inordinately long working hours, together with unsafe and unsanitary living and working conditions, are hardly a recipe for mental and physical well-being. The point is, rather, that this actual deterioration was inextricably bound up with other kinds of psychological suffering, as evidenced by strange complaints. The 'water in Europe', for instance, was blamed in conspiratorial or superstitious tones for this or that ailment, for hair loss and even shrinking libido. (Tahar Ben Jelloun's little-known (1977) study of sexual solitude among North African immigrant workers in France is a fascinating empirical work worth revisiting in order to understand these issues better; its relevance to contemporary discussions around race, gender, sexuality and the labour process is yet to be appreciated.)

The spending of vast sums of money on the building of mosque-mansions in villages like Chot Dheeran in Mandi Bahuddin might be seen, to some extent, as antidotes to the acute forms of disappointment, sexual deprivation and downward social mobility experienced in migration. The same is also true, arguably, of the proliferating mosques in Newham and elsewhere in Europe, where asexualised migrant communities flock to communal public prayers in search of meaning in an increasingly commodified, capitalised existence. Religious worship is, after all, following 'sex, the second oldest resource human beings have available to them for blowing their minds' (Sontag 2001 [1967]: 104), and not nearly so far removed from the pleasure principle as dominant discourse would have us believe.

Conclusion

To close the circle, let us return to Bataille, and the trope of returnee excess that drove an immobile individual to up and leave Punjab for an existence he now describes as bestial. Ego battered and bruised from the daily grind of despotic work regimes, Pakistan becomes a means of recovering self-esteem and social standing. The worse his situation, the greater the need to exaggerate his success; the logical corollary of big-spending returnees in sending contexts is a lifestyle and experience defined by the very opposite of lavish expenditure – by scrimping and saving that, in true dialectical fashion, is every bit as symbolic of masculine failure and weakness as excessive spending is of male potency. Mumtaz, a Prato-based middle-aged migrant from Lahore, explains:

> You try to reduce your food costs, and then you're spending less on coffee and cigarettes … so that you can save … This is the life here. You have to hide this from your clan. You tell them you're having a great time. This is our weakness: showing off …When you return, you put on good clothes even though you have no money left … You go to a bank here and get a loan for three, four thousand Euros … So you've stayed there a few days, rented a car, showed off a bit. Then you've come back here, you're scratching your head thinking, 'I can't find work and the bank wants its money'.

'Excess' and 'Loss' constitute two aspects of a singular process. Mumtaz's testimony reveals that the former image often obscures a reality of extreme frugality and desperation, underlining the need to disentangle ideology from truth in instances where 'excess' is a fiction – a performance that amounts to a willful distortion of actual circumstances. Again, the two are arguably linked: the more acute an individual's loss of self-esteem through social and sexual marginalisation in Europe, the greater his need for posturing as wealthy and potent upon return, an equation that goes some considerable way to explaining why, several decades since mass labour migration from Pakistan began, many continue to embark upon westward journeys in pursuit of fates that bear little resemblance to the realities which await them. In psychoanalytic terms, each new arrival, experience and subsequent disappointment on European shores is a product of 'erotic repetition' (Freud 2007 [1930]: 54-5). The conservative nature of the drives, that is to say, is manifested at a macro-economic level in the reproduction of an irrational migration system.

Thus we begin to understand how, despite the fact young Pakistani men might start off associating emigration with emancipation from patriarchal control, the migration system remains, in Bourdieusian terminology, 'doxic': the patriarchal norms that compose the established order remain largely naturalised to those who live them (Moi 1991: 1026, 1033). Pakistani diasporas can be distinguished from Latin American, East Asian and even some South Asian migration systems like Sri Lanka, where the male bread-winning model has been disrupted by independent female migration, and likened, in historical terms to the older predominantly male colonial labour migrations from South Asia sketched by Cohen (1997: 63) which were also characterised by gender imbalances that allowed the displacement of the costs of migration onto rural sending households which remained backward and dependent (Omvedt 1980: 185-212). Or indeed Northern Portugal, where women's exclusion from the emigratory economy reflected and reinforced the sexual divisions of labour: confined to working in the fields, their presence became so important their fathers would sometimes forbid them from marrying (1986: 95).

Manchuelle's (1997: 145) observations on life-cycle in Mossi migration from West Africa in the aftermath of slave emancipation are also salient here. Youthful men and boys considered too young to migrate occasionally defied their parents' opposition and left secretly to become sailors (Ibid: 199). So concerned were patriarchal elders about losing control over their young that they requested the French authorities for help. And yet, the rebellious instincts triggering these and other migrations from the region needn't have worried them: migrants displayed little inclination to challenge traditional authority over the course of their lives.

> Through migration, a young man could maintain a measure of emancipation from the traditional society simply by living abroad with independent financial resources, but these resources also allowed him to build up influence within his home society as the years went by. When he became older, he would return to his village and become a respected elder himself (Ibid: 176, 209).

Is anything at all learned in this process of disavowal, in which individuals' pasts evolve into palimpsestic presents? Since Gilgamesh, enduring loss has been an integral part of coming to terms with being human. Myths about heroic quests for the secrets of eternal life invariably conclude with an imperfect hero having to make do with the limited knowledge that comes with learning the miserable truths of lived experience and accepting the inevitability of death. Perhaps then, even melancholia can be thought of as a kind of wisdom; an understanding of life's limits that comes with the passage of time.

In his preface to *Phenomenology of Spirit*, Hegel makes a related point about the path taken by consciousness in its journey towards absolute understanding. Modernity's most celebrated philosopher of rationality and reason might seem an unusual choice with which to end a book about human folly such as this, but on questions of life, truth and experience, Hegel is critical of 'conventional opinion' which repudiates the mistakes, errors and wanderings astray that bring the *process* of thinking to its final outcome: 'The bud disappears when the blossom breaks through, and one might say that the former is refuted by the latter': a reified, 'false manifestation of the plant … the fruit now emerges as the truth instead' (Hegel 1979 [1807]: 2).

In receiving contexts such as Newham in East London, the migration process repudiates its origins and founding drives, its causes and consequences in prior miscalculations and desires. The Babas – now silver bearded patriarchs who assert their authority in mosques and households alike – bear little resemblance to the desirous young men they once were in Punjab and Mirpur; the frugality of Freshies in Florence is severed from their lavish spending on mosque-mansions in Pakistan. Across Europe, the sombre reality of human smuggling's outcomes broods in isolation from the optimistic imaginings that prevail in sending contexts. And yet, 'The ceaseless activity of their own inherent nature' makes all these moments in the migration process – buds and blossoms, causes and consequences – 'an organic unity' in which not only do the two 'not conflict, but in which one is necessary as the other'. This rather awkwardly phrased conceptualisation of *process* as singular and ongoing concludes the argument this book has sought to make about human smuggling and migration more generally. Like the forces that drive (and the bodies that experience) these phenomena, they are produced (and lived) simultaneously and relationally in sending and receiving contexts – dialectically, in ways that run contrary to the principle of balanced accounts.

Bibliography

Adam, B. (2004). *Time*. Cambridge, UK: Malden Polity Press.

Adam, B. and Loon, J. (2000). "Introduction", in Adam, B., Beck, U. and Loon, J. (eds) *The Risk Society Revisited*. London: Sage, 1-31.

Adams, C. (1987). *Across Seven Seas and Thirteen Rivers: Life Stories of Pioneer Sylhetti Settlers in Britain*. London: Thap Books.

Adam-Smith, D., Norris, G. and Williams, S. (2003). "Continuity or change in work", *Employment & Society*, 17(1), 29-47.

Afshar, H. and M. Maynard (2000). "Gender and ethnicity at the millennium: From margin to centre", *Ethnic and Racial Studies*, 23(5), 805-19.

Agarwal, B., Humphries, J. and Robeyns, I. (2005). "Introduction", in B. Agarwal, J. Humphries and I. Robeyns (eds) *Amartya Sen's Work and Ideas: A Gender Perspective*. Abingdon: Routledge, 3-13.

Agarwal, B. (1997). "Bargaining and gender relations: Within and beyond the household", *Feminist Economics*, 3(1), 1-51.

Aglietta, M. (1979 [1976]). *A Theory of Capitalist Regulation: The US Experience*. London: NLB.

Ahmad, A.N. (2001). "Whose underground? Asian cool and the poverty of hybridity", *Third Text*, Spring, (54), 71-84.

Ahmad, A.N. (2006). "The British Pakistanis", in Jones, A. (ed.) *Men of the Global South*. London: Zed Books.

Ahmad, A.N. (2007). "Le malaise sexuel des migrations de travail: réflexions socio-anthropologiques sur les pakistanais en Europe", in *Migrance*, (27).

Ahmad, A.N. (2008a). "Dead men working: Time and space in London's 'illegal' migrant economy", *Work, Employment and Society*, 22(2), 301-18.

Ahmad, A.N. (2008b). "Human smuggling and illegal labour: Pakistani migrants in London's informal economy", *Journal of Ethnic and Migration Studies*, 34(6), 853-74.

Ahmad, A.N. (2008c). "The romantic appeal of illegal migration: Gender masculinity and human smuggling from Pakistan", in Schrover, M., Leun, J., Lucassen, L. and Quispel, C. (eds) *Illegal Migration and Gender in Global and Historical Perspective*. Amsterdam: Amsterdam University Press.

Ahmad, A.N. (2008d). "Critical approaches to the study of masculinity: Gender and generation in Pakistani migration", in Ryan, L. and Webster, W. (eds) *Gendering Migration: Masculinity, Femininity and Ethnicity in Postwar Britain*. Aldershot: Ashgate.

Ahmad, A.N. (2009a). "The myth of arrival: Pakistanis in Italy", in Kalra, V. (ed.) *Pakistani Diasporas: Culture, Conflict, and Change*, in Pakistan Readings in Sociology and Social Anthropology. Karachi: Oxford University Press.

Ahmad, A.N. (2009b). "Bodies that (don't) matter: Desire, eroticism and melancholia in Pakistani labour migration", *Mobilities*, 4(3), 309-27.

Ahmad, A.N. (2010). "Pakistaníes en Italia: Los escencantos del 'vivir transactional'", in *Revista CIDOB d'Afers*. 92. Barcelona: CIDOB.

Ahmad, A.N. (forthcoming 2012). "The production of illegality in migration and diaspora: State policies and human smuggling from Pakistan", in Chatterji, J. and Washbrook, D. (eds) *The Routledge Handbook of the South Asian Diaspora*. London: Routledge.

Ahmed, S. (2004). *The cultural politics of emotion*. Edinburgh: Edinburgh University Press.

Al-Ali, N. and Koser, K. (2002). "Transnationalism, international migration and home", in Al-Ali, N. and Koser, K. (eds) *New Approaches to Migration? Transnational Communities and the Transformation of Home*. London: Routledge, 1-14.

Ali, W. (2004). "All roads lead to Gujrat". *The Dawn Review*. Lahore: October 20th.

Althusser, L. (1969). "Freud and Lacan", *New Left Review*, 64-101.

Althusser, L. (1994 [1970]). "Ideological state apparatus", in Eagleton, T. (ed.) *Ideology*. London: Longman, 89-111.

Anderson, B. (2007). *Battles in Time: The Relation between Global and Labour Mobilities*. Oxford: Centre on Migration Policy and Society. COMPAS working paper (55).

Andrijasevic, R. (2009). "Sex on the move: Gender, subjectivity and differential inclusion", *Subjectivity*, 29, 389-486.

Ansari, H. (2004). *The Infidel Within: Muslims in Britain since 1800*. London: Hurst & Company.

Anwar, M. (1979). *The Myth of Return*. London: Heinemann.

Anwar, M. (1995). "New Commonwealth migration to the UK", in Cohen, R. (ed.) *Cambridge Survey of World Migration*. Cambridge: Cambridge University Press, 274-78.

Arango, J. (2004). "Theories of international migration", in Joly, D. (ed.) *International Migration in the New Millennium*. Aldershot: Ashgate, 15-35.

Aurora, G. (1967). *The New Frontiersmen: A Sociological Study of Indian Immigrants in the United Kingdom*. Bombay: Popular Prakashan.

Balibar, E. and Wallerstein, I. (1991). *Race, Nation, Class*. London, New York: Verso.

Ballard, R. and Ballard, C. (1977). "The Sikhs: The development of South Asian settlements in England", in J. Watson (ed.) *Between Two Cultures*. Oxford: Basil Blackwell, 21-56.

Ballard, R. (1983). "The context and consequences of migration", *New Community*, 2 Autumn/Winter, 117-36.

Ballard, R. (1990). "Migration and kinship: The differential effect of marriage rules on the processes of Punjabi migration to Britain", in Clarke, C. (ed.) *South Asians Overseas: Migration and Ethnicity.* Cambridge: Cambridge University Press, 219-49.

Ballard, R. (2002). "The South Asian presence in Britain and its transnational connections", in Singh, H. and Vertovec, S. (ed.) *Culture and Economy in the Indian Diaspora.* London: Routledge.

Ballard, R. (2003). "A case of capital-rich development: The paradoxical consequences of successful transnational entrepreneurship from Mirpur", *Contributions to Indian Sociology,* 37(1&2), 49-81.

Barrett, M. (1991). *The Politics of Truth.* Cambridge: Polity Press.

Bataille, G. (1997). *Selected Writings from the Bataille Reader.* Botting, F. and Wilson, S. (eds). Oxford: Blackwell.

Bataille, G. (2001 [1962]). *Eroticism.* London: Penguin.

BBC (2006). *Canaries Migrant Death Toll Soars.* http://news.bbc.co.uk/2/hi/europe/6213495.stm, Last accessed: March 24, 2011.

Beck, U. (1992). *Risk Society: Towards a New Modernity.* London: Sage.

Beck, U. (2000). "Risk society revisited", in Adam, B., Beck, U. Van Loon, J. (eds) *The Risk Society Revisited.* London: Sage, 211-29.

Becker, G.S. (1976). *The Economic Approach to Human Behaviour.* Chicago: Chicago University Press.

Ben Jelloun, T. (1977). "La plus haute des solitudes". Paris: Seuil.

Benslama, F. (2009). *Psychoanalysis and the Challenge of Islam.* Bononno, R. (Translator). Minneapolis, MN: University of Minnesota Press.

Bhabha, H. (1994) *The location of culture.* London, New York: Routledge.

Bilger, V., Hofmann, M. and Jandl, M. (2006). "Human smuggling as a transnational service industry", *International Migration,* 44(4), 59-93.

Black, R. (2003). "Breaking the convention: Researching the 'illegal' migration of refugees to Europe", *Antipode,* 35(1), 34-54.

Blackaby, D., Leslie, D., Murphy, P., and O'Leary, N. (2005). "Born in Britain: How are native ethnic minorities faring in the British labour market?" *Economics Letters,* 88: 370-75.

Blokland, T. and Savage, M. (2001). "Networks, class and place", *International Journal of Urban and Regional Research,* 25: 221-6.

Bollas, C. (1987) *The shadow of the object: psychoanalysis of the unthought known.* London: Free Association Books.

Bonifazi, C. and F. Heins (2000). "Long-term trends of internal migration in Italy." *International Journal of Population Geography,* 6(2), 111-31.

Bourdieu, P. (1979). *Algeria 1960: The Disenchantment of the World, the Sense of Honour, the Kabyle House or the World Reversed.* Cambridge [Eng.], New York: Cambridge University Press.

Bourdieu, P. (1986). "The forms of capital", in Richardson, J. (ed.) *Handbook of Theory and Research for the Sociology of Education.* New York: Greenwood Press, 241-58.

Brah, A. (1996). *Cartographies of Diaspora: Contesting Identities*. London: Routledge.

Braudel, F. (1992 [1949]). *The Mediterranean and the Mediterranean World in the Age of Philip II*. Reynolds, S. (Translated). Abridged by Ollard, R. London: Harper Collins.

Brettell, C. (1979). "Emigrar para voltar: a Portuguese ideology of return migration", *Papers in Anthropology*, (20), 21-38.

Brettell, C. (1986). *Men Who Migrate, Women Who Wait*. Princeton, NJ: Princeton University Press.

Brettell, C. (2000). *Migration Theory*. New York: Routledge.

Burawoy, M. (1985). *The Politics of Production*. London: Verso.

Burton, A. (1996). "Making a spectacle of empire: Indian travellers in fin-de-siècle London", *History Workshop Journal*, 42, 126-46.

Butler, J. (1993). *Bodies that Matter*. New York: Routledge.

Caglar, A. (2001). "Constraining metaphors and the transnationalism of spaces in Berlin". *Journal of Ethnic and Migration Studies*, 27(4), 601-13.

Campbell, C. (1987). *The Romantic Ethic and the Spirit of Modern Consumerism*. Cambridge: Basil Blackwell.

Castells, M. and Portes, A. (1989). "World underneath: The origins, dynamics and effects of the informal economy", in *The Informal Economy: Studies in Advanced and Less Developed Countries*. Baltimore: John Hopkins University Press.

Charsley, K. (2005). "Unhappy husbands: Masculinity and migration in transnational Pakistani marriages", *The Journal of the Royal Anthropological Institute*, 11(1), 85-105.

Charsley, K. and Shaw, A. (2006). "South Asian transnational marriages in comparative perspective". *Global Networks*, 6(4), 331-44.

Chopra, R. (2004). "Encountering masculinity", in R. Chopra, Osella, F. and Osella, C. (eds) *South Asian Masculinities*, New Delhi: Women Unlimited/ Kali for Women, 36–59.

Cohen, R. (1997). *Global Diasporas*. London: UCL Press.

Colleyer, M. (2005). "When do social networks fail to explain migration?", *Journal of Ethnic and Migration Studies*, 31(4), 699-718.

Cornwall, A. (1997). "Men, masculinity and gender in development", *Gender and Development*, 5(2), 8-13.

Dahinden, J. (2005). "Contesting transnationalism? Lessons from the study of Albanian migration networks from former Yugoslavia", *Global Networks*, 5(2), 191-208.

Dahya, B. (1974). "Pakistani ethnicity in industrial cities in Britain", in A. Cohen (ed.) *Urban Ethnicity*. London: Tavistock, 77-119.

Davies, N. (1997). *Europe: A History*. London: Pimlico.

Davies, S. (1996). *Adaptable Livelihoods: Coping With Food Insecurity in the Malian Sahel*. London: Macmillan.

Delaney, E. (2001). "Gender and twentieth-century Irish migration, 1921-1971", in Sharpe, P. (ed.) *Women, Gender and Labour Migration*. London: Routledge, 209-23.

Dench, G., Gavron, K. and Young, M. (2006). *The New East End: Race, Kinship and Conflict*. London: Profile Books.

DeParle, J. (2010). *A World on the Move*. *New York Times* reprinted in *The Observer*. London: 4th July.

De Tapia, S. (2002). *New Patterns of Irregular Migration in Europe*, Council of Europe.

Devereux, S. (1999). *Making Less Last Longer: Informal Safety Nets in Malawi*. I.D.S. discussion paper, 373.

Direk, Z. (2007). "Erotic experience and sexual difference" in S.Winnubst (ed.) *Reading Bataille Now*. Bloomington and Indianapolis: Indiana University Press, 94-115.

Ditz, T.L. (2004). "The new men's history and the peculiar absence of gendered power: Some remedies from early American gender history", *Gender & History*, 16(1), 1-35.

Emirbayer, M. and Goodwin, J. (1994). "Network analysis, culture and the problem of agency", *American Journal of Sociology*, 99: 1411-54.

Endelman, T. (2004). *The Jews of Britain, 1656-2000*. Berkeley, CA: UCLA Press.

Edmundson, M. (2003 [1917]). "Preface", in Freud, S. *Beyond the Pleasure Principle: and Other Writings*. London: Penguin.

Freud, S. (2005 [1917]). *On Murder, Mourning and Melancholia*. London: Penguin.

Freud, S. (2007 [1930]). *Civilisation and its Discontents* (translated by David, M.). London: Penguin.

Faini, R., Galli, G., Gennari, P., and Rossi, F. (1997). "An empirical puzzle: Falling migration and growing unemployment differentials among Italian regions", *European Economic Review*, 41(3), 571-9.

Foner, N. (2001). *New Immigrants in New York*. New York: Columbia University Press.

Fontaine, L. (1996). *History of Peddlers in Europe*. Durham: Duke University Press.

Fontaine, L. and Schlumbohm, J. (2000). "Household strategies for survival", *International Review of Social History*, 45(8), 1-19.

Foti, A. (2004). "Precarity and North European identity", Interview with Alex Foti by Pepper, G. Reproduced in *Metamute: Culture and Politics after the Net* (2), *The Precarious Reader:* http://www.metamute.org/en/Precarity-european-Identity-Alex-Foti-ChainWorkers, Last accessed: 2 April, 2011.

Frank, R. and Cook, P. (1995). *The Winner Takes All Society*. New York: Free Press.

Freud, S. (2003 [1914]) "Remembering, repeating and working through" in *Beyond the pleasure principle and other writings*. London: Penguin, 31-42.

Freud, S. (2003 [1920]) "Beyond the pleasure principle" in *Beyond the pleasure principle and other writings*. London: Penguin, 42-102.

Gabaccia, D. (2001). "When migrants are men", in P. Sharpe (ed.) *Women, Gender and Labour Migration*. London: Routledge, 190-208.

Gardezi, H. (1995). *The Political Economy of Labour Migration: A Case Study of Pakistani Workers in Gulf States*. Lahore: Gautam.

Gardner, K. (1995). *Global Migrants, Local Lives*. Oxford: Clarendon Press.

Gerstle, G. (2003). "Pluralism and the war on terror", *Dissent*, Spring: 31-8.

Gilani, S.Z. (2001). "Personal and social power in Pakistan", in Weiss, A.M. and Gialani, S.Z. *Power and Civil Society in Pakistan*. Karachi: Oxford University Press, 49-64.

Glick-Schiller, N., Basch, L. and Szanton, B. (1992). *Towards a Transnational Perspective on Migration*. New York: New York Academy of Sciences.

Gosh, B. (1998). "Huddled masses and uncertain shores: Insights into irregular migration". *The Hague*/Boston: M. Nijhoff.

Granovetter, M. (1973). "The strength of weak ties", *American Journal of Sociology*, 78(6), 1360-80.

Granovetter, M (1985). "Economic action and social structure: The problem of embeddedness", *American Journal of Sociology*, 91(3), 481-510.

Graycar, A. (1999). "Trafficking in human beings", Paper presented at the *International Conference on Migration, Culture and Crime*, Israel, 7th July.

Grindon, G. (2010). "Alchemist of the revolution: The affective materialism of Georges Bataille", *Third Text*, 24(3), 305-17.

Grosfugel, R. (2003). *Colonial Subjects: Puerto Ricans in a Global Perspective*. Berkeley, CA: California University Press.

Grosfugel, R. and Cordero-Guzmán (1998). "International migration in a global context", *Diaspora*, 7(3).

Grosfugel, R. and Georas, C. (2000). "'Coloniality of power' and racial dynamics: Notes toward a reinterpretation of Latino Caribbeans in New York City", *Identities*, 7(1), 85-125.

Guarnizo, L. (2003). "The economics of transantional living", *International Review Migration*, 37: 667-90.

Guarnizo, L. and Smith, M. (1998). *Transnationalism from Below*. New Brunswick: NJ: Transaction Publishers.

Hall, P. and Soskice, D. (2001). *Varieties of Capitalism: The Institutional Foundations of Comparative Change*. Oxford: Oxford University Press.

Hall, S. (1997). *Representation: Cultural Representations and Signifying Practices*. London: Sage.

Hardt, M. and Negri, A. (2000). *Empire*. Cambridge, MA: Harvard University Press.

Harney, N. (2006). "Rumour, migrants in the informal economies of Naples, Italy", *International Journal of Sociology and Social Policy*, 26(9-10), 374-84.

Harvey, D. (2001). *Spaces of Capital: Towards a Critical Geography*. New York: Routledge.

Hegel, G. (1979). [1807] *Phenomenology of Spirit.* Translated by A.V. Miller. Oxford: Clarendon Press.

Held, D., McGrew, A., Goldblatt, D., Perraton, J. (1999). *Global Transformations.* Cambridge: Polity.

Helweg, A. (1979). *Sikhs in England.* Delhi: Oxford University Press.

Hill, A. (2004). "Saudis to boycott British universities." *The Observer.* London: 15th August.

Hiro, D. (1973). *Black British, White British.* London: Penguin.

Home Office (2002). "Secure borders, safe haven: Integration with diversity", in *Modern Britain.* The Stationery Office Ltd.

Home Office (2004). *Control of Immigration Statistics* (CM6690).

Hussein, A. (2000). *Émigré journeys.* London: Serpent's Tail.

Içduygu, A. (2003). *Irregular Migration in Turkey.* IOM: Geneva.

Jalalzai, M. (2002). *Women Trafficking and Prostitution in Pakistan and Afghanistan.* Lahore: Dua.

Jalalzai, M. (2003). *Children Trafficking in Pakistan.* Karachi: Royal Book Company.

Johnson, S. and Contreras, J. (2004). *The Migrant Economy*: Newsweek, January 19, 38-40.

Kakar, S. (1978). *The Inner World: A Psychoanalytic Study of Childhood and Society in Society in India.* New Delhi: Oxford University Press.

Kakar, S. (2001). *The Essential Writings of Sudhir Kakar.* New Delhi: Oxford University Press.

Kalra, V.S. (2000). *From Textile Mills to Taxi Ranks*. Ashgate: Aldershot.

Keeler, S.J. (2008). "'No job for a grown man': Transformations in labour and masculinity among Kurdish migrants in London", in Ryan, L. and Webster, W. (eds) *Gendering Migration: Masculinity, Femininity and Ethnicity in Post-War Britain.* Aldershot: Ashgate.

Kelman, H. (1972). "Power: The cultural approach of Karen Horney", in J.H. Masserman (ed.) *The Dynamics of Power.* New York: Grune and Stratton, 71-82.

Keohane, R. and Nye, J. (1971). *Transnational Social Relations and World Politics* Cambridge MA: Harvard University Press.

Kershen, A. (ed.) (1997). *London: The Promised Land?* Aldershot: Avebury.

Kershen, A. (1997a). "Introduction", in A. Kershen (ed.) *London: The Promised Land* Avebury: Aldershot, 1-9.

Kershen, A. (1997b). "Huguenots, Jews and Bangladeshis in Spittlefields and the spirit of capitalism", in A. Kershen (ed.) *London: The Promised Land?* Aldershot: Avebury, 66-90.

Khan, A. (2003). *Greek Tragedy Triggers Pakistani Drive Against Human Trafficking.* Volume, DOI: http://www.oneworld.net/article/view/68598/1/, Last accessed: April 2, 2011.

Khan, A.N. (2003). *Pakistanis Face Heat of 9/11 Afterburn.* http://www.oneworld.net/article/view/67844/1/, Last accessed: April 2, 2011.

Khan, V. (1976). "Purdah in the British situation", D. Barker and S. Allen (eds) *Dependence and Exploitation in Work and Marriage.* London: Longman, 225-45.

Khan, V. (1977). "The Pakistanis: Mirpuri villagers at home and in Bradford", in J. Watson (ed.) *Between Two Cultures.* Oxford: Basil Blackwell, 57-89.

Khan, V. (1979). "Migration and social stress", in V. Khan (ed.) *Minority Families in Britain: Social Stress.* London: Macmillan.

Khan, Z. (1982). "Immigration problems", in Centre for Pakistan Studies (ed.) *Pakistanis in Europe,* Manchester: New Century Publishers.

Khatibi, A. (2009 [1989]). Frontiers: Between psychoanalysis and Islam. *Third Text,* 23(6), 689-96.

King, R. (2002). "Towards a new map of European migration", *International Journal of Population Geography,* 8: 89-106.

Kloosterman, R., Leun, J.V.D. and Rath, J. (1999). "Mixed embeddedness: (In) formal economic activities and immigrant businesses in the Netherlands", *International Journal of Urban and Regional Research,* 23(2).

Kloosterman, R. and Rath, J. (2001). "Immigrant entrepreneurs in advanced economies: Mixed embeddedness further explored", *Journal of Ethnic and Migration Studies,* 27(2), 252-66.

Knights, D. and Wilmott, H. (1990). *Labour Process Theory.* London: Macmillan.

Knights, M. (1996). "Bangladeshi immigrants in Italy: From geopolitics to micro-politics", *Transactions of the Institute of British Geographers,* 21(1), 105-23.

Koser, K. (2006). *Human Smuggling: Theoretical and Empirical Perspectives from Pakistan, Afghanistan and the UK.* (17th March, 2006). Leverhulme Conference on Mobility, Ethnicity & Society University of Bristol.

Koser, K. and Lutz, H. (eds) *The New Migration in Europe: Social Constructions and Social Realities.* Basingstoke: Macmillan, 199-223.

Koser, K. (2008) "Why smuggling pays", *International Migration,* 46 (2), 3-26.

Kritz, M., Lim, L., Zlotnik, H. (1992). *International Migration Systems: A Global Approach.* Oxford: Clarenden.

Lacan, J. (2002 [1977]). *Ecrtis* (translated by Alan Sheridan). London: Tavistock.

Lahiri, S. (2000). *Indians in Britain.* London: Frank Cass.

Landholt, P. (2001). "Salvadoran economic transnationalism: Embedded strategies for household maintenance, immigrant incorporation and entrepreneurial expansion", *Global Networks,* 1(3), 217-41.

Lash, S. (2000). "Risk culture", in Adam, B., Beck, U. and Van Loon, J. (eds) *The Risk Society Revisited.* London: Sage, 47-62.

Lavenex, S. (2006). "Shifting Up and Out: The Foreign Policy of European Immigration Control". *West European Politics* 29 (2): 329–350.

Lesser J. (1992). "From peddlers to proprietors: Lebanese, Syrian and Jewish immigrants in Brazil", in Hourani, A. and Shehadi, N. (eds) *The Lebanese in the World: A Century of Emigration.* London and New York: I.B. Tauris and St. Martin's Press, 393-410.

Lefebvre, A. (1990). "International labour migration from two Pakistani villages with different forms of agriculture", *Pakistan Development Review*, Spring, 29(1), 59-89.

Leun, J.V.D. (2000). "Modes of incorporation: Undocumented migrants in an advanced welfare state: The case of the Netherlands", in Çinar, D., Gächter, A. and Waldrauch, H. (eds) *Irregular Migration: Dynamics, Impact, Policy Options*. Vienna The European Centre.

Leun, J. and Kloosterman, R. (2006). "Going underground: The labour market position of undocumented immigrants in the Netherlands", *Tijdschrift voor Economische en Sociale Gegrafie/Economic and Social Geography*, 97(1), 59-68.

Levitt, P. (2001). *The Transantional Villagers*. Los Angeles: UCLA Press.

Levitt, P., De Wind, J. and Vertovec, S. (2003). "Introduction", *International Migration Review*, 37, 565-75.

Liempt, I. and Doomernik, J. (2006). "Migrant's agency in the smuggling process: The perspectives of smuggled migrants in the Netherlands", *International Migration*, 44(4), 165-89.

Light, I. and Gold, S. (2000). *Ethnic Economies*. San Diego, CA: Academic Press.

Light, I. (2000). "Globalisation and migration networks", in J. Rath (ed.) *Immigrant Businesses*. Basingstoke: Macmillan Press, 162-81.

Linhart, R. (1985). "The assembly line", in C.R. Littler, *The Experience of Work*. Oxford: Oxford University Press.

London Chamber of Commerce and Industry (2001). *The Contribution of Asian Businesses to London's Economy*. London: GLA.

Lukács, G. (1971 [1968]). *History and Class Consciousness: Studies in Marxist Dialectics*. London: Merlin Press.

MacLean, R. (2006). *The Magic Bus: The Hippy Trail from Istanbul to India*. Viking: London.

MacMaster, N. (1997). *Colonial Migrants and Racism: Algerians in France, 1900-62*. London New York: Macmillan.

Mai, N. (2001). ''Italy is Beautiful'': the role of Italian television in the Albanian migratory flow to Italy', in R.King, and N.Wood (eds) *Media and Migration: Constructions of Mobility and Difference*. London: Routledge, pp. 95-109.

Mai, N. and King, R. (2009). "Introduction", *Mobilities [special issue on Love, Sexuality and Migration]*, 4(3), 295-307.

Manchuelle, F. (1997). *Willing Migrants: Sonike Labour Diasporas, 1848-1960*. Ohio: Ohio University Press.

Markovits, C. (2000). *The Global World of Indian Merchants, 1750-1947: Traders of Sind from Bukhara to Panama*. Cambridge: Cambridge University Press.

Marx, K. (1994 [1867]) Extract from *Das Capital* in (eds) Eagleton, T. *Ideology*. London: Longman, 25-28.

Massey, D., Arango, J., Hugo, G., Kouaouci, A., Pellegrino, A. and Taylor, J.E. (1998). *Worlds in Motion*. Oxford: Clarenden Press.

McClintock, A. (1995) *Imperial Leather*. New York: Routledge.

McKeown, A. (2004). "Global migration: 1846-1940", *Journal of World History*, 15(2), 155-89.

Meagher, K. (2005). "Social capital or analytical liability? Social networks and African informal economies", *Global Networks*, 5(3), 217-38.

Mercer, K. (1994) *Welcome to the Jungle*. London: Routledge.

Messina, A.M. (1996). "The not so silent revolution: Postwar migration to Western Europe", *World Politics*, 49(1), 130-54.

Mezzadra, S. (2001). *Diritto di fuga: Migrazioni, cittadinanza, globalizzazione* Verona: Ombre Corte.

Mezzadra, S. (2004). "Capitalismo, migrazioni e lotte sociali. Appunti per una teoria dell' autonomia delle migrazioni", in S. Mezzadra (ed.) *I confini della liberta: Per un' analisi politica delle migrazioni contemporanee*. Roma: Derive Approdi.

Mincer, J. (1978). "Family migration decisions", *Journal of Political Economy*, 86(5), 749-73.

Mitropoulos, A. (2005). "Precari-us?", in *Metamute: Culture and Politics after the Net (2)*, *The Precarious Reader*: http://www.metamute.org/en/Precari-us, Last accessed: 2nd April, 2011.

Moi, T. (1990). "Appropriating Bourdieu: Feminist theory and Pierre Bourdieu's sociology of culture", *New Literary History*, 22, 1017-49.

Morris, S. (2004). "Illegal migrants were smuggled into UK 'club class'", *The Guardian*. London, May 29th.

Moulier-Boutang, Y. (1998). *De l'esclavage au salariat. Économie historique du salariat bridé*. Paris: PUF.

Mulvey, L. (1975) "Visual Pleasure and Narrative Cinema," *Screen*, 16(3), 6-18.

Naseem, S.M. (2002). "The crisis of growth and economic management in Pakistan", in S. Naseem and K. Nadvi (eds) *The Post-colonial State and Social Transformation in India and Pakistan*. Karachi: Oxford University Press, 245-79.

Neske, M. (2006). "Human smuggling to and through Germany", *International Migration*, 44(4), 121-63.

The News (Jang). (2004a). *Pakistani Student Blows Whistle on Bogus Marriage Racket*. London edition, 18th August.

The News (Jang). (2004b). *Bogus Marriages Network Smashed*. London edition, 24th September.

The News, (Jang). (2004c). *Top British Firm to Implement Face Recognition in Pakistan's Smart Machine Readable Passport and National ID Cards*. London edition, 1st December.

The News, (Jang). (2004d). *28 Pakistanis Kept in Private Jail in Jordan, Arrive Home*. London edition, 20th February.

The News, (Jang). (2004e). *249 More Pakistani Prisoners Deported from Oman Arrive Home*. London edition, 12th August.

Noman, O. (1988). *The Political Economy of Pakistan, 1947-85*. London and New York: KPI.

Oakley, A. and Oakley, R. (1979). "Sexism in official statistics", in I. Miles and J. Evans (eds) *Demystifying Official Statistics.* London: Pluto Press.

Omvedt, G. (1980). "Migration in colonial India: The articulation of feudalism and capitalism by the colonial state", *Journal of Peasant Studies*, 7(2), 185-212.

ONS "National statistics". *International Immigration Series* MN, 31(28).

Osella, F. and Osella, C. (2000). "Migration, money and masculinity in Kerala", *Journal of the Royal Anthropological Institute*, 6(1), 117-33.

Paden, J. and Singer, P. (2003). "America slams the door (on its foot)", *Foreign Affairs*, 82(3), 8-14.

Panayi, P. (1994). *Immigration, Ethnicity and Racism in Britain 1815-1945.* Manchester: Manchester University Press.

Papadopoulou, A. (2002). "Kurdish asylum seekers in Greece", Paper given UNU/WIDER Conference on Poverty, International Migration and Asylum (September 2002), Helsinki, 27-28.

Pasha, M.K. (2001). "Savage capitalism and civil society in Pakistan", A.M. Weiss and S.Z. Gialani (eds) *Power and Civil Society in Pakistan.* Karachi: Oxford University Press, 18-45.

Pastore, F., Monzini, P, and Sciortino, G. (2006). "Schengen's soft underbelly? Irregular migration and human smuggling across land and sea borders to Italy", *International Migration*, 44(4), 95-119.

Patel, G. (2007). "Imagining risk care and security: Insurance and fantasy", *Anthropological Theory*, 7(1), 99-118.

Pessar, P. (1999). "Engendering migration studies", *American Behavioural Scientist*, 42(4), 577-600.

Pessar, P. and Mahler, S. (2003). "Transnational migration: Bringing gender in", *International Migration Review*, 37(3), 812-46.

Peter, F. (2005). "Gender and the foundations of social choice: The role of situated agency", in B. Agarwal, J. Humphries and I. Robeyns (eds) *Amartya Sen's Work and Ideas: A Gender Perspective.* Abingdon: Routledge, 15-34.

Pettman, J. (1996). *Worlding Women.* London and New York: Routledge.

Phizacklea, A. (1988). "Entrepreneurship, ethnicity and gender", in S. Westwood and P. Bachu (eds) *Enterprising Women: Ethnicity, Economy and Gender Relations.* London and New York: Routledge, 20-33.

Phizacklea, A. and Wolkowitz, C. (1993). *Homeworking Women: Gender, Racism and Class at Work.* London: Sage Publications.

Phizacklea, A. (2004). "Migration theory and migratory realities: A gendered perspective", in D. Joly (ed.) *International Migration in the New Millennium.* Aldershot: Ashgate.

Pieterse, J. (2003). "Social capital and migration", *Ethnicities*, 3(1), 29-58.

Poggi, G. (1993). *Money and the Modern Mind: George Simmel's Philosophy of Money* Los Angeles and London: UCLA Press.

Polanyi, K. (1985 [1944]). *The Great Transformation.* Boston: Beacon Press.

Portes, A. (1981). "Modes of structural incorporation and present theories of labor immigration", in M. Kritz, C. Keely and S. Tomasi (eds) *Global Trends in Migration: Theory and Research on International Population Movements.* Staten Island, NY: Center for Migration Studies.

Portes, A. (1994). "The informal economy and its paradoxes", in N.J. Smelser and R. Swedberg (eds) *Handbook of Economic Sociology* Princeton, NJ: Princeton University Press/Russell Sage Foundation, 426-49.

Portes, A. (1995). "Economic sociology and the sociology of immigration", in A. Portes (ed.) *The Economic Sociology of Immigration*. New York: Russell Sage Foundation.

Portes, A. (1999). "The study of transnationalism: Pitfalls and promises of an emergent research field", *Ethnic and Racial Studies*, 22(2), 217-37.

Portes, A. (2001). "Introduction: The debates and significance of immigrant transnationalism", *Global Networks*, 1(3), 181-93.

Portes, A. and Bach, R. (1985). *Latin Journey: Cuban and Mexican Immigrants in the United States*. Berkeley: University of California Press.

Portes, A. and Landholt, P. (2000). "Social capital: promise and pitfalls in its role in development", *Journal of Latin American Studies*, 32, 529-47.

Portes, A. and J. Sensenbrenner (1993). "Embeddedness and immigration. Notes on the social determinants of economic action", *American Journal of Sociology*, 98(6), 1320-50.

Rastrelli, R. (2003). "L'immigrazione a Prato fra società, istituzioni ed economia", in A. Ceccagno (ed.) *Migranti a Prato*. Milano, Franco Angeli, 69-104.

Raza, A. (2004). "FIA re-launches operation against human trafficking", *The News* (Daily Jang). Lahore: 3 September.

Raza, A. (2004b). "FIA's 'efficiency' not enough for human traffickers to trap youth", *The News* (Daily Jang). Lahore: 2 December.

Raza, S. (2004). "UK claims top figures involved in human trade", *The Dawn*. Lahore: 24 September.

Rees, G. and Fielder, S. (1992). "The services economy, subcontracting and the new employment relations: Contract catering and cleaning", in *Work, Employment and Society.* London: Sage.

Robinson, A. and Smallman, C. (2006). "The contemporary British workplace: A safer and healthier place?", *Work, Employment and Eociety*, 20(1), 87-107.

Robinson L., Schmid, A., and Siles, M.E. (2002). "Is social capital really capital?", in *Review of Social Economy*, 60(1), 1-24.

Rose, J. (2000). "Feminine sexuality", in P. du Gay, J. Evans and P. Redmond (eds) *Identity: A Reader.* London: Sage, 51-68.

Rose, J (2003). "Response to Edward Said", in *Freud and the Non-European.* London: Verso, 65-79.

Rosenau, J. (1980). *The Study of Global Interdependence.* London: Francis Pinter.

Ryan, L. and Webster W. (2008) *Gendering Migration.* Aldershot: Ashgate.

Said, E. (2003). *Freud and the Non-European.* London: Verso.

Salt, J. and Hogarth, J. (2000). *Migrant Trafficking and Human Smuggling in Europe: A Review of the Evidence*, Geneva: International Organisation for Migration.

Salt, J. and Stein, J. (1997). "Migration as a business: The case of trafficking", *International Migration*, 35(4), 467-94.

Salter, J. (1873). *The Asiatic in London.* London: Seeley.

Sarasúa, C. (2001). "Leaving Home to help the Family? Male and female temporary migrants in eighteenth- and nineteenth-century Spain" in P. Sharpe (ed) *Women, Gender and Labour Migration. Historical and Global Perspectives.* London: Routledge, 29-59.

Sassen, S. (1994). *Cities in a World Economy.* London: Sage.

Sayad, A. (1999). *La double absence: des illusions de l'émigré aux souffrances de l'immigré.* Paris, Éditions du Seuil.

Sayeed, A. (2002). "State society conjunctures and conjunctures", in Naseem, S.M. and Nadvi, K. (eds) *The Post-colonial State and Social Transformation in India and Pakistan* Karachi: Oxford University Press, 203-44.

Sayer, A. (2001). "For a critical, cultural political economy", *Antipode*, 33, 687-708.

Sayers, S. (1988). "The need to work: A perspective from philosophy", in E. Pahl (ed.) *On Work.* New York and Oxford: Basil Blackwell.

Scott, J. (1976). *The Moral Economy of the Peasant.* New Haven, CT: Yale University Press.

Scott, J.W. (1988). *Gender and the Politics of History.* New York: Columbia University Press.

Schrover, M., Leun, J., Lucassen, L. and Quispel, C. (2008). *Illegal Migration and Gender in Global and Historical Perspective.* Amsterdam: Amsterdam University Press.

Sen, A. (1985) "Well-being, agency and freedom". *Journal of Philosophy* 82 (4), 169-221.

Sen, A. (1990) "Gender and cooperative conflicts" in I.Tinker (ed.) *Persistent Inequalities.* New York: OU, 169-221.

Sennet, R. (1998). *The Corrosion of Character.* New York: Norton.

Sennet, R. and Cobb, J. (1993). *The Hidden Injuries of Class.* New York: Norton.

Sekher, T. (1999). "Integration of return migrants into the labour force", in Weil, S. (ed.) *Roots and Routes.* Jerusalem: The Magness Press, The Hebrew University, 191-204.

Seshadri-Crooks, K. (2000). *Desiring whiteness: A Lacanian analysis of race.* London: Routledge.

Shaheed, F. (2002). "Women's experiences of identity, religion and activism in Pakistan", in S.M. Naseem and K. Nadvi (eds) *The Post-colonial State and Social Transformation in India and Pakistan.* Karachi: Oxford University Press, 343-90.

Shahnaz, L. (2004). *A New Perspective on Poverty and Migration Issues in Pakistan.* DFID & RSPN: Quad-Azam-University.

Shaw, A. (2000 [1988]). *Kinship and Continuity: Pakistani Families in Britain.* Amsterdam, Abingdon, Marston: Harwood Academic.

Simmel, G. (1978). *The Philosophy of Money.* London: Routledge.

Smith, J., Wallerstein, I., and Evers, H. (1984). "Introduction", in Smith, J., Wallerstein, I., and Evers, H. (eds) *Explorations in the World Economy.* Beverly Hills, London, New Delhi: Sage, 7-16.

Smith, M.P. (2002). "Preface", in Al-Ali, N. and K. Koser (ed.) *New Approaches to Migration? Transnational Communities and the Tansformation of Home.* London: Routledge, xi-vv.

Smith, H. (2007). "An Idyllic Greek Island becomes the new frontier for African migrants", *The Guardian.*

Smith, H. (2009). "Greece struggles to cope as immigration tensions soar", *The Guardian.*

Sontag, S. (2001 [1967]). "The pornographic imagination", in G. Bataille, *Story of the eye.* London: Penguin, 83-118.

Stark, O. (1991). *The Migration of Labour.* Cambridge: Basil Blackwell.

Stark, O. and J.E. Taylor (1989). "Relative deprivation and international migration", *Demography*, 26(1), 1-14.

Stefani, G. (2004). "La presenza straniera nella provinica di Prato". *La società multiculturale: cambiamenti demografici ed integrazione sociale: l'immigrazione nella provincia di Prato*, Rapporto F. Bisogno, G. Marchetti, G. Stefani and V. Tesi. Provincia di Prato: Osservatorio immigrazione, 35-52.

Stokel, A. (2007). "Excess and depletion: Bataille's surprisingly ethical model of expenditure", in S. Winnubst (ed.) *Reading Bataille Now.* Bloomington and Indianapolis: Indiana University Press, 252-84.

Sutcliffe, B. (2004). "Crossing borders in the new imperialism", in Socialist Register: special issue entitled *The New Imperial Challenge*, edited by L. Panitch and C. Leys, 261-80.

Swift, J. (1989). *Why are Rural People Vulnerable to Famine?* IDS Bulletin, 20(2), 8-15.

Tendler, S. (2004). "Fake passport haul worth one million pounds seized", *The Times.* London. 17 January.

Tilly, C. (1990). "Transplanted networks", in V. Yans-MacLoughlin (ed.) *Immigration Reconsidered.* New York: Oxford University Press, 79-95.

Todaro, M. (1969). "A model of labour migration and urban unemployment in less developed countries", *The American Economic Review*, 59(1).

UNHCR (2001). *Statistical Year Book.*

Valenzuela García, H. (2007). *Pakistani Communities and Healthcare in Barcelona: An Ongoing Research on Ethnography and Applied Anthropology.* Paper presented at Pakistan Workshop, Lake District, May 11, 12.

Vertovec, S. (1999). "Conceiving and researching transnationalism", *Ethnic and Racial Studies*, 22(2), 447-77.

Vertovec, S. (2003). "Migration and other modes of transnationalism", in *International Review Migration*, 37, 641-65.

Vertovec, S. (2004). *Trends and Impacts of Migrant Transnationalism* (working paper: 04-03), COMPAS.

Visram, R. (1986). *Ayahs, Lascars and Princes: The Story of Asians in Britain 1700-1947*. London, Pluto.

Visram, R. (2002). *Asians in Britain: 400 Years of History*. London, Pluto.

Wallerstein, I. (1974). *The Modern World System.* New York: Academic Press.

Werbner, P. (1996). "Our blood is green: Cricket, identity and social empowerment among British Pakistanis", in J. Mac Clancey (ed.) *Sport, Identity and Ethnicity*. London: Berg.

Werbner, P. (1999). "Global pathways: Working-class cosmopolitans and the creation of transnational worlds", *Social Anthropology*, 7(1), 17-35.

Werbner, P. (2001). "Metaphors of spatiality and networks in the plural city: A critique of the ethnic enclave economy debate", *Sociology*, 35, 671-93.

Werbner, P. (2002 [1990 paperback edition]). *The Migration Process: Capital, Gifts and Offerings among British Pakistanis*. Oxford: Berg.

Wimmer, A. and Glick-Schiller, N.G. (2003) "Methodological nationalism, the social sciences, and the study of migration: An essay in historical epistemology", *International Review Migration*, 37(3), 576-610.

Wolfenstein, E.V. (1993). *Psychoanalytic-Marxism: Groundwork*. New York: The Guilford Press.

Woodbridge, J. (2005). "Sizing the unauthorised (illegal): Migrant population in the United Kingdom", in *2001 Home Office Online Report*.

Yinger, N. (2006) "Feminisation of Migration". Published online by the Population Reference Bureau and available at: http://www.prb.org/Articles/2006/TheFeminizationofMigration.aspx (last accessed 1 August 2011)

Appendices

Appendix I The old school (London)

Name	Age	District/ City/ Town/ Village	Ed.	Marital Status	Former Job in Pakistan	Mode of Migration	In UK since	Employment In UK (2004)	... Previous
Malik		Mirpur	None	S			1962	Self-employed (Carpet salesman)	Ford Factory Worker, Milk delivery business
Sarwar	63	Mirpur	None	S	Pupil at school		1963	Ford Factory Worker	Ford Factory Worker
Rashid	70	Jullunder Faislabad	Matric	M	Out of work	Work voucher	1965	Retired	Factory Worker
Bari	72	Jullunder Faislabad	Failed Matric	M	Out of work	Work voucher	1969	Self-employed (Leather store)	Leather worker, leather factory owner
Karim	65	Gujrat Karachi	Matric				Mid 60s	Retired	Ford Factory Worker
Zia		Amritsar Rawal- pindi			Airforce		1962	Retired	Self-employed (Butcher-grocer)
Anwar		Sialcot	BA	M	Physics teacher	Work voucher	1964	Retired	Factory Worker Physics teacher
Maqbool		Sialkot Lahore Cyprus	BA	S	Arms contract-or	Student	1961	Retired	Accountant

... **Continued**

Name	Age	City	Education	Sex			Year		
Sara	45	Jhelum City		M		Spouse	1978	None	Garment stitching (home worker)
Ayesha	44	Lahore		M		Spouse	1983	None	Ran a market stall. Sewed ready-made clothes
Nadia		Karachi		M		Spouse		None	
Seema		Rawal-pindi	BA	M		Spouse	1971	Works in family business (printers)	Family mini cab and Printing businesses
Bibi Maqbool				M		Spouse		None	

Raza		Jhelum	Matric	M	Time keeper in factory	Spouse	1975	Retired	Ford (quality control)
Nadir		Dinga	BA	M	Bank Manager	Work Permit	1971	Retired	Bank Manager
Tanvir	38	Jhelum		M	Student	Spouse	1984	Employer (owns grocery shop)	Truck driver / Pizza delivery
Irfan	44	Lahore	Failed A-Levels	M		Dependent	1973	Employer (Owns and runs two shops)	Worked in a newsagents
Asgahr	45	Jhelum		M		Dependent	1976	Meat-shop worker	
Saida		Lahore				Dependent		Dental nurse/ assistant	Retail worker
Shazia		Mirpur				Dependent			

Appendix II   Freshies (London)

Name	Age	District/City/Town/Village	Ed.	Marital Status	Former Job in Pakistan	Mode of migration	In UK since	Employment in UK (2004)	...Previous
Nasir	27	Bhawalpur	Matric	M*	Ran his own estate agency	Spouse	1998	Employer (meatshop)	Security guard, grocery store worker, meat shop worker
Ilyas	35	Karachi	BA	D	White collar job in Dubai	Spouse	1998	Auditing department of a hotel	WH Smiths
Rahat	29	Gujrat	BA	D		Spouse		Postal worker	McDonalds
Chotu	20	Bhawalpur	BA	S	Student	Student visa	2004	Meat shop worker	NONE
Nobil	26	FATA (Rural NWFP)	MA	S	Student	Student visa	2004	Part-time receptionist in a bank	Security guard, Credit card company
Talat	39	Gujuranwala	MA (LLB)	M	Student	Student visa	1991	Runs a grocery store	Waiter, Restaurant manager
MBA		Karachi	1st degree	S	Student	Student visa		Cost cutter	
Med student		Karachi	1st degree	S	Student	Student visa		NHS	Waiter

... Continued

Name	Age	Origin	Education	Status	Previous occupation	Entry	Year	Job	Job
Halim	25	Kohat	Matric	S	Un-employed	Visit visa	2004	Take-away shop worker	Casual restaurant work
Bacha	28	Peshawar	A-levels	S	Self-employed (ran a shop)	Visit visa	2004		
Hasan	50	Lahore		M	Self-employed (ran several shops)	Illegal Entry		Meat shop worker, garment factory	
Aaloo	28	Peshawar		M	Factory worker	Illegal Entry	2004	Take-away shop worker	
Khan Sahab	24	Kohat	FA	S	Un-employed	Illegal Entry	2002	Meat shop worker	Cash & carry worker
Wasim	30	Kabul	Matric	S	Self-employed (ran own shop)	Illegal Entry	2003	Restaurant worker	Construction
Asad	23	Peshawar	None	S	Ag	Illegal Entry	2003	Construction	none
Amir	33	Kabul	BA	S	State employee	Illegal Entry	1992	Skilled job in primary economy	
Saud	28	Lahore	BA	S	Property developer	Illegal Entry		Supermarket worker, newsagents	Grocery store, Food factory

Appendix III The Italians

Name	Age	District City/ Town/ Village	Ed	Marital Status	Former Job in Pakistan	Mode of Migration	Year of Emigration	In Italy Since	Employment In Italy (2006)	… Previous
Azum	38	Bhawal-poor	BA	M	Teacher	Illegal Entry	2001	2002	PC	Different PC
Kamran	23	Mandi	Matric	S	Un-employed	Illegal Entry	2003	2005	Unemployed	Painting and decorating
Salman	35	Mandi	Matric	M	Ag.	Illegal Entry	1995	1996	Factory	Different factory
Chima	31	Muridke (near La-hore)	FA	S	Student	Illegal Entry	1997	1998	Chef	Different restaurants PC
Farhad	39	Mandi	FSC	S	Un-employed	Illegal Entry	2002	2002	Unemployed	Fruit picking
Zubair	24	Mandi	None	S	Family business (Ag)	Dependent Visa	2000	2000	PC	Factory
Jaldi	38	Lahore	BA	M	Employee in City Bank	Illegal Entry	1996	2000	Factory	None
Abdul	54	Gujaran-wala	FA	S	Army	Illegal Entry	1978	1995	Factory	Different factory

Jameel	46	Gujrat	Inter-mediate	M	Self-employed (Chicken Farm)	Illegal Entry	1992	1998	Unemployed	Factory
Rafeeq	30	Mandi	metric	M	Ag	Illegal Entry	1995	1995	Factory/ PC	Different factory
Pela	42	Mandi	metric	M	Self-employed	Illegal Entry	1989	1990	Factory	Different factory
Bilal	39	Mandi	FSC	M	Ag	Visit visa	1994	1994	Factory	Different factory
Atif	35	Mandi	FSC	M	Un-employed	Illegal Entry	2000	2002	Restaurant/PC	Different restaurant
Sarfraz	31	Toba Tekh Singh	FA	M	Student	Illegal Entry	1994	1998	Unemployed	Restaurant PC
Faizal	43	Gujrat	matric	M	Un-employed	Visit visa	To Kuwait 1980	2002	Unemployed	Doner
Kamal	39	Rawal-pindi	MA	S	Teacher	Visit visa	1997	1997	Unemployed	PC Hotel receptionist
Mushtaq	34	Mandi	BA	M	Student	Illegal Entry	1995	1995	Factory	None
Hamza	40	Jhang	None	M	Middle East		2000	2001	Factory	None
Waqas	20	Mandi	BA	S	Self-employed (pesticide business)		1999	1999	Factory	None

Appendix IV Countries transited/previously settled by Pakistanis in Italy

Migrant	1st County transited/settled	Length of Stay	2nd Country transited (if applicable)	Length of Stay
Azum	Portugal	14 months	Germany	
Kamran	France	18 months		
Bilal	China	2 months	France	5 months
Chima	Russia*	3 months	Germany	3 years
Farhad	Russia*	1 month		
Jaldi	Portugal	1 month	Germany	5 years
Abdul	Libya	17 years	Malta	
Jameel	Norway	2 months	France	8 years
Salman	Germany	1 month	France	1 month
Pioneer	Austria	1 year	Switzerland	4 years
Saif	Kuwait	2 years	France	18 months
Atif	France	2 years		
Sarfraz	Africa**	6 months	Germany	3 years
Faizal	Kuwait	18 years	Greece	3 years
Mushtaq	Turkey	1 month		
Hamza	Middle East	Unknown	France	6 months

*   Failed attempt to migrate ending in deportation.

** Countries not specified.

Index